Forecasting with the Theta Method

Forecasting with the Theta Method

Theory and Applications

Kostas I. Nikolopoulos
Prifysgol Bangor University
Gwynedd, UK

Dimitrios D. Thomakos
University of Peloponnese
Tripolis, GR

Registered Offices
John Wiley & Sons, Inc., 111 River Street, Hoboken, NJ 07030, USA
John Wiley & Sons Ltd, The Atrium, Southern Gate, Chichester, West Sussex, PO19 8SQ, UK

Editorial Office
9600 Garsington Road, Oxford, OX4 2DQ, UK

For details of our global editorial offices, customer services, and more information about Wiley products visit us at www.wiley.com.

Library of Congress Cataloging-in-Publication Data applied for

ISBN: 9781119320760

Cover Design: Wiley
Cover Images: © Alexey Godzenko / Shutterstock; © arleksey / Shutterstock

Set in 10/12pt WarnockPro by SPi Global, Chennai, India
Printed in Singapore by C.O.S. Printers Pte Ltd

10 9 8 7 6 5 4 3 2 1

Kostas

I extend my deep and sincere gratitude to all those who have contributed to my post-DEng journey in academia from late 2002 onwards:

> First, my "father" Vasillis, and my big "brother" Dimitrios with his unbelievable capacity.
>
> Then, my younger "brother" Fotios who fortunately avoids the mistakes I made, and my oldest mate in the field Aris for the really great things we have done together.
>
> Also, my good old friends and frequent collaborators Kostas and Vicky.
>
> Always in debt to my wise mentors Shanti and Brian.
>
> Last but not least, unbelievably proud of my academic "children" to date: Nicolas, Vassilios, Sam, Vivian, Greg, Sama, Christina, Tolu, Azzam, Waleed, Ilias, Chris, and Axilleas.

Dimitrios

This volume is just a quick stop in a journey that began many years ago.

A heartfelt thank you to Kostas for sharing the road with me, and may we continue to nonlinear paths in the years to come. The intellectual curiosity and research support of my PhD students Lazaros Rizopoulos and Foteini Kyriazi in preparing the manuscript is gratefully acknowledged. This volume is dedicated to my parents, those who first allowed me to prosper freely in my endeavors.

Contents

Author Biography

Kostas I. Nikolopoulos is Professor of Business Analytics at Bangor Business School, UK. He is also the Director of *for*LAB, a forecasting laboratory, and former Director of Research for the College of Business, Law, Education, and Social Sciences. He received both his Engineering Doctorate Diploma in Electrical and his Computer Engineering (MEng) from the National Technical University of Athens, Greece. He is an expert in time series analysis and forecasting, forecasting support systems, and forecasting the impact of special events. Professor Nikolopoulos has published in a number of prestigious journals and is an Associate Editor of *Oxford IMA Journal of Management Mathematics* and *Supply Chain Forum: An International Journal*.

Dimitrios D. Thomakos is Professor of Applied Econometrics and Head of the Department of Economics at the University of Peloponnese, Greece, and Senior Fellow and Member of the Scientific Committee at the Rimini Center for Economic Analysis in Italy. Dimitrios holds an MA, MPhil, and PhD from the Department of Economics of Columbia University, USA. His research work has appeared in several prestigious international journals in economics and finance such as the *Review of Economics and Statistics*, the *Canadian Journal of Economics*, the *Review of International Economics*, and many others.

Kostas and Dimitrios have worked together extensively coauthoring in the *Journal of Management Mathematics* and the *Journal of Forecasting* among many other journals and recently coedited two volumes for Springer-Palgrave (*A Financial Crisis Manual* and *Taxation in Crisis*).

Preface

The Theta method is the most successful univariate time series forecasting technique of the past two decades, since its origination in the late 1990s. Jointly with the damped trend exponential smoothing, these are the two benchmarks that any newly proposed forecasting method aspires to outperform, so as to pass the test of time. This performance was originally demonstrated in the M3 competition in 2000 that the Theta method was the only method that outperformed Forecast Pro (www.forecastpro.com) and dominated a pool of 18 other academic methods and five more software packages.

The method originated in 1999 from Kostas and his supervisor Professor Vassilis Assimakopoulos, and was first presented in the International DSI 99[1] while the first full-fledged academic article and description came in 2000 in the *International Journal of Forecasting*. In the same journal came the first critique three years later, led by Professor Rob Hyndman and his team in Monash for the similarity of the basic model from the method to simple exponential smoothing (SES) with drift.

The journal made a mistake in that they had neither used our review on the paper (as our objections were left unanswered) nor had they offered us a commentary to be published along that article – that is a standard practice in similar situations. This created more confusion as an immediate clear answer from us and Vassilis could not see the light of day; and it took a few more years until we found the means and media to post our response. That 2003 argument is now dead and buried, as every year a new and different successful model is coming out from the Theta method; and none of them is an SES with drift. This was always our counterargument – that the method is much much broader and we cannot see the forest for the trees... But this is history; and actually that 2003 article has probably created even more interest in the method, so welcome it is even if it did not do justice to the method.

A few working papers from 2005 onward and an article of ours in 2011 in Springer LNEE have set the record straight; and from that point on, joint work

1 Assimakopoulos and Nikolopoulos (1999).

with Dimitrios in the IMA Journal of Management Mathematics[2] proved why the method works well for unit roots – that were the dominant data-generating processes (DGPs) in the M3 data – while more work in the *Journal of Forecasting* extended the method in the bivariate space, providing at the same time various successful extensions of it. This trend was picked up by research teams in Brazil, the United States, and, most notably, in the University of Bath and with Dr. Fotios Petropoulos – a scholar of the method – providing further extensions and optimizations. The same stands for the new students of Vassilis in the Forecasting and Strategy Unit (www.fsu.gr) in Greece who continue his legacy. When these lines are written, the original article of 2000 has achieved 209 citations in Google Scholar.

So now we know the method is far, far more than just SES with drift. It was not an easy journey to this point – but the forecasters' journey was never meant to be an easy one anyway from the very first day that the field was founded from Spyros Makridakis, Robert Fildes, and Scott Armstrong. From here onward, now that we have a fair share of the focus of the academic community – in forecasting and beyond – it is going to be a far more exciting one; and to kick start the process we proposed to Wiley – and the publishing house gladly and wisely accepted – to deliver the first book on the method that would capture the work done to date and, more importantly, lay the new theory and foundations for the years to come.

The book also includes a series of practical applications in finance, economics, and health care as well a contribution from Fotios on his honest view of what happened in the past and where things should go from now on. This is topped up by tools in MS Excel and guidance – as well as provisional access – for the use of R source code and respective packages.

When all is said and done, we do believe that this book is a valuable and useful tool for both academics and practitioners and that the potential of the method is unlimited. This is a forecast from forecasters and it comes with the usual caveat: the past success of the method does not guarantee the future one...but only time will tell!

February 2018   *Kostas & Dimitrios*

---

2 An article that for two years was reviewed in the *International Journal of Forecasting* (IJF) and never got published there – without a single mistake being found in it. We always took the stance that we should first submit in IJF – for historic reasons – any new work on the method, but that resulted in unnecessary delays in the publication process.

Part I

Theory, Methods and Models

1

The Θ-legacy

By Kostas I. Nikolopoulos and Dimitrios D. Thomakos

> *The laws of nature are but the mathematical thoughts of God*
>
> Euclid

1.1   The Origins...

(Written in first person by Kostas)

Once upon a time

There was a little boy keen on his (Euclidean) geometry...! It seems like yesterday...but actually it was 22 years ago – winter of 1996 – February of 1996. Me (Kostas), an eighth semester young and promising engineer-to-be, having completed a year ago my elective module in "Forecasting Techniques" and keen to start the (compulsory) dissertation in the National Technical University of Athens in Greece.

This is an endeavor students usually engage in during the 10th and last semester of MEng – but given that sufficient progress in my studies had been achieved to that point – I opted for an early start: this without being aware that it would mean moooore work; so a dissertation that usually takes 6 months to complete ended up an 18-month-long journey...

The topic "Nonparametric regression smoothing" or, in lay terms, time series smoothing (or filtering) with kernel methods – most notably nearest-neighbor approaches – would later on prove useful in my academic career as well, for forecasting time series. For a non-statistician – but math-bombarded engineer – this was quite a spin-off, but one that very much paid off intellectually and career-wise in the years to come.

And, yes, it took 18 months – no discounts there from Vassilis – damping my hopes for a relaxed have-nothing-to-do 10th semester. The reason was my Professor Vassilis Assimakopoulos and the fact that I was lucky enough to join

Forecasting with the Theta Method: Theory and Applications, First Edition.
Kostas I. Nikolopoulos and Dimitrios D. Thomakos.
© 2019 John Wiley & Sons Ltd. Published 2019 by John Wiley & Sons Ltd.

him in the best part of his academic journey, while he was still an Assistant Professor and had this hunger to climb the academic ladder as soon as possible – just like any other academic, although none of them will never admit it, so keen to publish and supervise young promising students like me – and modest (ha ha!). Hope he has not regretted it over the years, but ours is a relationship that is still alive and kicking. I still get the odd phone call wherever I am in the world, and I always find it very hard to say no to any of his academic requests. Vassilis is an extremely bright guy with amazing ideas, all of which you have to pursue until one or none flourishes; but this is a model that I was and still am happy to follow and live by. And, thus began my DEng journey.

The task was simple and bluntly disclosed – in the very words of my supervisor: build a new univariate forecasting method that would win the M3 competition (that was about to be launched). In Greece in the year 1997, in an Engineering school, outperform the entire academic forecasting community and win a blind empirical forecasting competition: probably Mission Impossible! The quest for a new method started with much experimentation – that is out of the scope of this book – and resulted in the "The Theta Model: A Decomposition Approach to Forecasting."

Earlier participatory attempts in the M3 competition along the lines of Theta-sm had been far simpler, non-versatile, and, as such, had never stood the test of time. But the big one had been achieved, and it was a brand new method... A method so versatile that it allowed for many new series to be created from the original data and each one of them could be extrapolated with any forecasting method, and the derived forecasts could be combined in all possible ways: the sky was the limit...

Any action brings on a reaction, inevitably so; in this case, it came from the same International Journal of Forecasting (IJF) with the article "Unmasking the Theta method" from Professor Rob J. Hyndman, who later became Editor-in-chief of the journal, and his student Baki Billah in Monash. I have extensively elaborated on this story in the Preface, but I reiterate here that despite that article not doing justice to the method, it did, however, add up to the discussion and kept the interest in the method alive. Looking back, it was an important thing because the next big set of results on the method was not published till 2008 and 2009 (in a series of working papers[1] and in the respective presentations in the International Symposium on Forecasting, ISF[2]), where attempts to mix the method with neural networks were made, results in financial time series were presented, as well as a new theory for unit root data-generating processes (DGPs) in 2009 – the early version of a paper published in the Institute of Mathematics and its Applications (IMA) and the superiority of the method was reconfirmed in the NN3 competition.

---

1 Nikolopoulos and Assimakopoulos (2005a).
2 Nikolopoulos and Assimakopoulos (2004, 2005b).

1.1.1 The Quest for Causality

Bring in then an econometrician ... Then came Dimitrios – switch to the year 2005...spring; I was well situated in North West United Kingdom doing my postdoc in Lancaster. What a guy...I have never seen such capacity in my life. A bright and hardworking academic, educated in Columbia in theoretical econometrics – an ideal scholar to throw light on the *why* and *when* the method works; a valuable friend always willing to give sharp and short advice, exactly what at that stage a not-so-young-any-more academic needed. Somehow he managed to find me in the Daedalian jungle of the School of Electrical and Computer Engineering building in the National Technical University of Athens, where the Forecasting and Strategy unit – that I was still loosely affiliated with and regularly visiting – was based. After that we worked closely, with him leading the research on the model from 2006 to late 2009, coauthoring a series of working papers.

The academic year 2009–2010 was the turning point: 10 years after publishing the method in a descriptive format, Dimitrios finally laid the foundations of the quest why and when it works – starting with how the method works on unit root DGPs. For two years the paper was in review for IJF without a single error being found in the analysis. In the end, we had to employ a third reviewer only to have him say – to still say that despite all the analysis done as requested by the reviewers these results were not interesting enough for the audience of IJF. Academic judgment is academic judgment...and as such we respected it, but this delayed the whole process by two years – the paper was already out as a working paper since 2009.

The paper took two more years to see the light of day, and in 2014 we finally had *why* the Theta method works for unit roots (that many of the M3 data series actually are), with the article being published in the Oxford IMA Journal of Management Mathematics. We also had a series of more results from local behaviors of the models, weight optimizations, single theta-line extrapolations, and many more. It was clear among the academic community that we were looking at a method that allowed for a series of models, to be developed within the same set of principles, more robust and accurate than the ETS or ARIMA family, but still equally or more versatile.

With the statement made and the road paved, the journey that followed was much easier. The year 2015 was another milestone, as the first multivariate extension was proposed: a bivariate Theta method that works very well. The results were presented in the JoF; special thanks go out to Editor Professor Derek Bunn for handling this submission so efficiently and for his personal attention to and handling of the paper.

The year 2016 was another important milestone as it was the first year that saw new results being presented by researchers other than Vassilis (and his team), me, and Dimitrios, or Rob (and his students). Fotios – that had in the past worked on the method with me and Vassilis – engaged in joint work with colleagues in Brazil led by Jose Fiorucci, as well as in the later stages of the project with Anne Koehler, provided further extensions and optimizations of the method and a link to state space models. This was the first time that a team – other than the aforementioned three – was using the method not just as a benchmark for evaluation purposes but was also developing a genuinely new theory.

That was the moment we decided it was about time for this book, and Wiley grabbed the opportunity. A book capturing progress in data but, more importantly, proposing a new and more complete theory on the method and many practical applications of it; with the dual scope of capturing the work done so far and emphatically and more prominently inspiring the next generations of forecasters to evolve the method onwards and upwards ...

Reflecting on the journey so far, I believe it is truly an extraordinary story – especially given that it started in the cemented basement of an engineering school in Greece and not in a luxurious Ivy League business school; forecasting is a fragmented field where the ability to improve accuracy per se is very small and differences in performance in between models very very small, at the limits of statistical error. So when out of the blue a new method comes out organically from an academic group and has been evolved and is still evolving after 20 years... it must be something.

1.2 The Original Concept: THETA as in THErmosTAt

Vassilis wanted to see time series behaving like materials under the sun: high temperature would dilate them, while low temperature would make them shrink. This natural process seems quite intuitively appealing for the time series, as through a parameter you could possibly amplify/dilate or constrict/shrink the (curvatures) of a series. In fact, he wanted through this parameter to actually control the ...temperature of the material: to control the dilation or shrinkage of the curvatures of the series; enacting exactly like a THErmosTAt. And this is how the name of the parameter came about: THETA or just the Greek letter Θ. The when and how to use, how to extrapolate, and combine those derived dilated/constricted series (the so-called Theta lines) was not decided in the first few months; and that is exactly what made Theta a method and not just a model. The ability to create as many as you want to (derived series), extrapolate with whatever method you want to, and combine them with whatever approach you want to – this is the true beauty and versatility of the original inception of the method.

In this section, we present more thoroughly the original foundations of the method as discussed for the first time in the proceedings of the International

DSI in Athens (1999 proceedings); and more rigorously in the IJF in 2000, from which article most of the following text in this section has been adopted.

1.2.1 Background: A Decomposition Approach to Forecasting

There have been many attempts to develop forecasts based directly on decomposition (Makridakis 1984). The individual components that are usually identified are the trend-cycle, seasonality, and the irregular components. These are projected separately into the future and recombined to form a forecast of the underlying series. This approach is not frequently used in practice. The main difficulties are in successfully isolating the error component as well as in producing adequate forecasts for the trend-cycle component. Perhaps the only technique that has been found to work relatively well is to forecast the seasonally adjusted data with a well-established extrapolation technique like, for example, using Holt's method (Makridakis 1998) or the damped trend method (Gardner 1985) and then adjust the forecasts using the seasonal components from the end of the data.

Assuming seasonally adjusted data, the Theta method proposes a second and different layer of decomposition: a decomposition of the seasonally adjusted series into short- and long-term components. The challenge for the proposed method was to increase the degree of exploitation of the embedded useful information in the data before the application of an extrapolation method, as this information has long- and short-term components. These components are captured from the theta lines and then extrapolated separately. The Theta method effectively mimics a magnifying glass through which the time series trends – short or long – are highlighted. The combination of the components and forecasts thus becomes more effective while retaining the benefits of combining.

Combining by and large is expected to improve forecasting accuracy (Clemen 1989) – at least in comparison to the combined elements. The reason lies in the averaging of errors that are produced by each individual forecasting method (Makridakis 1998). If there is an amount of useful information within the time series, then there is also an accompanying degree of exploitation of this information associated with each distinct forecasting method. In this sense, the Theta method can be seen as an alternative decomposition approach or/and as an extension to the concept of combining.

1.2.2 The Original Basic Model of the Theta Method

The method is based on the concept of modifying the curvatures of the time series via the Theta parameter (as a symbol is used the Greek letter Theta), applied directly to the second differences of the data:

$$X_{\text{new}}^{//}(\theta) = \theta \cdot X_{\text{data}}^{//}$$

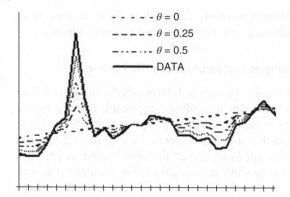

Figure 1.1 A randomly selected series from M3: Theta-model deflation.

The smaller the value of the Theta parameter from 1 (and positive), the larger the degree of shrinkage in the data, as shown in Figure 1.1. In the extreme case where Θ = 0, the time series is transformed into a straight line – the linear regression line of the data over time t. This process is like a filtering or smoothing process and gradually reveals the long-term trends in the data (Assimakopoulos 1995). Theta can also get negative values, and this will result in series that mirror the original data.

If, on the other hand, the value of the Theta parameter is increased over 1, then the time series is dilated, as shown in Figure 1.2, resulting in amplification of the short-term behavior.

The resulting time series in the previous two figures are called Theta lines, and these are the result of an ordinary least squares (OLS) minimization where the mean and the trend of the derived series remain identical to the original data (Assimakopoulos and Nikolopoulos 2000, Appendix A).

The original idea for the method was as follows: the original time series could be decomposed into a number of Theta lines. Each of the Theta lines

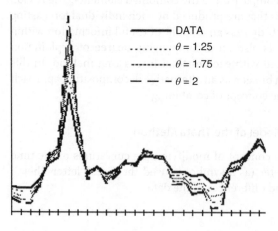

Figure 1.2 A randomly selected series from M3: Theta-model dilation.

would be extrapolated separately and the forecasts simply combined with equal weights. Any forecasting method can be used for the extrapolation of a Theta line according to existing experience (Fildes 1998) or via optimizing the out-of-sample accuracy performance over a holdout. In general, a different combination of Theta lines could be employed for each forecasting horizon.

In the majority of the M3 competition data – most notably for the 1428 monthly time series, two Theta lines were employed, i.e. $\Theta = 0$ and $\Theta = 2$:

$$Data = 1/2(L(\Theta = 0) + L(\Theta = 2))$$

The first Theta line ($\Theta = 0$) is the linear regression line of the data (Assimakopoulos and Nikolopoulos 2000, Appendix B) and the second one has double-second differences from the original data. The first line was extrapolated by just extending the straight line to the future, while the second one was originally via the damped exponential smoothing (DES): see Appendix 1.A at the end of the chapter for the original source code – originally in Vb3 and then transferred in VB6[3] that was used in the M3 competition. At later stages, Vassilis decided to switch from DES to simple exponential smoothing (SES) for the second Theta line as post hoc tests were indicating that most of the time the models ended up being non-trending models and also the average forecasting performance of the latter was on par with the former. However, SES was almost three times faster in terms of computational time as it was estimating only one parameter and thus a much better compromise even at the expense of some computational accuracy.

Back in those days in the late 1990s, this time was translated into a few hours in a top-spec computer, and so not something to ignore in a real-life operational and organizational setup. The difference was minimal in the provided forecasts with either extrapolation method, as the high noise of the inflated theta line (with theta parameter equal to 2) led to the DES very often collapsing to the SES model without trend.

In the monthly 1428 M3 series, SES was used for the extrapolation of Theta line 2 as reported in the respective IJF paper in the year 2000. This was not the case for the remaining M3 subsets as was reported in the 2011 paper by Nikolopoulos et al., the reason being to experiment with real blind data with the full potential of the method when other lines and other extrapolation techniques are employed. That created some confusion as full replicability of the

---

3 In 1999, a Pentium personal computer with maximum specification in terms of RAM given the motherboard was commercially available – would need a full weekend to get results for the 3003 series of the M3 competition – literally a weekend. And I had to call the security in the campus over phone once a day to see if there was any power cut; and if that was the case, I had to go back to the laboratory and restart the running of the experiment – a loop over the four subsets of the monthly, quarterly, yearly, and other data of the M3 competition. Today, in an i5 laptop with 4 GB of RAM, the same code runs in less than two minutes, while in the cloud with many cores available in just seconds.

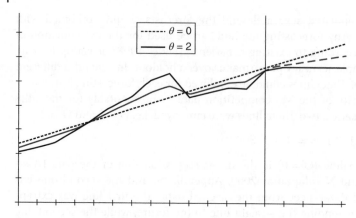

Figure 1.3 An example of a Theta-model extrapolation in an M3 series.

method was not easy to achieve. Mea culpa on that one; I have not clarified that entirely in the original paper. However, this has been communicated in many conferences and is clearly documented in the 2011 paper.

Irrespective of the exact extrapolation technique employed, at that stage the simple equal-weighted combination of the two separate forecasts was used in order to create the final forecast of the Theta model for the specific time series, as shown in Figure 1.3.

In the years that followed the original presentation of the method, many experimentations with different weights as well as with more Theta lines have been tried and reported in ISF conferences – usually leading to improvement in the forecasting accuracy over the M3 datasets – those, however, at that stage were not a blind competition anymore; and as such continuous iterative experimentation can always lead to forecasting accuracy improvements (for example, Nikolopoulos and Assimakopoulos (2004).)

1.2.3   How to Build and Forecast with the Basic Model

The full sequence of steps in order to provide forecasts from the basic model of the method – as described in the 2000 IJF paper – is as follows:

- Seasonality testing and, if need be, seasonal adjustment with the classical multiplicative decomposition method.
- Decomposition into two Theta lines for $\Theta = 0$ for $\Theta = 2$.
- Extrapolation with extending the straight regression line for the first theta line and employing either the DES or SES for the second one.
- Combination of the produced forecasts with equal weights.
- Re-seasonalization of the forecasts (if seasonality was present in the first place).

In terms of forecasting performance, this simple but intuitively appealing model was the big surprise in the M3 competition as it *won*, illustrating better accuracy than the 18 academic methods and 6 software packages including Forecast Pro; the latter to date is considered the most advanced and state-of-the-art off-the-shelf forecasting package/tool in the world (Makridakis and Hibon 2000, www.forecastpro.com).

From that point on, despite those ideas from scholars of the method not being picked up very fast, the way was paved for innovative extensions: for example, use of more than two theta lines, use of different Theta-line combinations for each forecasting horizon (Collopy and Armstrong 1992), and the utilization of different Theta lines for different time series in a "horses for courses" manner (Armstrong 1993; Petropoulos et al. 2014).

At this point, and before we close this section on the first manifestation of the method, I want also to personally[4] extend my special and sincere thanks to Professor Keith Ord, since he has edited and actually simplified the algebra for providing the theta lines in this 2000 IJF paper. He is a true academic; and this is something now widely known, that he actually activated and helped us on this far beyond what is expected of an Associate Editor in a journal.

1.2.4   SES with Drift

The arguments laid out in the next few paragraphs have been advocated since early 2005 in many conference presentations and working papers. However, it was not till 2011 when Nikolopoulos et al. gathered in one paper all the respective results that clarified the claim regarding the similarities in the basic Theta model used for the monthly M3 data and SES with drift.

Hyndman (2003) made the claim that the Theta model, as described in the 2000 IJF paper, is similar to SES with drift and in their analysis focused on the special case of the method where the decomposition is to the Theta line with $\Theta = 0$ and the Theta line with $\Theta = 2$.

The fact is that formula wise, the Theta model extrapolations in this specific case may look like SES with drift, i.e. like:

$$F_{t+1} = aY_t + (1 - a)F_t + \frac{b}{2}$$

where **a** is the smoothing parameter and **b**/2 the drift.

However, there are these two fundamental differences:

- The drift is predefined as being equal to half of the regression trend/slope **b**.
- The smoothing parameter **a** is optimized on the Theta line for $\Theta = 2$; not the original data, as is the standard practice in the SES-with-drift approach.

---

4 From Kostas.

This results in a model very different from SES with drift, because if **a** and **b** are different you will inevitably get different forecasts from the same – formula-wise – function. This very clear argument was never embedded in the 2003 Hyndman and Billah paper; and, as such, a lot of confusion was unnecessarily created.

No matter what the optimization technique employed, the SES-with-drift smoothing parameter is identical to the one obtained in the Theta model only by chance. This is simply because, in the case of the Theta model, the smoothing parameter **a** is calculated via a mean squared error (MSE) minimization procedure on a different time series: Theta line with $\Theta = 2$; *not on the original data.*

Furthermore, in any SES-with-drift approach, both the parameters **a** and **b** (for the drift **b**/2) are either set or optimized *simultaneously* in the original time series.

That is exactly the fundamental advantage of this specific Theta model. "Do not use the original data; use instead series containing reduced amounts of information"...such as the Theta line with $\Theta = 2$ in our case, a series with doubled local curvatures that captures the short-term trend of the series. In our approach, if you want to capture the short-term behavior, you just need to give emphasis to that (through Theta line with $\Theta = 2$) and at the same time use an extrapolation method that gives more weight to the most recent observations, (such as Exponential Smoothing or Naïve).

1.2.5 The Exact Setup in the M3 Competition

Yet again referring to the work in 2011 from Nikolopoulos et al. (2011), we provide an adapted version of Table 1 from that paper. In Table 1.1, we can see in the last row the exact Theta lines and extrapolation methods employed for the Theta method in the M3 competition.

Therefore, the following hold:

- *For the 1428 monthly series:* Two Theta lines for $\Theta = 0$ and $\Theta = 2$, with the latter extrapolated with SES;
- *For the 174 other series:* Two Theta lines for $\Theta = 0$ and $\Theta = 2$, with the latter extrapolated with DES;
- *For the 645 other series:* Two Theta lines for $\Theta = 0$ and $\Theta = 1.4$, with the latter extrapolated with DES, and that is why the published performance in M3 deviates a lot from SES with drift – in fact, the result in the M3 would have been even better if we had stuck to the same approach we had done for the monthly data for the entire M3 dataset;
- *For the 756 other series:* Two Theta lines for $\Theta = 0$ and $\Theta = 2$, with the latter extrapolated with DES for horizons 1 and 2; two Theta lines for $\Theta = 0$ and $\Theta = 1.9$, with the latter extrapolated with DES for horizons 3, 4, 5, and 6; two Theta lines for $\Theta = 0$ and $\Theta = 1,7$, with the latter extrapolated with DES for horizons 7 and 8.

Table 1.1 Theta lines and extrapolation methods employed for the Theta method in the M3 competition.

Source	Method	M3 Competition (Average symmetric MAPE)				
		Yearly	Other	Monthly	Quarterly	All-M3
Makridakis and Hibon (2000)	Single ES	17.82%	6.29%	15.32%	9.72%	14.32%
Makridakis and Hibon (2000)	**Theta model**	**16.90%**	**4.44%**	**13.85%**	8.96%	13.111%
Makridakis and Hibon (2000)	Top performer M3	16.42%	4.38%	13.85%	8.96%	13.01%
Makridakis and Hibon (2000)	#Series	645	174	1428	756	3003
Makridakis and Hibon (2000)	Horizon	6	8	18	8	18
Makridakis and Hibon (2000)	#Errors used	3870	1392	25 704	6048	37014
Current study	Theta lines/extrapolation methods that were used in M3	L(0), L(1.4) DES	L(0), L(2) DES	**L(0), L(2) SES**	L(0), L(2), L(1.9), L(1.7) DES	
Current study	Type of optimization in M3	Second Theta line	Extrapolation method	None	More Theta lines	

Bold indicates the published performance in the M3 competition.

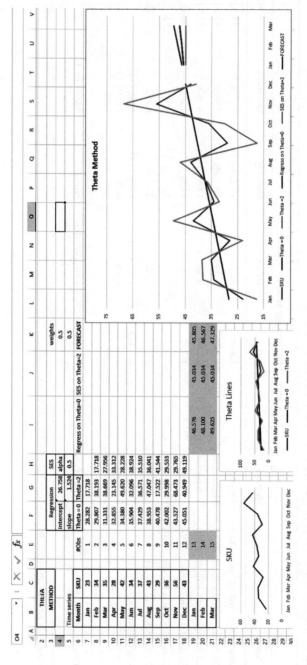

Figure 1.4 Microsoft Excel template for the basic model of the Theta method.

So we have experimented with different extrapolation methods and different theta lines for different forecasting horizons. These were optimized using a holdout equal to the required forecasting horizons of the M3 competition (6 for yearly data, 8 for quarterly data, and 18 for monthly data). All evaluations were done in a one-off extrapolation; and not rolling evaluations (sliding simulations).

1.2.6 Implementing the Basic Version in Microsoft Excel

For the basic model with two Theta lines for $\Theta = 0$ and $\Theta = 2$, then following the basic property of the (two) Theta lines (Assimakopoulos 2000; Nikolopoulos et al. 2011):

$$\text{Data} = \frac{1}{2} \text{ [Theta line with } \Theta = 0] + \frac{1}{2} \text{ [Theta Line with } \Theta = 2]$$

$$\Rightarrow \text{Data} = \frac{1}{2} \text{ [simple linear regression line over } t]$$

$$+ \frac{1}{2} \text{ [Theta line with } \Theta = 2]$$

$$\Rightarrow \text{[Theta line with } \Theta = 2] = 2 * \text{Data}$$

$$- \text{[simple linear regression line over } t] \tag{1.1}$$

Thus, in practice, the model can be easily implemented in Microsoft Excel as per the given screenshot (the XLS is provided via the electronic companion of the book and/or through contacting the authors directly at kostas@fortank.com) (Figures 1.4–1.6):

In order to build the worksheet, the following steps need to be implemented:

1. *Step 1*: Apply simple linear regression to nonseasonal data and prepare as follows:
   The [Theta Line with $\Theta = 0$] = [Simple Linear Regression Line over t] and also forecasts for the respective horizon. You can employ the standard functions =Intercept() and =Slope() in MS Excel for the aforementioned task as follows:
   For the intercept and the slope of the regression line
   (a) G4 = INTERCEPT(C7:C18, E7:E18)
   (b) G5 = SLOPE(C7:C18, E7:E18)
   For the Theta line with $\Theta = 0$
   (a) F7 = G4 + G5 * E7
2. *Step 2*: Calculate [Theta line with $\Theta = 2$] with (Eq. (1.1)) as follows:
   For Theta line with $\Theta = 2$
   (a) G7 = 2 * C7−F7
3. *Step 3*: Extrapolate [Theta line with $\Theta = 2$] with the inbuilt MS Excel function "Exponential Smoothing" or by implementing the recursive formula in the respective cells. In the simplest version, the smoothing parameter is not

| G7 | ▼ | ⋮ | ✕ ✓ *fx* | =2*C7-F7 | | | |

	A	B	C	D	E	F	G	H
2		**THETA**						
3		**METHOD**				**Regression**		**SES**
4						intercept	26.758	alpha
5		**Time series**				slope	1.524	0.5
6		**Month**	**SKU**		**#Obs**	Theta = 0	Theta =2	
7		Jan	23		1	28.282	17.718	
8		Feb	34		2	29.807	38.193	17.718
9		Mar	35		3	31.331	38.669	27.956
10		Apr	28		4	32.855	23.145	33.312
11		May	42		5	34.380	49.620	28.228
12		Jun	34		6	35.904	32.096	38.924
13		Jul	37		7	37.429	36.571	35.510
14		Aug	43		8	38.953	47.047	36.041
15		Sep	29		9	40.478	17.522	41.544
16		Oct	36		10	42.002	29.998	29.533
17		Nov	56		11	43.527	68.473	29.765
18		Dec	43		12	45.051	40.949	49.119
19		Jan			13			
20		Feb			14			
21		Mar			15			

Figure 1.5 Theta-line calculations.

optimized rather than just set by the user; however, this can be optimized if you employ the Solver as well and minimize the MSE over the fitting period. You can also use a simpler extrapolation method, such as a Moving Average or even a Naïve (Figures 1.7 and 1.8)

   (a) H5 set the smoothing parameter to whatever value you want between 0 and 1
   (b) H8 = G7
   (c) H9 = (1−H5) * G8 + H5 * H8
   (d) K4, K5 set the weight for the combination of the Theta lines
   (e) I19 = G4 + G5 * E19
   (f) J19 = (1−H5) * G18 + H5 * H18
   (g) K19 = K4 * I19 + K5 * J19

5. *Step 4*: Combine with equal weights the derived forecasts from the two Theta lines. These latter weights can also be optimized by the Solver.

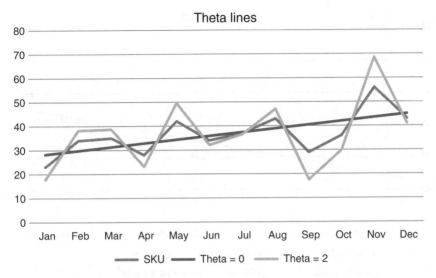

Figure 1.6 Theta-line graph.

Figure 1.7 Theta-line extrapolations.

	I	J	K
			weights
			0.5
			0.5
	Regress on Theta=0	SES on Theta=2	FORECAST
	46.576	45.034	45.805
	48.100	45.034	46.567
	49.625	45.034	47.329

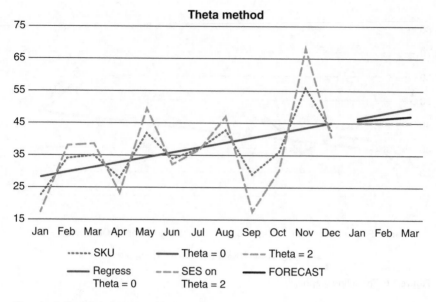

Figure 1.8 Template in MS Excel: main graph.

1.2.7 The FutuRe is Written in R

There are many implementations nowadays for the Theta method in R, but all cover only the basic version or the optimized version of Fiorucci et al. All these functions and respective packages are detailed in Chapter 6, which is the contribution of my good friend and student Dr. Fotios Petropoulos. We are also more than happy to provide the R code for the new theory and respective variations of the method in our past papers with Dimitrios (Thomakos and Nikolopoulos 2014, 2015) or in the current book, upon request at kostas@fortank.com

1.A Appendix

```
Public Sub THETA()

'Implements theta for two theta lines and with equal weights
combination; Damped
Exponential Smoothing used for extrapolation

    'Variables

        'the necessary variables hereafter used are defined here

        'this section is omitted
```

```
'Initialisations

    'the variables are initialised in this section

    'this section is omitted

'Theta parameter 0

'Sets the theta parameter

k_parameter2 = 0

'Solve the respective system and creates the Theta line

System_Theta_to_Xi

'extrapolates the Theta Line with Damped Exponential Smoothing

f_method X(), N


For k = 1 To h

  X(N + k) = f_forecasts(k)

  k1_forecasts(k) = X(N + k)

Next k

  'Theta parameter 2

k_parameter2 = 2

System_Theta_to_Xi

f_method X(), N

For k = 1 To h

  X(N + k) = f_forecasts(k)

  k2_forecasts(k) = X(N + k)

Next k


  'Linear combination of forecasts

For k = 1 To h
```

```
        final_forecasts(k) = 0.5 * k1_forecasts(k) + 0.5 *
          k2_forecasts(k)

    Next k


    'Check for negative values

    For i = 1 To h

      If final_forecasts(i) < 0 Then

          final_forecasts(i) = 0

      End If

    Next i


    'Visualise time series

    For i = 1 To N

        FORECAST_DATA(i) = Y(i)

    Next i


    For i = 1 To h

        FORECAST_DATA(i + N) = final_forecasts(i)

    Next i


End Sub
Public Sub System_Theta_to_Xi()


Dim c, sum As Double

Dim c1, c2 As Double

Dim l1, l2, l3, l4, l5, l6, l44 As Double


For i = 2 To (N - 1)

          thn(i) = k_parameter2 * th(i)

Next i
```

```
c1 = Sumarray(ORIGINALDATAY(), N)


c = trend(t(), ORIGINALDATAY(), N)


c = c * ((SumSqarray(t(), N) / N) - (meanvalue(t(), N)   2))

c = c + meanvalue(t(), N) * meanvalue(ORIGINALDATAY(), N)

c2 = c * N


l1 = (N - 1) / 2

l1 = l1 * N

l1 = -l1

l2 = N - 1

l2 = l2 * (N - 2)

l2 = l2 / 2

l2 = l2 - 1


sum = 0

For k = 2 To (N - 1)

        For i = 1 To (N - k)

                sum = sum + i * thn(k)

        Next i

Next k

l3 = sum - c1


l4 = 0

l4 = N

l4 = l4 * (N - 1)
```

```
l4 = l4 * (2 * N - 1) / 6

l44 = N

l44 = l44 * (N - 1)

l44 = l44 / 2

l4 = l4 + l44

l4 = -l4


l5 = (N - 1)

l5 = l5 * (N - 2)

l5 = l5 * (2 * N - 3) / 6

l55 = (N - 1)

l55 = l55 * (N - 2)

l55 = l55 - 1

l5 = l5 + l55


sum = 0

For k = 2 To (N - 1)

For i = 1 To (N - k)

sum = sum + i * (i + k) * thn(k)

Next i

Next k

l6 = sum - c2


system2x2 l1, l2, l3, l4, l5, l6

X(1) = x2

X(2) = x1
```

```
'Here we can replace it with a faster recursive algorithm

For k = 3 To N

        sum = 0

        For i = 1 To (k - 2)

                sum = sum + i * thn(k - i)

        Next i

        X(k) = sum + (k - 1) * X(2) - (k - 2) * X(1)

Next k


End Sub

Public Sub f_method(Y#(), ByVal N)


Static keep_back1, tasi_back1 As Double

Static synt(8) As Double


Dim gh1_1, gh1_2, gh1_final As Double 'smoothing parameters

Dim gh2_1, gh2_2, gh2_final As Double 'smoothing parameters

Dim gF_1, gF_2, gf_final As Double 'smoothing parameters


Dim g_for, g_s As Double


ReDim gx(N, 8) As Double

ReDim GX_ERROR(N, 8) As Double

ReDim TASI1(N, 8) As Double


Dim gp, gi, gj, gk, gl As Integer 'counters

Static gsum(8), gprevsum, gminsum As Double 'sums

Static gsummean(8), gvar(8) As Double

Dim hflag As Integer 'boolean
```

```
'Initialisations

synt(1) = 0.17

synt(2) = 0.17

synt(3) = 0.08

synt(4) = 0.04

synt(5) = 0.02

synt(6) = 0.015

synt(7) = 0.0005

synt(8) = 0.0001


'code

'InitiaLISATIONS

 hflag = False

 gprevsum = 1000

 gp = 0

 gh1_final = 0.5

 gh2_final = 0.5


 gf_final = 0.5

 g_for = 0

 gminsum = 0


Do Until hflag = True

  'Increase the counter

   gp = gp + 1
```

```
'Setting values to the three parameters

   gh1_1 = gh1_final - synt(gp)

   gh1_2 = gh1_final + synt(gp)


   gh2_1 = gh2_final - synt(gp)

   gh2_2 = gh2_final + synt(gp)


   gF_1 = gf_final - synt(gp)

   gF_2 = gf_final + synt(gp)


For gk = 1 To 8

   gx(1, gk) = Y(1)

Next gk

For gk = 1 To 8

  TASI1(1, gk) = Y(2) - Y(1)

Next gk


For gi = 2 To N

   'gF_1,gh1_1,gh2_1

   g_for = gx(gi - 1, 1) + gF_1 * TASI1(gi - 1, 1)

   GX_ERROR(gi, 1) = Y(gi) - g_for

   gx(gi, 1) = gx(gi - 1, 1) + gF_1 * TASI1(gi - 1, 1) + gh1_1 *
      GX_ERROR(gi, 1)

   TASI1(gi, 1) = gF_1 * TASI1(gi - 1, 1) + gh2_1 * GX_ERROR(gi, 1)

   'gF_2,gh1_1,gh2_1

   g_for = gx(gi - 1, 2) + gF_2 * TASI1(gi - 1, 2)

   GX_ERROR(gi, 2) = Y(gi) - g_for
```

```
gx(gi, 2) = gx(gi - 1, 2) + gF_2 * TASI1(gi - 1, 2) + gh1_1 *
   GX_ERROR(gi, 2)

TASI1(gi, 2) = gF_2 * TASI1(gi - 1, 2) + gh2_1 * GX_ERROR(gi, 2)

'gF_1,gh1_2,gh2_1

g_for = gx(gi - 1, 3) + gF_1 * TASI1(gi - 1, 3)

GX_ERROR(gi, 3) = Y(gi) - g_for

gx(gi, 3) = gx(gi - 1, 3) + gF_1 * TASI1(gi - 1, 3) + gh1_2 *
   GX_ERROR(gi, 3)

TASI1(gi, 3) = gF_1 * TASI1(gi - 1, 3) + gh2_1 * GX_ERROR(gi, 3)

'gF_2,gh1_2,gh2_1

g_for = gx(gi - 1, 4) + gF_2 * TASI1(gi - 1, 4)

GX_ERROR(gi, 4) = Y(gi) - g_for

gx(gi, 4) = gx(gi - 1, 4) + gF_2 * TASI1(gi - 1, 4) + gh1_2 *
   GX_ERROR(gi, 4)

TASI1(gi, 4) = gF_2 * TASI1(gi - 1, 4) + gh2_1 * GX_ERROR(gi, 4)

'gF_1,gh1_1,gh2_2

g_for = gx(gi - 1, 5) + gF_1 * TASI1(gi - 1, 5)

GX_ERROR(gi, 5) = Y(gi) - g_for

gx(gi, 5) = gx(gi - 1, 5) + gF_1 * TASI1(gi - 1, 5) + gh1_1 *
   GX_ERROR(gi, 5)

TASI1(gi, 5) = gF_1 * TASI1(gi - 1, 5) + gh2_2 * GX_ERROR(gi, 5)

'gF_2,gh1_1,gh2_2

g_for = gx(gi - 1, 6) + gF_2 * TASI1(gi - 1, 6)

GX_ERROR(gi, 6) = Y(gi) - g_for

gx(gi, 6) = gx(gi - 1, 6) + gF_2 * TASI1(gi - 1, 6) + gh1_1 *
   GX_ERROR(gi, 6)

TASI1(gi, 6) = gF_2 * TASI1(gi - 1, 6) + gh2_2 * GX_ERROR(gi, 6)

'gF_1,gh1_2,gh2_2
```

```
g_for = gx(gi - 1, 7) + gF_1 * TASI1(gi - 1, 7)

GX_ERROR(gi, 7) = Y(gi) - g_for

gx(gi, 7) = gx(gi - 1, 7) + gF_1 * TASI1(gi - 1, 7) + gh1_2 *
   GX_ERROR(gi, 7)

TASI1(gi, 7) = gF_1 * TASI1(gi - 1, 7) + gh2_2 * GX_ERROR(gi, 7)

'gF_2,gh1_2,gh2_2

g_for = gx(gi - 1, 8) + gF_2 * TASI1(gi - 1, 8)

GX_ERROR(gi, 8) = Y(gi) - g_for

gx(gi, 8) = gx(gi - 1, 8) + gF_2 * TASI1(gi - 1, 8) + gh1_2 *
   GX_ERROR(gi, 8)

TASI1(gi, 8) = gF_2 * TASI1(gi - 1, 8) + gh2_2 * GX_ERROR(gi, 8)

Next gi


'Creating sum of errors , MSE

For gk = 1 To 8

  gsum(gk) = 0

Next gk

For gk = 1 To 8

  For gi = 2 To N

    gsum(gk) = gsum(gk) + ((GX_ERROR(gi, gk))  2)

  Next gi

Next gk

For gk = 1 To 8

   gsum(gk) = gsum(gk) / (N - 1)

Next gk


'Finding min
```

```
gsummin = gsum(1)

For gk = 2 To 8

  If gsum(gk) < gsummin Then

  gsummin = gsum(gk)

  End If

Next gk

'Keeping best values

Select Case gsummin

  Case gsum(1)

    ONE_STEP_FORECAST_ERROR_VARIANCE = gvar(1)

    gf_final = gF_1

    gh1_final = gh1_1

    gh2_final = gh2_1

    If gp = 8 Then

     hflag = True

     keep_back1 = gx(N, 1)

     tasi_back1 = TASI1(N, 1)

    Else

     gprevsum = gsum(1)

    End If

  Case gsum(2)

    ONE_STEP_FORECAST_ERROR_VARIANCE = gvar(2)

    gf_final = gF_2

    gh1_final = gh1_1

    gh2_final = gh2_1

    If gp = 8 Then
```

```
    hflag = True

    keep_back1 = gx(N, 2)

    tasi_back1 = TASI1(N, 2)

  Else

    gprevsum = gsum(2)

  End If

Case gsum(3)

  ONE_STEP_FORECAST_ERROR_VARIANCE = gvar(3)

  gf_final = gF_1

  gh1_final = gh1_2

  gh2_final = gh2_1

  If gp = 8 Then

    hflag = True

    keep_back1 = gx(N, 3)

    tasi_back1 = TASI1(N, 3)

  Else

    gprevsum = gsum(3)

  End If

  Case gsum(4)

  ONE_STEP_FORECAST_ERROR_VARIANCE = gvar(4)

  gf_final = gF_2

  gh1_final = gh1_2

  gh2_final = gh2_1

  If gp = 8 Then

    hflag = True

    keep_back1 = gx(N, 4)
```

```
      tasi_back1 = TASI1(N, 4)

  Else

    gprevsum = gsum(4)

  End If

Case gsum(5)

  ONE_STEP_FORECAST_ERROR_VARIANCE = gvar(5)

  gf_final = gF_1

  gh1_final = gh1_1

  gh2_final = gh2_2

  If gp = 8 Then

    hflag = True

    keep_back1 = gx(N, 5)

    tasi_back1 = TASI1(N, 5)

  Else

    gprevsum = gsum(5)

  End If

  Case gsum(6)

    ONE_STEP_FORECAST_ERROR_VARIANCE = gvar(6)

    gf_final = gF_2

    gh1_final = gh1_1

    gh2_final = gh2_2

    If gp = 8 Then

      hflag = True

      keep_back1 = gx(N, 6)

      tasi_back1 = TASI1(N, 6)

    Else
```

```
  gprevsum = gsum(6)

  End If

Case gsum(7)

  ONE_STEP_FORECAST_ERROR_VARIANCE = gvar(7)

  gf_final = gF_1

  gh1_final = gh1_2

  gh2_final = gh2_2

  If gp = 8 Then

   hflag = True

   keep_back1 = gx(N, 7)

   tasi_back1 = TASI1(N, 7)

  Else

   gprevsum = gsum(7)

  End If

Case gsum(8)

  ONE_STEP_FORECAST_ERROR_VARIANCE = gvar(8)

  gf_final = gF_2

  gh1_final = gh1_2

  gh2_final = gh2_2

  If gp = 8 Then

   hflag = True

   keep_back1 = gx(N, 8)

   tasi_back1 = TASI1(N, 8)

  Else

   gprevsum = gsum(8)

  End If
```

```
    End Select


Loop


For gj = 1 To HORIZON

 f_forecasts(gj) = 0

 For gi = 1 To gj

  f_forecasts(gj) = f_forecasts(gj) + ((gf_final)  gi) * tasi_back1

 Next gi

 f_forecasts(gj) = f_forecasts(gj) + keep_back1

Next gj


End Sub

Public Function SumMparray(a() As Double, B() As Double, ByVal num
    As Integer) As Double

        Dim sum As Double

        Dim cntr As Integer


        sum = 0


        For cntr = 1 To num

                sum = sum + a(cntr) * B(cntr)

        Next cntr

        SumMparray = sum


End Function


Public Function meanvalue(a() As Double, ByVal num As Integer) As
    Double
```

```
        Dim sum As Double

        Dim cntr As Integer


        sum = 0


        For cntr = 1 To num

                sum = sum + a(cntr)

        Next cntr


        If num <> 0 Then

                meanvalue = sum / num

        Else

                MsgBox "N must be <> 0 ."

        End If

End Function

Public Function trend(a() As Double, B() As Double, ByVal num As
   Integer) As Double


        Dim ar, par, HELPB As Double

        Dim cntr As Integer


        ar = (SumMparray(a(), B(), num) / num) - (meanvalue(a(),
           num) * meanvalue(B(), num))

        par = (SumSqarray(a(), num) / num) - (meanvalue(a(), num)
           2)


        If par <> 0 Then

                trend = ar / par

                HELPB = ar / par

        Else
```

```
                    trend = 1000000000

        End If


        b_of_trend = meanvalue(B(), num) - HELPB * meanvalue(a(),
          num)

        intercept = b_of_trend

End Function

Public Sub system2x2(ByVal a1!, ByVal a2!, ByVal a3!, ByVal b1!,
  ByVal b2!, ByVal b3!)


        Dim det, detx1, detx2 As Double


        det = a1 * b2 - b1 * a2

        detx1 = a3 * b2 - b3 * a2

        detx2 = a1 * b3 - b1 * a3

        If det = 0 Then

                    MsgBox "System Impossible"

        Else

                    x1 = detx1 / det

                    x2 = detx2 / det

        End If

End Sub

Public Function SumSqarray(a() As Double, ByVal num As
  Integer) As Double


        Dim sum As Double

        Dim cntr As Integer


        sum = 0


        For cntr = 1 To num
```

```
                sum = sum + a(cntr) * a(cntr)

        Next cntr


        SumSqarray = sum

End Function
Public Function Sumarray(a() As Double, ByVal num As Integer)
  As Double

        Dim sum As Double

        Dim cntr As Integer


        sum = 0

        For cntr = 1 To num

                sum = sum + a(cntr)

        Next cntr


        Sumarray = sum

End Function
```

2

From the θ-method to a θ-model

By Dimitrios D. Thomakos and Kostas I. Nikolopoulos

2.1 Stochastic and Deterministic Trends and their DGPs

In our analysis of the properties of the θ-method, we focus on the general "signal + noise" model, whereas the original time series[1] Y_t is decomposed into a "trend" or "signal" or a slowly varying component denoted by $\mathcal{T}_t$ and a "noise" or "error" or "residual" component denoted by S_t. This class of models is very broad and allows for great flexibility in specifying various data-generating processes (DGPs) on it. Therefore, we start with the following representation:

$$Y_t \overset{\text{def}}{=} \mathcal{T}_t + S_t \tag{2.1}$$

The particular context of analysis will shape the form that the trend/signal component will take and whether we would be interested in accurately extracting this component or just using a particular approximation to it in order to forecast the original time series. In most of what follows, the discussion focuses more on the latter and we are interested in analyzing the properties of the θ-method when the trend/signal component is approximated by a suitable function of time or of past observations of the series itself.

Concentrating then on the case where we take $\mathcal{T}_t$ as the trend component, we first note that various forms of trend functions, such as moving averages, for smoothing can be nested into the following generic representation:

$$\mathcal{T}_t = Y_0 + \sum_{j=0}^{M} \lambda_j f_{t-j}(Y_{t-j}; \alpha) \tag{2.2}$$

where M is the degree of smoothing, the λ_j are a first set of smoothing parameters, and $f_{t-j}(\cdot)$ are known deterministic functions of time which may or may not

---

1 The terminology "series" will be used interchangeably with that of "process."

Forecasting with the Theta Method: Theory and Applications, First Edition.
Kostas I. Nikolopoulos and Dimitrios D. Thomakos.

depend on the past values of the series itself and/or another set of parameters in the vector α. For example, when $\lambda_0 = \lambda_1 = \cdots = \lambda_M = 1/(M+1)$ and $f_{t-j}(x) \equiv x$, then the usual, simple moving average smoother is obtained; when $\lambda_0 = \lambda_1 = \cdots = \lambda_M = 1$ and $f_{t-j}(Y_{t-j}, \alpha) \equiv \alpha(1-\alpha)^j Y_{t-j}$, the exponential moving average with scalar parameter α is obtained (for M large enough to have a negligible effect from the starting value of the associated recursion). The linear trend and, of course, the polynomial trends are part of the abovementioned scheme; and since we are going to be using the linear trend in what follows, we note that when $M = 0$, $\lambda_0 = \mu$, and $f_t(x) = t$ the simple linear trend representation is obtained as

$$T_t = Y_0 + \mu t \tag{2.3}$$

The properties of the second component, the "error" or "residual" or "noise" S_t, are also important in understanding the properties of the θ-method under different DGPs. We are mostly interested in two types of representation for S_t, one that generates a nonstationary series and one that generates a stationary series. This representation can be compactly written in the following way:

$$S_t \stackrel{\text{def}}{=} \sum_{j=1}^{t} \kappa_j \eta_j = \left\{ \begin{array}{ll} \eta_t & \text{when} \quad \kappa_1 \kappa_2 = \cdots \kappa_{t-1} = 0, \kappa_t = 1 \\ \sum_{j=1}^{t} \eta_j & \text{when} \quad \kappa_1 = \kappa_2 = \cdots \kappa_t = 1 \end{array} \right\} \tag{2.4}$$

that is, as a backward weighted sum of the stationary series η_t with weights given by the sequence of constants κ_j. At this stage, we only need to impose the assumptions that $E[\eta_t] = 0$, $\text{Var}[\eta_t] = \sigma_\eta^2$ and we make no other assumptions about the autocorrelation of the properties of η_t. Now, if we take it that S_t has the first formulation in the given equation, we will have a DGP corresponding to a "trend-stationary" representation, because if we remove the T_t trend component from the original series, then the remainder would be a stationary series. If we take, however, the second formulation in the equation, we have a DGP corresponding to a "stochastic trend" representation, for even if we remove the T_t trend component from the original series the remainder will still be a nonstationary process.

In the next sections, we explore the properties that the θ-method has, in a forecasting context, when we assume that the underlying DGP is either a "stochastic trend" or is of the "trend-stationary" variety.

2.2 The θ-method Applied to the Unit Root with Drift DGP

2.2.1 Main Results

We begin by considering the "stochastic trend" DGP. Letting $X_t \stackrel{\text{def}}{=} Y_t - Y_0$ denote the series after removing the initial conditions, we consider the following DGP representation:

$$X_t \overset{\text{def}}{=} \mu t + S_t \equiv \mu + X_{t-1} + \eta_t \tag{2.5}$$

This is in the form of a "random walk with drift" model, μ being the drift term, or in econometrics parlance in the form of a "unit root with drift" model – the unit root referring to the root of the characteristic polynomial of the difference equation.[2] This class of models is popular in economics and finance and is a special case of linear autoregressive models. What makes this class of models interesting is the simplicity of their mean-squared error (MSE)-based forecast function, their ability to model well the trending times series (even when these series do not correspond to the DGP), and their use as forecasting benchmarks: the MSE-based forecast from this class of models is the so-called Naíve forecast. To illustrate, let $\mathcal{F}_t \overset{\text{def}}{=} \sigma(X_t, X_{t-1}, \dots)$ denote the information set/σ-field to which we assume that the process of the DGP is adapted to and denote by $E[X_{t+1}|\mathcal{F}_t]$ the conditional expectation (projection) operator on $\mathcal{F}_t$. Then, we immediately have that the minimum MSE-based forecast is given by

$$E[X_{t+1}|\mathcal{F}_t] \overset{\text{def}}{=} \underset{g_t \in \mathcal{F}_t}{\text{argmin}} E[X_{t+1} - g_t]^2 \equiv \mu + X_t + E[\eta_{t+1}|\mathcal{F}_t] \tag{2.6}$$

and, therefore, the forecast is completely determined by the properties of the η_t series. If this series is a martingale difference process[3] and thus $E[\eta_{t+1}|\mathcal{F}_t] = 0$, then we have the Naíve forecast given by

$$F^N_{t+1} \equiv E[X_{t+1}|\mathcal{F}_t] = \mu + X_t \tag{2.7}$$

i.e. the last observed value plus the drift. We are interested in examining the θ-method in the context of the unit root DGP and to compare its forecasting performance to that of the minimum MSE-based forecast, under this DGP.

We begin by defining the θ-line, the original concept behind the application of the θ-method. In its more general formulation, the θ-line is a linear combination of the last value of the time series and its trend component as in

$$Q_t(\theta) \overset{\text{def}}{=} \theta X_t + (1 - \theta)\mathcal{T}_t \tag{2.8}$$

---

2 Let B denote the backward or lag operator such as $B^k X_t \overset{\text{def}}{=} X_{t-k}$ for integer k. Then the model of the DGP can be written as $(1 - \phi B)X_t = \mu + \eta_t$, where ϕ is the autoregressive coefficient. Solving the characteristic polynomial $1 - \phi z = 0$ for ϕ, we find that $z = 1/\phi$, which is equal to one when $\phi = 1$. Thus, the name "unit root" model.

3 A martingale difference process obeys $E[\eta_{t+1}|\mathcal{F}_t] = 0$ which also implies, by the law of iterated expectations, that $E[\eta_{t+k}\eta_t] = 0$ for all k, thus having no autocorrelation. We often call such a process an "innovation" as it conveys only new information and has no memory. When this assumption about the memory of η_{t+1} does not hold, we can write $E[\eta_{t+1}|\mathcal{F}_t] = m_t(\beta)$ for some functional parametric form $m_t(\cdot)$ with parameter vector β. Examples of $m_t(\cdot)$ include the standard ARMA(p, q) family of models.

where $\theta \in [0, 1]$ is the θ-parameter. Under the unit root DGP, this simplifies to

$$Q_t(\theta) = \theta X_t + (1 - \theta)\mu t \tag{2.9}$$

The motivation behind the original θ-line formulation was given in previous chapters and thus here we provide another way of looking at the θ-line. We know that a convex combination of two real numbers is their weighted sum with the weights being nonnegative and summing to one. A convex combination connects two points of an unknown function in a line and can, therefore, approximate the curvature of the function by that line. How suitable this approximation will be depends on the structure of the function and the local slopes that it has at the points of approximation. In our discussion, the function is the time series that we wish to forecast and the convex combination is the θ-line: the properties of the θ-line depend on the evolution of the two components of the time series T_t and S_t and the weights that we give to each. If we wish to use the θ-line as a forecasting device, then it should have some desirable probabilistic properties related to its ability to project close to the minimum MSE-based forecast. It is easy to see that if we define as the forecast the projection of the θ-line, we have

$$F_{t+1}^L \equiv \mathsf{E}[Q_{t+1}(\theta)|\mathcal{F}_t] \stackrel{\text{def}}{=} \theta(\mu + X_t) + (1 - \theta)\mu(t + 1) = \mu + Q_t(\theta) \tag{2.10}$$

when we assume that η_{t+1} follows a martingale difference process and L denotes the "levels" θ-line. We can compute the difference between the minimum MSE-based forecast and the forecast based on the θ-line as in

$$F_{t+1}^N - F_{t+1}^L = (1 - \theta)S_t \tag{2.11}$$

and we can see that this difference implies that the θ-method has accounted only for the presence of the linear trend, i.e. the mean of the series $\mathsf{E}[X_t] \stackrel{\text{def}}{=} \mu t$, thus leaving out of the forecast function the stochastic trend component. The corresponding forecast error from the use of the θ-line is given as

$$e_{t+1}^L \stackrel{\text{def}}{=} \mu(t + 1) + S_{t+1} - \mu - \theta X_t - (1 - \theta)\mu t = S_{t+1} - \theta S_t \tag{2.12}$$

i.e. it forms an autoregressive model in the stochastic trend component. We can immediately see that (i) the levels forecast error is possibly a nonstationary process, unless θ is equal to 1, or we assume that this quasi-differenced process is stationary for any positive value of θ; (ii) the levels forecast error is unbiased since $\mathsf{E}[S_{t+1}] = 0$ by the assumptions already made for η_{t+1}. Known results from the theory of unit root processes imply that if we try to minimize the MSE of the forecast with respect to θ, that is

$$\min_{\theta} \mathsf{E}[S_{t+1} - \theta S_t]^2 \tag{2.13}$$

we will find the optimal estimate being given by $\theta^{*,L} \overset{\text{def}}{=} E[S_{t+1}S_t]/E[S_t^2] \equiv 1$ and that its sample counterpart $\hat{\theta}^{*,L}$ is super-consistent[4] for $\theta^{*,L}$. Thus, the levels forecast function of the θ-line is not going to provide us with a forecast different from the minimum MSE-based forecast for the DGP, when η_{t+1} is a martingale difference process – as we have been assuming so far.

These results suggest that the natural next step is to consider the θ-line, and the analysis so far, in differences and not in levels. We can easily compute the difference[5] of the projection of the levels θ-line and the projection of the differenced θ-line as given here:

$$\Delta E[Q_{t+1}(\theta)|\mathcal{F}_t] = \Delta Q_t(\theta) = \theta \Delta X_t + (1-\theta)\mu \tag{2.14}$$

being the difference of the levels projection, and the projection of the differenced θ-line as in

$$E[\Delta Q_{t+1}(\theta)|\mathcal{F}_t] \overset{\text{def}}{=} \theta(\mu + E[\eta_{t+1}|\mathcal{F}_t]) + (1-\theta)\mu = \mu \tag{2.15}$$

which, as expected, equals to μ if η_{t+1} is a martingale difference process. Combining these two equations, we can express the difference of the levels projection as

$$\Delta E[Q_{t+1}(\theta)|\mathcal{F}_t] = \Delta Q_t(\theta) = \theta \Delta X_t + (1-\theta)E[\Delta Q_{t+1}(\theta)|\mathcal{F}_t] \tag{2.16}$$

that is, the difference of the levels projection is a convex combination of the difference of the series and the projection of the differenced θ-line. Following the practice of ARIMA(p, d, q)-type models, we can next construct a θ-forecast from the above-given equation as follows:

$$F_{t+1}^D \overset{\text{def}}{=} X_t + \Delta E[Q_{t+1}(\theta)|\mathcal{F}_t] = X_t + \Delta Q_t(\theta) = \mu + X_t + \theta(\Delta X_t - \mu) \tag{2.17}$$

which is in the form of an ARIMA$(1, 1, 0)$ forecast function. The associated forecast error of the abovementioned forecast is given by

$$e_{t+1}^D = \mu(t+1) + S_{t+1} - \mu t - S_t - \mu - \theta(\mu + \eta_t) - (1-\theta)\mu \tag{2.18}$$

$$= \eta_{t+1} - \theta\eta_t$$

And, as we can now easily see, the differences forecast error is both stationary and unbiased by construction. We also immediately obtain that the

---

4 Converging in probability to $\theta^{*,L}$ at a rate faster than $\sqrt{T}$, T being the sample size used in estimation.

5 The difference operator is defined in terms of the backward operator B as $\Delta \overset{\text{def}}{=} 1 - B$.

MSE-optimal value of θ is given by

$$\theta^{*,D} = \underset{\theta}{\arg\min}\, E[\eta_{t+1} - \theta\eta_t]^2 = \sigma_\eta(1)/\sigma_\eta^2 \overset{def}{=} \rho_\eta(1) \tag{2.19}$$

where $\sigma_\eta(1) \overset{def}{=} E[\eta_{t+1}\eta_t]$ and where $\rho_\eta(1)$ is the first-order serial correlation of the η_{t+1} process and the MSE-optimal θ is this first-order autocorrelation of the innovations of the DGP. This will of course be zero if the η_{t+1} is a martingale difference process; but if it is not, then we see that the differenced-based θ-forecast will improve upon the Naíve forecast. Two results of practical usefulness thus emerge from our analysis: (i) we can construct feasible θ-line forecast functions in both levels and differences and we can easily find the properties of the resulting forecast errors, which are unbiased in both cases; (ii) the θ-line forecast based on differences can account for first-order serial correlation in the η_{t+1} process "automatically" if we use the MSE-optimal value of θ. This second finding can potentially explain the excellent performance of the original θ-method in the M3 forecasting competition: for trending time series, with deterministic and stochastic trends, if the underlying DGP is one of the unit roots with drift type, the θ-line forecast can be close to the MSE-optimal forecast under certain assumptions for the η_{t+1} process and that the ARIMA(1, 1, 0) form representation implies a very popular, compact, and powerful (in performance) forecast function. Thus, the θ-based forecast will be a top contender, in terms of forecasting performance, for any type of trending time series that has deterministic and or stochastic trends, with or without serial correlation. Furthermore, these results do provide support for the term "method" rather than "model" since the applicability of the method is not related (although it can be explained) by the DGP.

2.2.2 Alternative Trend Functions and the Original θ-line Approach

A question that naturally arises is whether one can consider a different form for the trend function, instead of the one dictated by the unit root DGP, and what the forecast function and properties of the forecast error might be in this case. A possible approach, which is also adopted in general in the next section, is to proxy the trend by a moving average – the question of the length of the moving average being open to consideration. Here, we provide a suggestive approach suited to both the use of moving averages for assessing trends and also for short-term forecasting. To this end, let the trend function be approximated by the shortest possible moving average of length 2, i.e. by $0.5(X_t + X_{t-1})$, and take the levels forecast function to obtain

$$F_{t+1}^{MA} \overset{def}{=} \theta X_t + (1 - \theta)0.5(X_t + X_{t-1})$$
$$= 0.5\theta\Delta X_t + 0.5(X_t + X_{t-1}) \tag{2.20}$$

where we see the desirable result, that the first differences of the original series enters along with the moving average component. This is suggestive of possible better properties for the corresponding forecast error than the plain levels forecast function we have seen before. Computing the forecast error under the DGP we get

$$
\begin{aligned}
e_{t+1}^{MA} \overset{\text{def}}{=} & \ \mu(t+1) + S_t + \eta_{t+1} \\
& - 0.5\theta(\mu + \eta_t) - 0.5\left[\mu t + S_{t-1} + \eta_t + \mu(t-1) + S_{t-1}\right] \\
= & \ 0.5\mu(3 - \theta) + \eta_{t+1} - 0.5\eta_t(\theta + 1)
\end{aligned}
\tag{2.21}
$$

and is immediately obvious that the forecast error is biased by $E[e_{t+1}^{MA}] = 0.5\mu(3 - \theta)$, but otherwise has a form similar to the differences forecast function. The presence of θ in the forecast error bias does not create a practical problem since we can obtain the bias-adjusted form of the forecast function as

$$
F_{t+1}^{MA,BA} \overset{\text{def}}{=} 0.5\theta\Delta X_t + 0.5(X_t + X_{t-1}) + 0.5\mu(3 - \theta)
\tag{2.22}
$$

and then proceed as before with the unbiased forecast error, i.e. $e_{t+1}^{MA,BA} = \eta_{t+1} - 0.5\eta_t(\theta + 1)$, from which we can obtain the minimum MSE-optimal value of θ for this case as in

$$
\theta^{*,MA} \overset{\text{def}}{=} \underset{\theta}{\arg\min} \ E[\eta_{t+1} - 0.5\eta_t(\theta + 1)]^2 = 2\sigma_\eta(1)/\sigma_\eta^2 - 1
\tag{2.23}
$$

where the condition for $\theta < 1$ is satisfied not only by the stationarity of η_t but also by the construction of the estimator. Thus, there is at least one possible alternative for the trend function under this DGP that provides an unbiased θ-based forecast for which an optimal value of the θ-parameter can be obtained.

We next turn our attention to the θ-method applied by Assimakopoulos and Nikolopoulos on the M3 forecasting competition data. In that case, the method was one where the forecast is formed as an equally weighted combination of two projected θ-lines, usually with $\theta = 0$ and with $\theta = 2$. Denoting the weighted combination of the two lines as

$$
Q_t(\theta_1, \theta_2, w) = wQ_t(\theta_1) + (1 - w)Q_t(\theta_2)
\tag{2.24}
$$

we can easily establish that the following holds for $w = 0.5$:

$$
\begin{aligned}
E\left[Q_{t+1}(0, 2, 0.5)|\mathcal{F}_t\right] = & \ 0.5E\left[Q_{t+1}(0)|\mathcal{F}_t\right] + 0.5E\left[Q_{t+1}(2)|\mathcal{F}_t\right] \\
= & \ 0.5\left[\mu + Q_t(0)\right] + 0.5\left[\mu + Q_t(2)\right] \\
= & \ 0.5\mu(t+1) + 0.5\left(\mu + 2X_t - \mu t\right)
\end{aligned}
\tag{2.25}
$$

and upon completing the algebra on the last line, we can immediately see that the forecast is given by $E\left[Q_{t+1}(0, 2, 0.5)|\mathcal{F}_t\right] = \mu + X_t$, i.e. the equally weighted θ-lines forecast coincides with the optimal, under the DGP, minimum MSE forecast, maintaining the assumption that η_{t+1} is the martingale difference process (but note that this result holds more generally upon noting that all that is required is that $w\theta_1 + (1 - w)\theta_2 = 1$). This could explain the success of the θ-method which was implemented by Assimakopoulos and Nikolopoulos in the M3 forecasting competition almost as in the earlier discussion, and where the majority of the dataset was made of trending series. It is immediate that the abovementioned result will also hold when the η_{t+1} process has some form of a parametric model, for that accounts for serial correlation and this is taken into account in the derivations – of course, this comes at the cost of removing the simplicity of the method as it will revert things to full parametric modeling.[6]

We can derive another interesting result based on the unit root DGP that relates to the original application of the θ-method. Suppose that instead of using the optimal value of the θ-parameter, one combines the two θ-lines with $\theta_1 = 0$ and $\theta_2 = 2$, and then optimizes the weight attached to each one of the lines. Thus, consider the following forecast function:

$$F^C_{t+1}(0, 2, w) = w[\mu + Q_t(0)] + (1 - w)[\mu + Q_t(2)]$$

$$= w\mu(t + 1) + (1 - w)(\mu + 2X_t - \mu t) \tag{2.26}$$

$$= \mu[(2w - 1)t + 1] + 2(1 - w)X_t$$

and optimize the value of the weight parameter w by minimizing the MSE of the first difference of the forecast function as in

$$\min_w \mathrm{E}[\Delta X_{t+1} - \Delta F^C_{t+1}(0, 2, w)]^2 \tag{2.27}$$

and upon expanding the expression within the above-given MSE we can arrive at

$$\Delta X_{t+1} - \Delta F^C_{t+1}(0, 2, w) = \Delta X_{t+1} - \mu(2w - 1) - 2(1 - w)\Delta X_t$$

$$= \mu + \eta_{t+1} - \mu(2w - 1) - 2(1 - w)(\mu + \eta_t)$$

$$= \eta_{t+1} - 2(1 - w)\eta_t \tag{2.28}$$

which has the immediate solution $w^* = 1 - 0.5\rho_\eta(1)$. Inserting back this optimal value for the weight parameter into the forecast function in first differences, we next obtain

$$\Delta F_{t+1}(0, 2, 1 - 0.5\rho_\eta(1)) = \mu[2(1 - 0.5\rho_\eta(1)) - 1]$$

$$+ 2(1 - 1 + 0.5\rho_\eta(1))\Delta X_t\mu + \rho_\eta(1)(\Delta X_t - \mu) \tag{2.29}$$

which is identical to the θ-forecast in differences using $\theta^{*,D}$.

---

6 A comment should be made at this juncture about the generality of our results compared to Hydman and Billah. In the context of our discussion, we start off with a much more general DGP than the special case of the Hydman and Billah results: in our case, the η_{t+1} can take the form of an arbitrary, zero-mean stationary process with more complicated characteristics than those assumed in Hydman and Billah. It should be clear from the presentation so far that one should not confuse our illustrative special case of having η_{t+1} as a martingale difference (which *is* a special case of Hydman and Billah) with the full generality that is allowed to η_{t+1}.

2.2.3 Implementing the θ-method under the Unit Root DGP

Our presentation so far has been on the theoretical properties of the θ-method and with parameters set to their optimal theoretical/expected values. The transition to practical application is, for this DGP, really straightforward. To this end, we assume that a sample of T observations $\{X_t\}_{t=1}^{T}$ is available for estimation and we proceed in the following steps, for the two θ-forecast functions that was said to be viable in applications.

1. Difference the series to obtain ΔX_t and compute the sample mean that corresponds to the drift parameter, i.e. $\hat{\mu} = (T-1)^{-1} \sum_{t=2}^{T} \Delta X_t$.
2. Compute the first-order serial correlation coefficient from the demeaned differenced series, i.e. take $\hat{\eta}_t = \Delta X_t - \hat{\mu}$ and estimate $\hat{\rho}_{\hat{\eta}}(1) = \sum_{t=2}^{T-1} \hat{\eta}_{t+1}\hat{\eta}_t / \sum_{t=2}^{T} \hat{\eta}_t^2$.
3. Depending on the selected forecast function, obtain the optimal value of θ as either $\hat{\theta}^{*,D} = \hat{\rho}_{\hat{\eta}}(1)$ or as $\hat{\theta}^{*,MA} = 2\hat{\rho}_{\hat{\eta}}(1) - 1$.
4. Compute the appropriate θ-line either as $\Delta Q_T(\hat{\theta}^{*,D}) = \hat{\theta}^{*,D}\Delta X_T + (1 - \hat{\theta}^{*,D})\hat{\mu}$ or as $Q_T(\hat{\theta}^{*,MA}) = \hat{\theta}^{*,MA}X_T + (1 - \hat{\theta}^{*,MA})0.5(X_T + X_{T-1})$.
5. Compute the final forecasts as either $\hat{F}_{T+1}^{D} = X_T + \Delta Q_T(\hat{\theta}^{*,D})$ or as $\hat{F}_{T+1}^{MA,BA} = Q_T(\hat{\theta}^{*,MA}) + 0.5\hat{\mu}(3 - \hat{\theta}^{*,MA})$.

Further discussion on the empirical application of these steps can be found in the chapter that follows.

2.3 The θ-method Applied to the Trend-stationary DGP

In this section, we expand our presentation so far to the case of the trend-stationary DGP. Here, we have to address both the modifications needed to the θ-line and associated forecast functions and also to the implications that might arise from the more generic trend function that enters in the computations. We start by the appropriate θ-line, taking the standard form as before:

$$Q_{t+1}(\theta) \overset{\text{def}}{=} \theta X_{t+1} + (1 - \theta)\mathcal{T}_{t+1} \tag{2.30}$$

where the trend function component $\mathcal{T}_{t+1}$ remains, as yet, unspecified. Projecting one period ahead under the DGP we easily obtain that:

$$E\left[Q_{t+1}(\theta)|\mathcal{F}_t\right] \overset{\text{def}}{=} E\left[\mathcal{T}_{t+1}|\mathcal{F}_t\right] + \theta E\left[\eta_{t+1}|\mathcal{F}_t\right] \tag{2.31}$$

and under the assumption that the innovations are from a martingale difference process we immediately have that $E\left[Q_{t+1}(\theta)|\mathcal{F}_t\right] = E\left[\mathcal{T}_{t+1}|\mathcal{F}_t\right]$, i.e. the ex ante projection of the θ-line coincides with the trend projection. In this case, it is easy to also see that

$$E[X_{t+1}(\theta)|\mathcal{F}_t] \equiv E[Q_{t+1}(\theta)|\mathcal{F}_t] \tag{2.32}$$

i.e. the ex ante projection of the θ-line coincides with the minimum MSE forecast. To maintain consistency with our previous results, on the unit root DGP, we thus define the (single) θ-line forecast function as

$$F_{t+1}^s \overset{\text{def}}{=} \theta X_t + (1-\theta)\mathcal{T}_{t+1} \tag{2.33}$$

with the trend function extrapolated one period ahead, and note that it follows that

$$E[F_{t+1}^s|\mathcal{F}_t] = E[\mathcal{T}_{t+1}|\mathcal{F}_t] + \theta(X_t - E[\mathcal{T}_{t+1}|\mathcal{F}_t]) \tag{2.34}$$

which simplifies to $E[F_{t+1}^s|\mathcal{F}_t] = E[X_{t+1}|\mathcal{F}_t] + \theta(X_t - E[X_{t+1}|\mathcal{F}_t])$ under the assumption of martingale differences for η_{t+1}. That is, the projection of the single θ-line forecast is a linear combination of the last observation and the minimum MSE forecast. As we have remarked before, the usefulness of the method lies in the fact that we cannot possibly know ex ante whether the η_{t+1} series is a martingale difference process. Thus, the simplicity of the proposed forecast function attempts to cover the contingencies arising from both the unknown trend function and the serial correlation properties of the error series. Defining the forecast errors as

$$e_{t+1}^s \overset{\text{def}}{=} X_{t+1} - F_{t+1}^s \tag{2.35}$$

and taking into account the DGP, we easily find that

$$\begin{aligned} e_{t+1}^s &= \mathcal{T}_{t+1} + \eta_{t+1} - \theta\mathcal{T}_t - \theta\eta_t - \mathcal{T}_{t+1} + \theta\mathcal{T}_{t+1} \\ &= \eta_{t+1} - \theta\eta_t + \theta\Delta\mathcal{T}_{t+1} \end{aligned} \tag{2.36}$$

which implies that "single" θ-line forecast is biased since $E[e_{t+1}^s] = \theta E[\Delta\mathcal{T}_{t+1}]$, which is different from zero in general. Noting, however, that the change in the trend function corresponds to a drift term (e.g. in the case of a linear trend, this would be the slope parameter), we can construct a bias-adjusted forecast function that performs smoothing and forecasting at the same time:

$$F_{t+1}^{s,\text{BA}} \overset{\text{def}}{=} F_{t+1}^s + \theta\Delta E[\mathcal{T}_{t+1}] \tag{2.37}$$

so that we implement a "slope" correction and the forecast error becomes unbiased and now has the form:

$$e_{t+1}^s = (\eta_{t+1} - \theta\eta_t) + \theta(\Delta\mathcal{T}_{t+1} - \Delta E[\mathcal{T}_{t+1}]) \tag{2.38}$$

which is now unbiased. In applications, the bias correction can easily be implemented as the sample mean of the first difference of any chosen trend function (taken over the window of observations used for training the data). Given this form of the forecast error, we can easily get the MSE-optimal value of θ for this case as follows:

$$\theta^{*,s} = \underset{\theta}{\mathrm{argmin}}\ \mathrm{E}[(\eta_{t+1} - \theta\eta_t) + \theta(\Delta\mathcal{T}_{t+1} - \Delta\mathrm{E}\,[\mathcal{T}_{t+1}])]^2 = \sigma_\eta(1)/(\sigma_\eta^2 - \sigma_\tau^2)$$

(2.39)

where it is assumed that the error series η_{t+1} is orthogonal to the trend function and where the variance of the differenced trend function is given by $\sigma_\tau^2 \overset{\text{def}}{=} \mathrm{E}[\Delta\mathcal{T}_{t+1} - \Delta\mathrm{E}\,[\mathcal{T}_{t+1}]]^2$. For a positive value of θ, we thus require that the variance of the innovations is higher than the variance of the difference in the trend. If the trend is completely deterministic with no unknown parameters, then we can easily see that $\sigma_\tau^2 = 0$ and the optimal value of θ is again the first-order autocorrelation of the error series. If we were to repeat this analysis by taking as the forecast function the θ line itself we will find, after redoing the algebra, that the new forecast error would be of the form $e_{t+1}^s \overset{\text{def}}{=} (\eta_{t+1} - \theta\eta_t) + \Delta\mathcal{T}_{t+1}$, i.e. the θ would be absent in front of the difference of the trend function. Thus, the same discussion as made earlier applies i.e. a bias correction via the mean of the first difference of the trend and an MSE-optimal value of θ that corresponds again to $\rho_\eta(1)$ without the presence of σ_τ^2. In applications, either of these two approaches can be used.

However, in the applications we have to use an estimate of the trend function, say $\widehat{\mathcal{T}}_t$, and it is instruction to explore what difference – if any – this will make in our abovementioned derivations. Substituting for $\mathcal{T}_{t+1}$ with $\widehat{\mathcal{T}}_{t+1}$, in the abovementioned expression for the unbiased forecast function, and doing the algebra again, we can write the new forecast error as

$$\widehat{e}_{t+1}^{s,\mathrm{BA}} = (\mathcal{T}_{t+1} - \widehat{\mathcal{T}}_{t+1}) + (\eta_{t+1} - \theta\eta_t) - \theta(\mathcal{T}_t - \widehat{\mathcal{T}}_t)$$

(2.40)

where, in contrast to what we had before, there are now two terms with differences between the actual and the estimated trend. If, however, the expectation of the trend estimate coincides with the expectation of the trend function, i.e. $\mathrm{E}\,[\widehat{\mathcal{T}}_{t+1}] = \mathrm{E}\,[\mathcal{T}_{t+1}]$, then this new forecast error will be unbiased as well. Note that in all our derivations so far we have not imposed unbiasedness of the trend function itself, for if we have that $\mathrm{E}\,[\widehat{\mathcal{T}}_{t+1}] = \mathrm{E}\,[\mathcal{T}_{t+1}] = \mathcal{T}_{t+1}$ then the same results do obtain as well and in simpler form. Thus, substituting into the expression of the forecast function, the estimated value of the trend function does not alter the unbiasedness of the forecast error.

The θ-line can be used as a smoother for the observations, as we next illustrate, and this provides us with the basis for developing the double θ method as follows. Define the residuals after smoothing the observations by the θ-line as $h_t(\theta)$ and write

$$h_t(\theta) = X_t - Q_t(\theta) = (1 - \theta)\eta_t$$

(2.41)

with resulting residual variance given by $\mathsf{Var}[h_t(\theta)] \stackrel{\text{def}}{=} \sigma_h^2 = (1-\theta)^2\sigma_\eta^2$. Given the DGP, the corresponding proportion of variance explained by smoothing is then given by

$$\frac{\sigma_h^2}{\sigma_\eta^2} = (1-\theta)^2 \tag{2.42}$$

and thus θ takes on another interpretation, that of a variance ratio, and furthermore one can choose θ by a desired proportion of explained variances. That is, $\theta^s \stackrel{\text{def}}{=} 1 - (\sigma_h/\sigma_\eta)$, and if one wants to explain $q\%$ of total variance then we will have that $\theta^s = 1 - q$.

If smoothing is considered a valid first part of the analysis, and interest in forecasting rests with the trend component mainly, we can propose a "double" θ forecasting function as follows: take the θ-line as the data (using a first θ-parameter, say θ_1) and apply the θ-forecast function to the differences of the smoother (using a second θ-parameter, say θ_2), to have

$$F_{t+1}^d(\theta_1,\theta_2) \equiv F_{t+1}^d = Q_t(\theta_1) + \theta_2\Delta Q_t(\theta_1) + (1-\theta_2)\delta \tag{2.43}$$

where δ is to be determined by the properties of the resulting forecast error. Note that the abovementioned forecast function is in the form of a forecast function in differences, as seen in the previous section for the unit root DGP, and thus consistent with the use of the smoother as the data. With the same approach as before, we find that the forecast error now becomes

$$e_{t+1}^d = (\Delta\mathcal{T}_{t+1} - \theta_2\Delta\mathcal{T}_t) + (\eta_{t+1} - \theta_1\eta_t) - \theta_1\theta_2\Delta\eta_t - (1-\theta_2)\delta \tag{2.44}$$

which is unbiased if we take $\delta \stackrel{\text{def}}{=} \mathsf{E}[\Delta\mathcal{T}_{t+1}] = \mathsf{E}[\Delta\mathcal{T}_t]$, i.e. δ should be the mean of the change in the forecast function and constant. This is more restrictive than before because it precludes polynomial trends or trends that deviate a lot from linearity (e.g. exponential trends). As before, the forecast function still produces an unbiased forecast error when we substitute the estimated trend function in place of the unknown trend. Under our maintained assumption that $\mathsf{E}[\widehat{\mathcal{T}}_{t+1}] = \mathsf{E}[\mathcal{T}_{t+1}]$ and that the mean of the change in the trend is constant and equal to δ, the forecast error is still unbiased. To see this:

$$\begin{aligned}\widehat{e}_{t+1}^d = (T_{t+1} - \widehat{\mathcal{T}}_t) - \theta_1(T_t - \widehat{\mathcal{T}}_t) - \theta_1\theta_2\Delta\mathcal{T}_t \\ - \theta_2(1-\theta_1)\Delta\widehat{\mathcal{T}}_t - (1-\theta_2)\delta + (\eta_{t+1} - \theta_1\eta_t) - \theta_1\theta_2\Delta\eta_t\end{aligned} \tag{2.45}$$

and straightforward application of the $\mathsf{E}[\cdot]$ expectation operator shows that we maintain unbiasedness. The effective, computable forecast function for double θ now becomes

$$\widehat{F}_{t+1}^d(\theta_1,\theta_2) \equiv \widehat{F}_{t+1}^d \stackrel{\text{def}}{=} \widehat{Q}_t(\theta_1) + \theta_2\Delta\widehat{Q}_t(\theta_1) + (1-\theta_2)\widehat{\delta} \tag{2.46}$$

where $\widehat{\delta}$ is estimated using the sample mean of the differences of the trend. Now the "optimal" two θ parameters can easily be found by numerical optimization on the unit square on a set of training data.

2.3.1 Implementing the θ-method under the Trend-stationary DGP

The choice of the trend function $\mathcal{T}_t$ is of course crucial in the forecasting performance of the method in the current context. There is a plethora of ways that this can be specified and we outline these here. Subject matter considerations and previous knowledge of the type of trend should, of course, be incorporated into the trend selection process.

1. Polynomial trends, $\mathcal{T}_t \overset{\text{def}}{=} \sum_{j=0}^{M} \beta_j t^j$, or some form of polynomial basis (e.g. Bernstein polynomials).
2. Moving averages, as explained in the beginning of the chapter, such as simple or exponential moving averages.
3. Singular spectrum analysis (SSA) trends; SSA is a well-established method for trend extraction, smoothing, and forecasting and can provide an additional benchmark to compare the θ-method with.
4. Unobserved component (UC) model trends, as the popular local level model, i.e. to consider the form of the DGP as being

$$\mathcal{T}_t \overset{\text{def}}{=} \mathcal{T}_{t-1} + \epsilon_t \tag{2.47}$$

with $\mathcal{T}_T$ being unobserved, ϵ_t be the trend innovation, independent of η_t and with $\text{Var}[\epsilon_t] \overset{\text{def}}{=} \sigma_\epsilon^2$ and to ignore the resulting state-space model for forecasting[7] but use it purely for extracting the slowly varying component of X_t. We note that the relationship $\sigma_\epsilon^2 < \sigma_\eta^2$ is a requirement of the trend to be "smoother" than the data.

Given an estimate for the trend $\widehat{\mathcal{T}}_t$, we can outline the steps for the implementation of the θ-method in the case of the trend-stationary DGP as follows:

1. Compute the residual series $\widehat{\eta}_t \overset{\text{def}}{=} X_t - \widehat{\mathcal{T}}_t$ and the mean of the difference in the estimated trend $\widehat{\delta} = T^{-1} \sum_{t=1}^{T} \Delta \widehat{\mathcal{T}}_t$.
2. Compute the variance and first-order autocovariance coefficients from the residual series, i.e. take $\widehat{\sigma}_{\widehat{\eta}}(1) = \sum_{t=2}^{T-1} \widehat{\eta}_{t+1} \widehat{\eta}_t$ and $\widehat{\sigma}_{\widehat{\eta}}^2 = \sum_{t=2}^{T} \widehat{\eta}_t^2$.
3. Depending on the selected forecast function, obtain the optimal value of θ as either $\widehat{\theta}^{*,s} = \widehat{\rho}_{\widehat{\eta}}(1) = \widehat{\sigma}_{\widehat{\eta}}(1)/\widehat{\sigma}_{\widehat{\eta}}^2$ or as $\widehat{\theta}^{*,s} = \widehat{\sigma}_{\widehat{\eta}}(1)/(\widehat{\sigma}_{\widehat{\eta}}^2 - \widehat{\sigma}_\tau^2)$ for the single θ-line approach, or as the pair $(\widehat{\theta}_1^{*,d}, \widehat{\theta}_2^{*,d})$ for the double θ-line approach (the latter obtained through numerical optimization). Here,

---

7 It is well known that the minimum MSE forecast function for X_t under this form of the trend is that of an ARIMA(0, 1, 1) model.

$\hat{\sigma}_\tau^2 = T^{-1} \sum_{t=1}^{T} (\Delta \hat{\mathcal{T}}_t - \hat{\delta})^2$ is the estimated variance of the difference of the trend.

4. Compute the appropriate θ-line for the single θ-line forecast as $Q_T(\hat{\theta}^{*,s}) = \hat{\theta}^{*,s} X_T + (1 - \hat{\theta}^{*,s}) \hat{\mathcal{T}}_{T+1}$, where the estimated trend can be extrapolated to $T+1$ depending on its form or else it is set to the last available value at T.

5. Compute the final forecasts as either $\hat{F}_{t+1}^{s,\text{BA}} = Q_T(\hat{\theta}^{*,s}) + \hat{\theta}^{*,s} \hat{\delta}$ or $\hat{F}_{t+1}^{s,\text{BA}} = Q_T(\hat{\theta}^{*,s}) + \hat{\delta}$ for the single θ-line approach (again depending on whether we extrapolate the trend component of the θ-line or not) or as $\hat{F}_{T+1}^d = \hat{Q}_T(\hat{\theta}_1^{*,d}) + \hat{\theta}_2^{*,d} \Delta \hat{Q}_T(\hat{\theta}_1^{*,d}) + (1 - \hat{\theta}_2^{*,d}) \hat{\delta}$ for the double θ-line approach.

We elaborate on the empirical implementation of these steps in the chapter on applications that follows.

2.3.2 Is the AR(1)-forecast a θ-forecast?

Finally, before closing this chapter, it is instructive to illustrate as to why the trend-stationary θ-forecast can be effective even in a time series that does not have a trend, i.e. is stationary to begin with. Consider an AR(1) model with a constant term, i.e.

$$X_t = \alpha_0 + \alpha_1 X_{t-1} + \eta_t \tag{2.48}$$

whose parameters are to be estimated by least squares. Then, the out-of-sample, one-step-ahead forecast becomes $\hat{X}_{T+1} = \hat{\alpha}_0 + \hat{\alpha}_1 X_T$ where $\hat{\alpha}_0 = \overline{X}_{T,2} - \hat{\alpha}_1 \overline{X}_{T,1}$, where $\overline{X}_{T,j} \overset{\text{def}}{=} (T-1)^{-1} \sum_{t=j}^{T-2+j} X_t$ are the sample means of the dependent variable and its first lag, respectively. Now, for a large sample we should have that $\overline{X}_{T,2} \approx \overline{X}_{T,1}$, both being equal to the sample mean $\overline{X}_T$. We can thus write the AR(1) forecast as

$$\hat{X}_{T+1} = (\overline{X}_T - \hat{\alpha}_1 \overline{X}_T) + \hat{\alpha}_1 X_T \tag{2.49}$$

which is easily seen to be equivalent to

$$\hat{X}_{T+1} = \hat{\alpha}_1 X_T + (1 - \hat{\alpha}_1) \overline{X}_T \tag{2.50}$$

which is in the form of both the single θ-forecast function for the trend-stationary DGP case but also in the form of the levels θ-forecast function in the unit root DGP case; here, the sample mean estimates the "trend" (the constant level of the series) and, by design, the α_1 parameter is the θ-parameter for the stationary region of $\alpha_1 \in [0, 1]$. Thus, the θ-method is, in the end, not just suited for trended series but also for the stationary series; and for them it will resemble the most important time series benchmark, the simple AR(1) model.

3

The Multivariate θ-method

By Dimitrios D. Thomakos and Kostas I. Nikolopoulos

3.1 The Bivariate θ-method for the Unit Root DGP

In this chapter, we explore the extensions of the univariate θ-method to the case where we have more than one time series under study. One would not be amiss in thinking that the initial conceptual simplicity of the method will lend itself to a straightforward multivariate extension. It turns out that there are some useful implications to be discovered when dealing with the multivariate case. We explore these implications in what follows.

We start with the basics and the $(K \times 1)$ vector of time series $X_t \stackrel{\text{def}}{=} [X_{t1}, X_{t2}, \dots, X_{tK}]^\top$. The properties of the individual series are yet left unspecified and we write the multivariate θ-line as in

$$Q_t(\Theta) = \Theta X_t + (I - \Theta)\mathcal{T}_t \tag{3.1}$$

where Θ is the $(K \times K)$ matrix of the θ-parameters and $\mathcal{T}_t$ is the $(K \times 1)$ vector of the trend functions. If we assume that X_t follows a multivariate random walk/unit root model with drift vector μ, that is

$$X_t = \mu t + S_t \tag{3.2}$$

with $S_t \stackrel{\text{def}}{=} \sum_{j=1}^{t} \eta_t$ being the multivariate analog of the univariate case, then we can correspondingly write

$$Q_t(\Theta) = \Theta X_t + (I - \Theta)\mu t \tag{3.3}$$

To better understand the potential implications of the multivariate θ-line, we next turn our attention to the bivariate case $K = 2$ and, for exploiting potential co-movement components, assume that the multivariate unit root model noted earlier holds. Then, we can write explicitly the two equations that form $Q_t(\Theta)$ as in

$$Q_{t1}(\theta_{11}, \theta_{12}) = \theta_{11}X_{t1} + \theta_{12}X_{t2} + (1 - \theta_{11})\mu_1 t - \theta_{12}\mu_2 t$$

$$Q_{t2}(\theta_{21}, \theta_{22}) = \theta_{21}X_{t1} + \theta_{22}X_{t2} - \theta_{21}\mu_1 t + (1 - \theta_{22})\mu_2 t \tag{3.4}$$

where the positioning of the indices in θ_{ij} follows standard matrix algebra practice. This expression can be informatively rewritten as

$$Q_{t1}(\theta_{11}, \theta_{12}) = Q_{t1}(\theta_{11}) + \theta_{12}(X_{t2} - \mu_2 t)$$

$$Q_{t2}(\theta_{21}, \theta_{22}) = Q_{t2}(\theta_{22}) + \theta_{21}(X_{t1} - \mu_1 t) \tag{3.5}$$

We see, therefore, that in extending from the univariate to the bivariate θ-line we are merging the univariate component with an additional one which has an interpretation similar to that of *causality*. That is, the bivariate θ-line would be different from the univariate for at least one of the two time series if and only if $\theta_{ij} \neq 0$, $i \neq j$, for at least one of the off-diagonal parameters. When this (these) condition(s) hold, we have that the bivariate θ-line is different from the univariate one and that one might expect different forecasting performances between the univariate and bivariate approaches.

For the bivariate unit root data-generating process (DGP), we can easily extend the univariate results for the two forecasting functions, in levels and in differences. As one might expect in the bivariate case under this DGP, the forecast functions are similar to a first-order vector autoregression (VAR). As we show in what follows, there are some interesting twists to discuss in the current context, as the case of cointegrated series enters the picture. To continue, we then write the two forecast functions, in levels and in differences, as

$$F_{t+1}^L \overset{\text{def}}{=} \mu + Q_t(\Theta)$$

$$= \mu(t + 1) + \Theta(X_t - \mu t) \tag{3.6}$$

with associated forecast error vector given by

$$e_{t+1}^L = S_{t+1} - \Theta S_t \tag{3.7}$$

which is in the form of levels, first-order VAR or $VAR(1)$ model. Similarly, when we take the differences forecast function, we easily have that

$$F_{t+1}^D \overset{\text{def}}{=} X_t + \Delta F_{t+1}^L$$

$$= X_t + \Delta Q_t(\Theta) \tag{3.8}$$

$$= \mu + X_t + \Theta(\Delta X_t - \mu)$$

and the corresponding forecast error now becomes

$$e_{t+1}^D = \eta_{t+1} - \Theta \eta_t \tag{3.9}$$

also being a $VAR(1)$ model in the model error series.

While in the univariate case the forecast function in levels F_{t+1}^L was not the preferred one, we can see that here we cannot immediately dismiss it because of the possible presence of cointegration in the detrended series, which would make the forecast error series a stationary one.[1] We can thus have the special case of a nonstationary, potentially cointegrated model where the linear deterministic trend is not annihilated by the cointegrating relationship. This, in accordance with the related literature, naturally dictates that one can consider a reduced rank regression in order to estimate the parameter matrix Θ. To make this argument more transparent, consider the usual decomposition of the Θ-matrix as $\Theta = \alpha\beta^\top$, where α is the $(K \times 1)$ vector of the loading parameters and β is the $(K \times 1)$ vector of the cointegrating parameters. Thus, we can express the component ΘX_t as follows:

$$\Theta X_t = \alpha\beta^\top \mu t + \alpha\beta^\top S_t \tag{3.10}$$

We can easily see that in order for the bivariate θ-method to work as presented so far, and using a reduced rank cointegrating regression (i.e. a vector error correction model, VECM) to estimate the Θ-matrix, we should have that $\beta^T \mu \neq 0$, so that the cointegrating vector does not annihilate the trend, as stated previously. This implies that the trend is part of the cointegrating relationship as in $Z_t = \beta^T (X_t - \mu t) = \beta^T S_t$, and in contrast to the standard case of $Z_t = \beta^T X_t - \gamma t$, for a scalar parameter γ. If this is not the case, we cannot expect, *a priori*, that the use of a reduced rank regression would offer performance improvements for estimating Θ or for forecasting. In addition, we would also require that the $VAR(1)$ is implicitly formed in the forecast error specified (e.g. one lag might not be sufficient) for cointegration estimation; for if it is not, then one can have misspecification problems that will result in decreased forecasting performance. Finally, note that under the assumed unit root DGP we can estimate Θ consistently from the forecast errors of the difference-based forecast function without reference to the potential cointegration in levels.

But even more can be glimpsed on the potential improvement of the bivariate θ-method over the univariate one if we consider the forecast error that comes from the forecast function in differences we also presented earlier. For the mean squared error (MSE) function for the first of the two equations, in the bivariate case, can now be written as

$$\text{MSE}_1(\theta_{11}, \theta_{12}) = \text{E}[\eta_{t+1,1} - \theta_{11}\eta_{t1} - \theta_{12}\eta_{t2}]^2$$

$$= \text{E}[\eta_{t+1,1} - \theta_{11}\eta_{t1}]^2 + \text{E}[\theta_{12}\eta_{t2}]^2 - 2\theta_{12}\text{E}[\eta_{t+1,1}\eta_{t2}] + 2\theta_{11}\theta_{12}\text{E}[\eta_{t1}\eta_{t2}]$$

$$= \text{MSE}_1(\theta_{11}) + \text{E}[\theta_{12}\eta_{t2}]^2 - 2\theta_{12}\text{E}[\eta_{t+1,1}\eta_{t2}] + 2\theta_{11}\theta_{12}\text{E}[\eta_{t1}\eta_{t2}]$$

$$\tag{3.11}$$

---

1 The reader unfamiliar with the notion of cointegration among series that exhibit stochastic trends can think of the concept of cointegration as a linear combination of the variables in X_t such that it forms a stationary series.

which is the sum of the univariate θ-method MSE and extra components that depend on the serial and cross-correlations of the two series. If we find the value of θ_{12} that minimizes the extra components in the previous equation, we have that

$$\theta_{12}(\theta_{11}) = (\mathsf{E}[\eta_{t+1,1}\eta_{t2}] - \theta_{11}\mathsf{E}[\eta_{t1}\eta_{t2}])/\mathsf{E}[\eta_{t2}^2] \overset{\text{def}}{=} [\sigma_{\eta,12}(1) - \theta_{11}\sigma_{\eta,12}(0)]/\sigma_{\eta,2}^2$$

(3.12)

We can easily see that θ_{12} will be different from zero if the series of errors η_{t1} and η_{t2} are either contemporaneously correlated and $\theta_{11} \neq 0$ or are first-order cross-correlated with series 2 leading series 1 (and θ_{11} can take any value including zero) or both. Thus, the bivariate θ-method applied in differences should provide smaller forecast errors than the univariate one for series which have some degree of linear codependence. Only if the error series are contemporaneously and serially uncorrelated would we need to use the univariate method.

There is no real need for a detailed description of the estimation of the unknown parameters in the multivariate case under the unit root DGP; the steps are essentially the same as those in the univariate case and straightforward. The drift terms are estimated by the sample means of the first differenced series, i.e. $\hat{\mu} = n^{-1} \sum_{t=2}^{T} \Delta X_t$. Then, the detrended/demeaned series are formed as $\hat{S}_t = X_t - \hat{\mu}t$ and $\hat{u}_t = \Delta X_t - \hat{\mu}$ and the Θ-matrix is estimated either via reduced rank regression or via multivariate least squares, respectively (of course, we can use multivariate least squares in both levels and differences). Note that as far as possible and cointegration is concerned, we do not pretest on the type of trend, with all the caveats made in our earlier discussion. This is part of the simplicity of the method and the type of forecast function we consider, and it should not be seen as a methodological drawback – the θ-approach is after all not a model but a forecasting method.

3.2 Selection of Trend Function and Extensions

Going from the unit root DGP to the trend-stationary DGP in the multivariate case, we follow the same approach as in the univariate case, and most results pass through without major modifications – either with respect to the presentation of the previous section or with respect to the univariate case. The same conditions for forecasting improvements hold for this DGP as well, with the same parameter restrictions as previously discussed. In this section, we thus concentrate on the various extensions that one can consider for the case where we either do not want to extract the trend function by smoothing and proceed as in the univariate case or we would like to address the possibility of co-movement but without entering into the complications arising from possible cointegration; that was dealt with in the previous section.

Let us therefore discuss the practically relevant case where we believe that $\boldsymbol{T}_t$ has only one component and we can write $\boldsymbol{T}_t \overset{\text{def}}{=} \lambda f_t$, where λ is a (2×1) vector of unknown parameters[2] and f_t is the common component of the trend function, also unknown. This structure can be treated easily with existing results in time series factor analysis methods, but we discuss the (potentially) simpler alternative here. We start off with a standard factor model as given:

$$X_t \overset{\text{def}}{=} \lambda f_t + \boldsymbol{\eta}_t \tag{3.13}$$

where f_t is, as earlier, the unknown common trend factor of the two series and λ is the corresponding factor loading vector of dimension (2×1). The parameter vector can easily be estimated by a covariance decomposition such as principal components or other factor analysis methods and then the unknown factor can be extracted by rotation of the original data series or by regression. However, the treatment of the statistical properties of the resulting parameter estimator and the extracted factor do depend on the assumptions that one makes about both the factor itself and the data. As our interest lies in maintaining the simplicity of the θ-method, we proceed under the simplest of assumptions of positing that $\lambda \equiv e$ the unit vector. This is not a (too) farfetched assumption for variables that are measured on the same units and have about the same scale (examples are given in the following chapters). It simply says that the data have a main common component on which there is added noise, and no further assumptions are made with respect to the properties of this component. We thus can write

$$X_t \overset{\text{def}}{=} e f_t + \boldsymbol{\eta}_t \tag{3.14}$$

This model forms a natural benchmark as we now illustrate. First, note that since the parameter vector here is known to be e, the objective of estimation becomes the unknown factor f_t. Direct application of least squares, as is done in factor analysis proper, using the full sample model of

$$X = Fe^\top + H \Rightarrow \text{vec}(X) = (e \otimes I_T)\text{vec}(F) + \text{vec}(H) \tag{3.15}$$

where X is the $(T \times 2)$ data matrix, F is the $(T \times 1)$ factor vector, and H is the $(T \times 2)$ error matrix, results in the vectorized solution of

$$\text{vec}(\widehat{F}) = (0.5 \otimes I_T)\text{vec}(Xe) \tag{3.16}$$

which simply implies that $\widehat{f}_t \overset{\text{def}}{=} 0.5(X_{t1} + X_{t2})$. Under the assumption of a common component in both series, this result is of practical use (if not significance): if the DGP is one of stochastic/trend nonstationarity driven by the common trend factor, then this is preserved in its estimate $\widehat{f}_t$ which is also nonstationary; if the DGP is one of stationarity, then the common factor also preserves

---

2 We continue discussing the bivariate case in this section.

it. Furthermore, we can derive some interesting results on the application of the θ-method given this estimate of the trend function. First, note that we can extrapolate $\hat{f}_{t+1}$ by applying the univariate θ-method to each series and average them; then, apply the bivariate θ-method to obtain the final forecasts. Second, we can extrapolate $\hat{f}_{t+1}$ by applying the univariate θ-method directly, say, with a third parameter θ_f, and then apply the bivariate θ-method for another set of final forecasts. Of course, any other method/model can be used to extrapolate $\hat{f}_{t+1}$.

We can easily find how the form of the Θ-line looks like when we adopt the abovementioned approach for modeling/estimating the trend function; in fact, what we present in this paragraph holds for any common trend approach. Substituting $\mathcal{T}_t = ef_t$ into the Θ-line, we obtain for the first of the two equations:

$$\theta_{11}X_{t1} + \theta_{12}X_{t2} + f_t(1 - \theta_{11} - \theta_{12}) \tag{3.17}$$

which shows, as anticipated, that the Θ is a linear combination of the two series and the offset of the common trend component, this offset being determined by the *sum* of the two θ-parameters. If we furthermore consider the corresponding forecast function, we can easily find the resulting forecast error. First, when we do not project the trend component (as in the univariate case), we obtain

$$e_{t+1}^{L,CT} \overset{\text{def}}{=} f_{t+1} + \eta_{t+1,1} - \theta_{11}(f_t + \eta_{t1}) + \theta_{12}(f_t + \eta_{t2}) - f_t(1 - \theta_{11} - \theta_{12})$$
$$= \eta_{t+1,1} - \theta_{11}\eta_{t1} - \theta\eta_{t2} + \Delta f_{t+1} \tag{3.18}$$

where CT stands for *common trend*; this is in the same format as in the forecast error for the forecast function in differences we saw before, the forecast error being biased but easily made unbiased and, thus, the optimal Θ-matrix is estimated easily by least squares from the residuals after smoothing. That is, under the common trend assumption, the forecast function becomes

$$F_{t+1}^{L,CT-BA} \overset{\text{def}}{=} \Theta X_t + (I - \Theta)ef_t + E[\Delta f_{t+1}] \tag{3.19}$$

and a similar discussion as in the univariate case applies. Next, we take the trend component projected one period ahead and thus we obtain

$$e_{t+1}^{L,CT} \overset{\text{def}}{=} f_{t+1} + \eta_{t+1,1} - \theta_{11}(f_t + \eta_{t1}) + \theta_{12}(f_t + \eta_{t2}) - f_{t+1}(1 - \theta_{11} - \theta_{12})$$
$$= \eta_{t+1,1} - \theta_{11}\eta_{t1} - \theta\eta_{t2} + \Delta f_{t+1}(\theta_{11} + \theta_{12}) \tag{3.20}$$

where again the form of the biased forecast error is as in the univariate case and we can easily generalize to the unbiased forecast function as in

$$F_{t+1}^{L,CT-BA} \overset{\text{def}}{=} \Theta X_t + (I - \Theta)ef_t + \Theta e E[\Delta f_{t+1}] \tag{3.21}$$

and we can expand on the univariate results with some additional algebra. However, as in the univariate case, in applications we do not have to work with the projected trend component and thus use the simpler form of the first of the two forecast functions which relies on having the Θ-line itself as the forecast.

Whether, however, the proposed common trend function is consistent with the data is a matter of empirical analysis, but we have shown that there exists at least one case of the "trend-stationary" DGP that will give us the same forecast error as the forecasting function of the unit root DGP.

Other forms of the trend function are of course possible, but we would not want to move too far away from the original simplicity of the θ-method. We thus close this section by showing how the multivariate Θ-method works when we use a simple moving average for each of the individual series. Take, therefore, as $\widehat{f}_{t+1,i}^{MA} \stackrel{def}{=} M^{-1} \sum_{j=0}^{M-1} X_{t-j,i}$ for $i = 1, 2$ suppose that we assume that the trend function is slowly varying and that it is approximately constant over a window of M observations. Then, assuming that $f_{t+1,i}$ slowly varies over a window of M observations so that approximately $f_{t+1,i} \approx f_{t,i} = f_{s,i}$, constant for $t - M + 1 \leq t_s \leq t + 1$, we take that $\widehat{f}_{t+1,i}^{MA} \approx f_{s,i}$ and show that the forecast error is of the same format as in the case of the common trend approach illustrated earlier:

$$e_{t+1,1}^{L,MA} \stackrel{def}{=} f_{s,1} + \eta_{t+1,1} - \theta_{11}(f_{s,1} + \eta_{t1}) - (1 - \theta_{11})f_{s,1} - \theta_{12}(f_{s,2} + \eta_{t2} - f_{s,2})$$

$$= \eta_{t+1,1} - \theta_{11}\eta_{t1} - \theta_{12}\eta_{t2} \tag{3.22}$$

We close this section by summarizing, as in the univariate case, the practical implementation of the bivariate Θ-method when we consider having a generic trend function $\mathcal{T}_t$ – and taking into account our previous discussion. We therefore have

1. Select an estimation/approximation approach for the trend function, i.e. obtain $\widehat{\mathcal{T}}_t$ and the corresponding residuals $\widehat{\eta}_t$.
2. Compute $\widehat{\Theta}$ by least squares using a first-order autoregression on the residual series $\widehat{\eta}_t$.
3. Form the appropriate Θ-line and compute the corresponding forecast. For the cases treated in the text earlier, we can have the following cases:
   (a) For the common trend case, obtain the bias-adjusted forecast as $\widehat{F}_{t+1}^{L,CT-BA} \stackrel{def}{=} Q_t(\widehat{\Theta}) + \widehat{\delta}$, where $Q_t(\widehat{\Theta}) = \widehat{\Theta}X_t + (I - \widehat{\Theta})\widehat{ef}_t$, $\widehat{f}_t = 0.5(X_{t1} + X_{t2})$ and $\widehat{\delta} \stackrel{def}{=} T^{-1} \sum_{t=1}^{T} \widehat{ef}_t = 0.5e(\overline{X}_{T1} + \overline{X}_{T2})$.
   (b) For the moving average case, obtain the (possibly unbiased) forecast as $\widehat{F}_{t+1}^{L,MA} \stackrel{def}{=} Q_t(\widehat{\Theta})$, where $Q_t(\widehat{\Theta}) = \widehat{\Theta}X_t + (I - \widehat{\Theta})\widehat{f}_t$, $\widehat{f}_t \stackrel{def}{=} M^{-1} \sum_{j=0}^{M-1} X_{t-j}$.
   Note that in the case where the locally constant assumption about the trend function, when using the moving average, does not hold, we can add the bias correction of the common trend approach to the forecast.

Part II

Applications and Performance in Forecasting Competitions

4

Empirical Applications with the θ-method

By Dimitrios D. Thomakos and Kostas I. Nikolopoulos

4.1   Setting up the Analysis

4.1.1   Sample Use, Evaluation Metrics, and Models/Methods Used

In this chapter, we go through several real-life series and present empirical applications for the material of the previous chapters. The aim here is to examine not only the relative forecasting performance of the proposed methods, against some well-known benchmarks, but also to understand how the forecasting performance of the θ- or Θ-based forecasts changes when we change the data-generating process (DGP), the trend function, and other parameters used in the forecast functions of the methods. Our approach is the standard rolling window training/evaluation approach that appears in the literature, where we generate genuine, out-of-sample rolling forecasts and then evaluate them over a number of periods.

Consider therefore a sample split of $T_0 + T_1 = T$ total observations. We say that T_0 is the rolling window on which we estimate model parameters and compute the forecasts, the latter to be evaluated on the remaining T_1 observations. In common forecasting parlance, we have that T_0 is the in-sample or training window and that T_1 is the out-of-sample or evaluation window. Moving the T_0 rolling window across the T_1 evaluation window one observation at a time, we end up with T_1 forecasts and the corresponding forecast errors which we can pass on to several forecast evaluation statistics and compare methods and models. For the rest of our discussion, we take the following conventions. Let $\widehat{X}_{t+1}^m$ and $\widehat{e}_{t+1}^m \overset{\text{def}}{=} X_{t+1} - \widehat{X}_{t+1}^m$ denote the mth model/method forecasts and forecast error, respectively. Then we define our forecast evaluation measures that include the (root) mean-squared error (RMSE), the mean absolute error

(MAE), Theil's information criterion (U1, unscaled, and U2, scaled), and the sign success ratio (SSR) as follows:

$$\text{RMSE}(m, T_1) \stackrel{\text{def}}{=} \sqrt{T_1^{-1} \sum_{t=T_0+1}^{T} \widehat{e}_t^{m,2}}$$

$$\text{MAE}(m, T_1) \stackrel{\text{def}}{=} \sum_{t=T_0+1}^{T} |\widehat{e}_t^m|$$

$$\text{U1}(m, T_1) \stackrel{\text{def}}{=} \sqrt{\sum_{t=T_0+2}^{T} (\widehat{e}_t^m)^2 / \sum_{t=T_0+2}^{T} (\Delta X_t)^2} \tag{4.1}$$

$$\text{U2}(m, T_1) \stackrel{\text{def}}{=} \sqrt{\sum_{t=T_0+2}^{T} (\widehat{e}_t^m / X_{t-1})^2 / \sum_{t=T_0+2}^{T} (\Delta X_t / X_{t-1})^2}$$

$$\text{SSR}(m, T_1) \stackrel{\text{def}}{=} T_1^{-1} \sum_{t=T_0+1}^{T} [\text{sign}(\widehat{X}_t^m - X_{t-1}) = \text{sign}(X_t - X_{t-1})]$$

We concentrate on using these measures in our discussion and purposefully avoid the use of model comparison test statistics; our focus here is to illustrate that the θ- or Θ-based forecasts are on average on par or better than the benchmarks based on these evaluation measures and thus can be successful members of a forecasters toolbox. Given the simplicity of all the proposed θ-methods, they can easily serve as the new benchmarks to beat in any forecasting exercise. Note that the RMSE and MAE values will always be expressed as ratios to the Naíve forecasting benchmark, as explained here.

The benchmark models/forecasts we use in comparing forecasting performance with the θ- and Θ-based forecasts are the following:

1. The Naíve forecast $\widehat{X}_{t+1}^{Naive} \stackrel{\text{def}}{=} X_t$;
2. The AR(1) model forecast, $\widehat{X}_{t+1}^{AR} \stackrel{\text{def}}{=} \widehat{\phi}_0 + \widehat{\phi}_1 X_t$, with the (ϕ_0, ϕ_1) parameters estimated by least squares (LS);
3. The simple exponential smoothing (SES) forecast, $\widehat{X}_{t+1}^{SES} \stackrel{\text{def}}{=} \alpha X_t + (1 - \alpha)\widehat{X}_t^{SES}$, with automatic smoothing constant estimation;
4. The Hyndman and Billah (2003), HB, θ-forecast adaptation, $\widehat{X}_{t+1}^{HB}$;
5. The ARIMA(1, 1, 0) model forecast, $\widehat{X}_{t+1}^{ARIMA} \stackrel{\text{def}}{=} X_t + \widehat{\phi}_0 + \widehat{\phi}_1(X_t - X_{t-1})$, with the parameters estimated by LS;
6. The auto-ARIMA(1 : 2, 1, 1 : 2) model forecast, $\widehat{X}_{t+1}^{auto}$, where the model's forecast is selected among all possible combinations of orders in the model via the bias-corrected AIC criterion;

7. The VAR(1) model forecast, $\hat{X}_{t+1}^{\text{VAR}}$, the multivariate analog of the AR(1) model forecast.

In Tables 4.1 and 4.2, we present the nomenclature of all the models that are used in our empirical applications, with their correspondence to notation that appeared in previous chapters. Table 4.1 contains all the θ- and $\boldsymbol{\Theta}$-based forecasts and Table 4.2 repeats the benchmarks we just described. Note that in the presentation of the results later we omit from the relevant tables the bivariate model notation when discussing univariate analysis.

Table 4.1 Model nomenclature used in empirical applications, θ- and $\boldsymbol{\Theta}$-based.

UR1	Unit root DGP θ-forecast, $\hat{F}_{T+1}^{D} = X_T + \Delta Q_T(\hat{\theta}^{*,D})$
UR2	Unit root DGP θ-forecast, SMA, and bias correction
	$\hat{F}_{T+1}^{\text{MA,BA}} = Q_T(\hat{\theta}^{*,\text{MA}}) + 0.5\hat{\mu}(3 - \hat{\theta}^{*,\text{MA}})$
TS1	Trend-stationary DGP θ-forecast, SMA, ignores bias in $\hat{\theta}^*$
	$\hat{F}_{t+1}^{s,\text{SMA}} = Q_T(\hat{\theta}^{*,s})$
TS1-BC1	Trend-stationary DGP θ-forecast, SMA, and first bias correction, ignores bias in $\hat{\theta}^*$
	$\hat{F}_{t+1}^{s,\text{BA}} = Q_T(\hat{\theta}^{*,s}) + \hat{\delta}$
TS1-BC2	Trend-stationary DGP θ-forecast, SMA, and second bias correction, ignores bias in $\hat{\theta}^*$
	$\hat{F}_{t+1}^{s,\text{BA}} = Q_T(\hat{\theta}^{*,s}) + \hat{\theta}^{*,s}\hat{\delta}$
TS2	As in TS1, but takes into account the bias in $\hat{\theta}^*$
TS2-BC1	As in TS1-BC1, but takes into account the bias in $\hat{\theta}^*$
TS2-BC2	As in TS1-BC2, but takes into account the bias in $\hat{\theta}^*$
TS-DBL	Trend-stationary DGP θ-forecast, double θ approach
	$\hat{F}_{T+1}^{d} = \hat{Q}_T(\hat{\theta}_1^{*,d}) + \hat{\theta}_2^{*,d}\Delta\hat{Q}_T(\hat{\theta}_1^{*,d}) + (1 - \hat{\theta}_2^{*,d})\hat{\delta}$
BUR-L	Bivariate, unit root DGP $\boldsymbol{\Theta}$-forecast, estimation of $\boldsymbol{\Theta}$ matrix from levels of time series
	$\hat{\boldsymbol{F}}_{t+1}^{L} = \hat{\mu} + \boldsymbol{Q}_t(\hat{\boldsymbol{\Theta}})$
BUR-RR	As in BUR-L, but estimation of $\boldsymbol{\Theta}$ matrix from reduced rank regression
BUR-D	As in BUR-L, but estimation of $\boldsymbol{\Theta}$ matrix from differences of time series
	$\hat{\boldsymbol{F}}_{t+1}^{D} = \boldsymbol{X}_t + \Delta\hat{\boldsymbol{F}}_{t+1}^{L}$
BCT	Bivariate common trend DGP forecast
	$\hat{\boldsymbol{F}}_{t+1}^{L,\text{CT-BA}} = \hat{\boldsymbol{\Theta}}\boldsymbol{X}_t + (\boldsymbol{I} - \hat{\boldsymbol{\Theta}})\boldsymbol{ef}_t + \mathsf{E}[\Delta f_{t+1}]$
BMA	Bivariate, trend-stationary DGP, SMA, and bias correction
	$\hat{\boldsymbol{F}}_{t+1}^{L,\text{MA}} = \boldsymbol{Q}_t(\hat{\boldsymbol{\Theta}})$
BMA-BC	Bivariate, trend-stationary DGP, SMA, and bias correction
	$\hat{\boldsymbol{F}}_{t+1}^{L,\text{MA}} = \boldsymbol{Q}_t(\hat{\boldsymbol{\Theta}}) + \hat{\mu}$

Table 4.2 Model nomenclature used in empirical applications, benchmarks.

Naíve	Naíve forecast, $\hat{X}_{t+1}^{\text{Naíve}} \overset{\text{def}}{=} X_t$
AR(1)	The AR(1) model forecast, $\hat{X}_{t+1}^{\text{AR}} \overset{\text{def}}{=} \hat{\phi}_0 + \hat{\phi}_1 X_t$
SES	The simple exponential smoothing forecast, $\hat{X}_{t+1}^{\text{SES}} \overset{\text{def}}{=} \alpha X_t + (1-\alpha)\hat{X}_t^{\text{SES}}$
HB	The Hyndman and Billah (2003), HB, θ-forecast adaptation, $\hat{X}_{t+1}^{\text{HB}}$
ARIMA (1,1,0)	The ARIMA(1,1,0) model forecast, $\hat{X}_{t+1}^{\text{ARIMA}} \overset{\text{def}}{=} X_t + \hat{\phi}_0 + \hat{\phi}_1(X_t - X_{t-1})$
Auto-ARIMA	The auto-ARIMA($1:2, 1, 1:2$) model forecast, $\hat{X}_{t+1}^{\text{auto}}$
VAR	The VAR(1) model forecast, $\hat{X}_{t+1}^{\text{VAR}}$

4.1.2 Data

Our group of economic time series consists of $S_1 = 6$ members, four of which are univariate and two are bivariate. These series were selected to reflect different underlying economic conditions, different structures, different countries, and different frequencies. All data were obtained from the Federal Reserve Bank of Saint Louis online database (FRED) and are easily retrievable. Our data list is thus the following:

- *Series "CREDIT"*: Total Credit to General Government, Adjusted for Breaks, for Greece, Percentage of GDP, Quarterly, Not Seasonally Adjusted, sample range from Q4 of 1997 to Q1 of 2017; series ID in FRED is QGRGAM770A.
- *Series "UNRATE"*: Civilian Unemployment Rate for the United States, Percent, Monthly, Seasonally Adjusted, sample range from January of 2000 to October of 2017; series ID in FRED is UNRATE.
- *Series "EXPIMP"*: Ratio of Exports to Imports for China, Percent, Monthly, Seasonally Adjusted, sample range from January of 2000 to August of 2017; series ID in FRED is XTEITT01CNM156S.
- *Series "TRADE"*: Current Account Balance, Total Trade of Goods for Germany US Dollars, Sum Over Component Subperiods, Quarterly, Seasonally Adjusted, sample range Q2 of 1986 to Q1 of 2014; series ID in FRED is BPBLTD01DEQ637S.
- *Series "JOBS"*: Bivariate series: (i) Job Openings, Retail Trade Rate, Monthly, Seasonally Adjusted, sample range from December of 2000 to September 2017; series ID in FRED is JTS4400JOR; (ii) Job Openings, Manufacturing, Rate, Monthly, Seasonally Adjusted, sample range from December of 2000 to September of 2017; series ID in FRED is JTS3000JOR.
- *Series "FINANCE"*: Bivariate series: (i) Foreign Exchange Rate of the British pound with respect to the US dollar, sample range from January of 1999 to November of 2017; series ID in FRED is EXUSUK; (ii) Foreign Exchange Rate of the Euro with respect to the US dollar, sample range from January of 1999 to November of 2017; series ID in FRED is EXUSEU.

For each of these series, we considered $S_2 = 4$ transformations of the data onto which we applied our forecasting exercise, the levels of the data, their logarithms, the first differences of the logarithms, and the seasonal differences for the logarithms as given here:

$$X_t, \ \log X_t, \ \Delta \log X_t, \ \Delta_{12} \log X_t \qquad (4.2)$$

where $s = 4$ for the quarterly series and $s = 12$ for the monthly series. The rolling windows were set to $T_0 = [30, 60]$ for the quarterly series and to $T_0 = [60, 90, 120]$ for the monthly series. Moving average lengths of $M = [3, 4, 6, 12, 24, 36]$ were used for the computation of the trend functions in the trend-stationary DGP forecasting models, either in the univariate or in the bivariate case. The total number of forecasting exercises thus computed was $S_1 \times S_2 \times \mathcal{N}(T_0), \mathcal{N}(M)$, which comes to 240 (quarterly) or 360 (monthly) outcomes. The total number of results is available on request, but we cannot possibly present them all. We thus present a selection that illustrates the conditions under which the θ- or Θ-based forecasts works as a guide to the reader and the forecasting practitioner. We note that all tables with results that we present in the results section have the same caption format, i.e. "SERIES NAME-Transformation Type-Length of Moving Average-Rolling Window."

4.2 Series CREDIT

We begin our empirical applications with the analysis of the CREDIT series. The time series plots of the four different transformations appear in Figure 4.1 and the main descriptive statistics for the full sample and two subsamples appear in Tables 4.3–4.5.

This series reflects the evolution of the credit made available to the general government in Greece and it has three distinct periods that can be seen: the period that the series remains relatively flat before the first memorandum of understanding (MoU) that the then government signed with the International Monetary Fund (IMF) and its European partners, the high rise after the MoU was signed, and the stabilization at a higher level after 2015. The increasing variance in the series can be seen in the lower two panels of the plot. These characteristics can be read through from the corresponding statistics in the relevant tables. This series has a number of exogenous structural changes and is thus suitable to consider for examining forecasting performance.

For this series, we present results for six different combinations of data transformations, rolling window size, and moving average length. We start off with Table 4.6 where the length of the rolling window is 60 observations, the series is at its level, and the length of the moving average for trend computations is 3 observations. The table immediately reveals that only three methods provide better forecasts than the Naíve model, based on a combination of results from

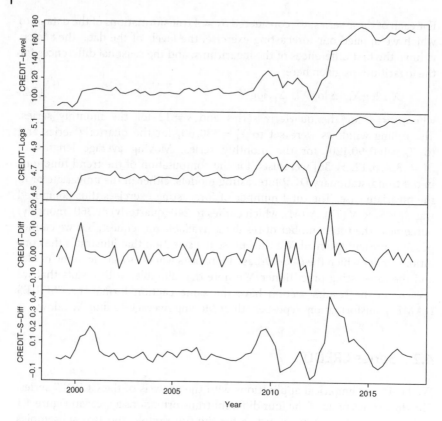

Figure 4.1 Time series plots of series CREDIT.

Table 4.3 Full sample statistics, 1997–2017, series CREDIT.

	Mean	Standard Deviation	Minimum	Maximum	Skewness	Kurtosis
CREDIT-Level	123.012	27.554	88.200	178.200	0.985	2.348
CREDIT-Logs	4.790	0.207	4.480	5.183	0.839	2.227
CREDIT-Diff	0.009	0.047	−0.130	0.201	0.609	6.653
CREDIT-S-Diff	0.034	0.103	−0.160	0.432	1.527	6.076

all evaluation measures, the double θ-line forecast, the θ adaptation by HB, and the ARIMA$(1, 1, 0)$-forecast.

The latter forecast dominates here, especially because of its larger SSR which is at 64.3% vs. 50% of the other models. What is interesting here, however, is that two out of three methods that beat the simplest possible forecast are indeed

Table 4.4 Subsample statistics, 1997–2013, series CREDIT.

	Mean	Standard Deviation	Minimum	Maximum	Skewness	Kurtosis
CREDIT-Level	111.570	15.217	88.200	165.700	1.881	6.932
CREDIT-Logs	4.707	0.124	4.480	5.110	1.416	5.626
CREDIT-Diff	0.010	0.051	−0.130	0.201	0.541	5.835
CREDIT-S-Diff	0.035	0.111	−0.160	0.432	1.503	5.518

Table 4.5 Subsample statistics, 2014–2017, series CREDIT.

	Mean	Standard Deviation	Minimum	Maximum	Skewness	Kurtosis
CREDIT-Level	172.050	4.295	164.000	178.200	−0.566	2.076
CREDIT-Logs	5.147	0.025	5.100	5.183	−0.599	2.100
CREDIT-Diff	0.003	0.024	−0.049	0.034	−0.480	2.091
CREDIT-S-Diff	0.027	0.064	−0.083	0.132	−0.125	1.891

Table 4.6 CREDIT-1-60-3.

	RMSE	MAE	U1	U2	SSR
Naíve	1.000	1.000	1.000	1.000	0.000
UR1	1.007	1.006	0.999	1.007	0.500
UR2	1.517	1.303	1.521	1.517	0.500
TS1	1.198	1.128	1.202	1.198	0.429
TS1-BC1	1.177	1.109	1.177	1.177	0.429
TS1-BC2	1.179	1.112	1.180	1.179	0.429
TS2	1.198	1.128	1.202	1.198	0.429
TS2-BC1	1.177	1.109	1.177	1.177	0.429
TS2-BC2	1.179	1.112	1.180	1.179	0.429
TS-DBL	0.991	0.991	0.986	0.991	0.500
AR(1)	1.053	1.016	1.041	1.053	0.500
SES	1.000	1.000	1.000	1.000	0.500
HB	0.996	1.007	0.993	0.996	0.500
ARIMA (1, 1, 0)	0.970	0.975	0.972	0.970	0.643
Auto-ARIMA	1.000	0.996	0.991	1.000	0.500

Table 4.7 CREDIT-1-60-36.

	RMSE	MAE	U1	U2	SSR
Naíve	1.000	1.000	1.000	1.000	0.000
UR1	1.007	1.006	0.999	1.007	0.500
UR2	1.517	1.303	1.521	1.517	0.500
TS1	1.041	1.001	1.045	1.041	0.571
TS1-BC1	1.023	0.993	1.024	1.023	0.571
TS1-BC2	1.024	0.993	1.025	1.024	0.571
TS2	2.213	2.177	2.177	2.213	0.500
TS2-BC1	2.320	2.293	2.283	2.320	0.500
TS2-BC2	2.345	2.318	2.307	2.345	0.500
TS-DBL	1.007	1.005	1.008	1.007	0.571
AR(1)	1.053	1.016	1.041	1.053	0.500
SES	1.000	1.000	1.000	1.000	0.500
HB	0.996	1.007	0.993	0.996	0.500
ARIMA (1, 1, 0)	0.970	0.975	0.972	0.970	0.643
Auto-ARIMA	1.000	0.996	0.991	1.000	0.500

θ-methods. Moving on to Table 4.7, where the length of the moving average is increased to 36 observations, we note an interesting result: the SSR statistic of the trend-stationary DGP θ-forecasts and that of the double θ-forecast all rise by 7%, from 50% to 57.1%.

This implies that the trend estimation/smoothing inherent in these θ-forecasts is (more) successful in capturing the series changes in direction. The next two tables present the results of the logarithms of the series. Both in Table 4.8 and in Table 4.9 the SSR statistics tell the story: while we cannot find a performance improvement with the other four measures in any of the forecasts, compared to the Naíve benchmark, we can see that the SSR of the θ-based forecasts appears to be the best.

Specifically, in Table 4.8, where the rolling window is of size 30 observations and the length of the moving average is 24 observations, we can see that highest SSR, at 63.6% and 61.4%, respectively, is given by the bias-corrected trend-stationary DGP θ-forecasts of the first kind, the third and fourth best SSR at 59.1% is given by the HB-forecast, and the trend-stationary DGP θ-forecasts are again of the first kind.

That is, in terms of correct sign predictions, the top four forecasts come from θ-based methods. In Table 4.9, the results are even more pronounced in favor of a single θ-forecast, the double θ. Here, only this forecast produces an SSR of 57.1%, while all other forecasts are spot on at 50%.

Table 4.8 CREDIT-2-30-24.

	RMSE	MAE	U1	U2	SSR
Naíve	1.000	1.000	1.000	1.000	0.000
UR1	1.039	1.023	1.039	1.039	0.523
UR2	1.486	1.476	1.478	1.486	0.568
TS1	1.103	1.004	1.097	1.103	0.591
TS1-BC1	1.088	0.968	1.083	1.088	0.636
TS1-BC2	1.092	0.975	1.087	1.092	0.614
TS2	28.449	8.831	27.098	28.449	0.545
TS2-BC1	28.458	8.833	27.106	28.458	0.545
TS2-BC2	28.631	8.926	27.271	28.631	0.545
TS-DBL	0.995	0.994	0.994	0.995	0.432
AR(1)	1.007	0.984	1.006	1.007	0.545
SES	1.041	1.039	1.042	1.041	0.500
HB	1.039	1.034	1.040	1.039	0.591
ARIMA $(1, 1, 0)$	1.068	1.063	1.071	1.068	0.091
Auto-ARIMA	1.041	1.026	1.041	1.041	0.500

Table 4.9 CREDIT-2-60-36.

	RMSE	MAE	U1	U2	SSR
Naíve	1.000	1.000	1.000	1.000	0.000
UR1	1.027	1.008	1.025	1.027	0.500
UR2	1.570	1.340	1.571	1.570	0.500
TS1	1.152	1.107	1.154	1.152	0.500
TS1-BC1	1.093	1.072	1.095	1.093	0.500
TS1-BC2	1.096	1.075	1.097	1.096	0.500
TS2	3.530	3.536	3.524	3.530	0.500
TS2-BC1	3.685	3.721	3.679	3.685	0.500
TS2-BC2	3.734	3.770	3.728	3.734	0.500
TS-DBL	1.013	1.009	1.013	1.013	0.571
AR(1)	1.039	1.010	1.037	1.039	0.500
SES	1.000	1.000	1.000	1.000	0.500
HB	0.997	1.007	0.996	0.997	0.500
ARIMA $(1, 1, 0)$	0.894	0.883	0.894	0.894	0.500
Auto-ARIMA	1.014	0.990	1.012	1.014	0.500

Table 4.10 CREDIT-3-30-24.

	RMSE	MAE	U1	U2	SSR
Naíve	1.000	1.000	1.000	1.000	0.000
UR1	0.836	0.866	1.310	0.836	0.705
UR2	1.327	1.185	3.061	1.327	0.705
TS1	0.803	0.804	0.963	0.803	0.727
TS1-BC1	0.802	0.799	0.959	0.802	0.750
TS1-BC2	0.804	0.806	0.962	0.804	0.727
TS2	1.084	0.943	0.999	1.084	0.750
TS2-BC1	1.083	0.943	0.995	1.083	0.773
TS2-BC2	1.088	0.947	0.999	1.088	0.750
TS-DBL	1.000	1.001	0.997	1.000	0.500
AR(1)	0.762	0.745	0.966	0.762	0.750
SES	0.749	0.729	0.925	0.749	0.773
HB	0.773	0.776	0.933	0.773	0.705
ARIMA $(1, 1, 0)$	0.856	0.879	1.242	0.856	0.682
Auto-ARIMA	0.840	0.864	1.333	0.840	0.727

We next turn to results that apply to the first and seasonal log-differences of the series CREDIT. Tables 4.10 and 4.11 contain the results on the first log-differences of the series. Here, of course, we anticipated that the benchmark models will possibly be better performers, but the results are again quite surprising. In Table 4.10, we have a rolling window of length 30 observations and a moving average of 24 observations. On the one hand, the SES-forecast, along with the HB and AR(1)-forecasts, have the lowest RMSE and MAE, and correspondingly low values of their U1 and U2 statistics, but in terms of the SSR statistic we find that again the θ-forecasts perform very well.

Specifically, note that the best overall θ-based forecasts are the HB and the bias-corrected trend-stationary θ-forecast of the first kind; however, these two forecasts do not have the highest SSR value, which is given by the bias-corrected trend-stationary DGP of the second kind at 77.3% – and this is on par with the best performer, which is the SES-forecast. What is interesting here is that the improvement in the SSR comes from a model that beats the benchmark Naíve model only in terms of the MAE from the other statistics, but uses the bias correction in the estimation of the θ-parameter of the forecast function.

Turning to Table 4.11, where the rolling window is now 60 observations and the length of the moving average is 36 observations, we can immediately see that the θ-forecasts dominate not only the Naíve benchmark but also other

Table 4.11 CREDIT-3-60-36.

	RMSE	MAE	U1	U2	SSR
Naíve	1.000	1.000	1.000	1.000	0.000
UR1	0.904	0.896	1.493	0.904	0.571
UR2	1.453	1.340	2.850	1.453	0.571
TS1	0.887	0.832	0.768	0.887	0.714
TS1-BC1	0.881	0.832	0.759	0.881	0.714
TS1-BC2	0.887	0.833	0.768	0.887	0.714
TS2	0.889	0.842	0.771	0.889	0.714
TS2-BC1	0.883	0.841	0.761	0.883	0.714
TS2-BC2	0.890	0.843	0.771	0.890	0.714
TS-DBL	1.003	0.999	0.996	1.003	0.500
AR(1)	0.808	0.818	0.861	0.808	0.714
SES	0.857	0.841	0.821	0.857	0.714
HB	1.010	0.862	0.840	1.010	0.714
ARIMA $(1, 1, 0)$	0.839	0.806	1.467	0.839	0.714
Auto-ARIMA	0.898	0.881	1.500	0.898	0.571

models. Note the following in the table: the lowest value of the U1 statistics is given by the bias-corrected trend-stationary DGP θ-forecast of the first kind and has an SSR value of 71.4%; this is the top model in terms of the U1 statistic, and the top four positions go to other θ-forecasts of the trend-stationary DGP of both the first and the second kind.

These forecasts have the same SSR value as the top performer and are contenders along with the benchmarks on the rankings of the U2 statistic. Thus, no single model dominates across all statistics, but the θ-forecasts are ranked at the top in terms of their U1 and SSR values.

The remaining two tables, Tables 4.12 and 4.13, contain the forecast evaluation results for the case where the series is expressed as a seasonal log-difference. For Table 4.12, where the rolling window is 30 observations and the moving average length is 12 observations, the results are not in favor of any model/method forecast save for the AR(1)-forecast that slightly beats the Naíve benchmark. However, note that as in previous tables there is one θ-forecast, the double θ one, that provides the second highest, after the AR(1) model, value for the SSR at 59.1% vs. 63.6% of the AR(1)-forecast.

This is another illustration of the ability of θ-based forecasts to predict direction well. Next, turning to Table 4.13, where the rolling window is 60 observations and the moving average length is 36 observations, we can see that while the AR(1)-forecast is ranked at the top, we have all the trend-stationary

Table 4.12 CREDIT-4-30-12.

	RMSE	MAE	U1	U2	SSR
Naíve	1.000	1.000	1.000	1.000	0.000
UR1	1.078	1.087	0.836	1.078	0.568
UR2	1.387	1.561	2.131	1.387	0.318
TS1	1.018	0.969	1.030	1.018	0.591
TS1-BC1	1.029	0.972	0.983	1.029	0.568
TS1-BC2	1.026	0.972	1.001	1.026	0.591
TS2	1.020	1.013	1.455	1.020	0.568
TS2-BC1	1.025	1.011	1.394	1.025	0.477
TS2-BC2	1.024	1.012	1.397	1.024	0.477
TS-DBL	1.004	0.994	0.919	1.004	0.591
AR(1)	0.994	0.921	1.000	0.994	0.636
SES	1.021	1.036	1.019	1.021	0.295
HB	1.028	1.042	0.988	1.028	0.432
ARIMA $(1, 1, 0)$	1.008	1.021	1.011	1.008	0.000
Auto-ARIMA	1.088	1.090	0.775	1.088	0.545

Table 4.13 CREDIT-4-60-36.

	RMSE	MAE	U1	U2	SSR
Naíve	1.000	1.000	1.000	1.000	0.000
UR1	1.007	0.998	0.841	1.007	0.643
UR2	1.481	1.655	2.129	1.481	0.286
TS1	0.845	0.877	0.746	0.845	0.643
TS1-BC1	0.848	0.879	0.736	0.848	0.643
TS1-BC2	0.847	0.879	0.739	0.847	0.643
TS2	1.020	0.978	0.940	1.020	0.643
TS2-BC1	1.026	0.989	0.930	1.026	0.571
TS2-BC2	1.026	0.989	0.931	1.026	0.571
TS-DBL	1.005	1.010	0.990	1.005	0.357
AR(1)	0.810	0.814	0.985	0.810	0.786
SES	1.000	1.000	1.000	1.000	0.286
HB	1.004	1.005	0.983	1.004	0.357
ARIMA $(1, 1, 0)$	1.000	1.000	1.000	1.000	0.000
Auto-ARIMA	1.003	0.987	0.828	1.003	0.643

DGP θ-forecasts of the first kind outperforming the Naíve benchmark and perform well in terms of their statistics compared to the AR(1)-forecast, with only their SSR being at 64.3% vs. 78.6% of the AR(1)-forecast.

4.3   Series UNRATE

The next series UNRATE is a well-known one and has been the subject of several papers. Besides its obvious economic significance, the unemployment series has characteristics that made it amenable to more complicated, model-based analysis that might include nonlinearities and explanatory variables. The time series plots of the four different transformations appear in Figure 4.2 and the main descriptive statistics for the full sample and two subsamples appear in Tables 4.14–4.16.

The series exhibits the structural break of the increase in unemployment because of the 2008 crisis and the subsequent negative trend as a result of the

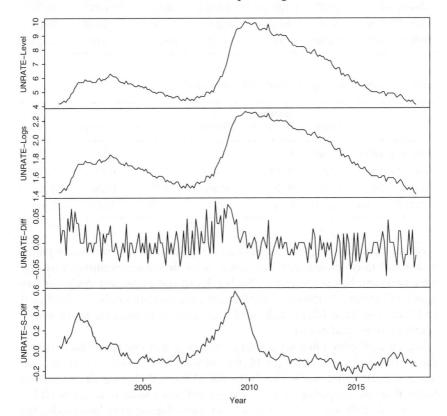

Figure 4.2 Time series plots of series UNRATE.

Table 4.14 Full sample statistics, 2000–2017, series UNRATE.

	Mean	Standard Deviation	Minimum	Maximum	Skewness	Kurtosis
UNRATE-Level	6.260	1.725	4.100	10.000	0.815	2.303
UNRATE-Logs	1.800	0.259	1.411	2.303	0.555	2.001
UNRATE-Diff	0.000	0.027	−0.078	0.077	0.421	3.270
UNRATE-S-Diff	0.007	0.178	−0.234	0.588	1.408	4.285

Table 4.15 Subsample statistics, 2000–2005, series UNRATE.

	Mean	Standard Deviation	Minimum	Maximum	Skewness	Kurtosis
UNRATE-Level	5.428	0.530	4.200	6.300	−0.728	2.709
UNRATE-Logs	1.687	0.102	1.435	1.841	−0.913	3.031
UNRATE-Diff	0.004	0.025	−0.038	0.074	0.662	3.064
UNRATE-S-Diff	0.050	0.143	−0.122	0.379	0.682	2.304

Table 4.16 Subsample statistics, 2006–2017, series UNRATE.

	Mean	Standard Deviation	Minimum	Maximum	Skewness	Kurtosis
UNRATE-Level	6.612	1.925	4.100	10.000	0.365	1.578
UNRATE-Logs	1.847	0.289	1.411	2.303	0.175	1.453
UNRATE-Diff	−0.001	0.028	−0.078	0.077	0.386	3.235
UNRATE-S-Diff	−0.011	0.188	−0.234	0.588	1.681	4.931

economic policies adapted, the so-called nonconventional monetary policy with quantitative easing, and the return to low levels of unemployment that were prevalent before the crisis. This break can also be seen at the lower two panels of the plot. As the series exhibits the characteristics of both a level shift and local trends, it is also suitable for comparing forecasting performance across methods and models.

We start off with Table 4.17, where the rolling window is 60 observations, the moving average is of length 24 observations, and the series is at its level. The best performing model here is the ARIMA$(1, 1, 0)$, having all its statistics better than all competing models. The second best model in terms of RMSE is the trend-stationary DGP $θ$-forecast, with a tie for the third best model, the unit root DGP $θ$-forecast and Auto-ARIMA-forecast.

Table 4.17 UNRATE-1-60-24.

	RMSE	MAE	U1	U2	SSR
Naíve	1.000	1.000	1.000	1.000	0.254
UR1	0.980	1.019	0.985	0.980	0.408
UR2	1.506	1.565	1.486	1.506	0.373
TS1	0.959	1.027	0.998	0.959	0.317
TS1-BC1	1.020	1.110	1.015	1.020	0.345
TS1-BC2	1.017	1.105	1.013	1.017	0.338
TS2	13.157	4.272	9.571	13.157	0.310
TS2-BC1	13.197	4.360	9.591	13.197	0.345
TS2-BC2	13.774	4.446	9.928	13.774	0.338
TS-DBL	1.078	1.123	1.058	1.078	0.275
AR(1)	1.032	1.096	1.007	1.032	0.380
SES	1.004	1.005	1.003	1.004	0.380
HB	1.024	1.071	1.010	1.024	0.394
ARIMA $(1,1,0)$	0.922	0.970	0.939	0.922	0.458
Auto-ARIMA	0.979	1.016	0.983	0.979	0.408

The two models in third place have the same SSR as well, while the trend-stationary DGP forecast does not perform as well in terms of detecting the direction of the time series. Increasing the length of the rolling window, and keeping the same length for the moving average, we can see in Table 4.18 that all the three models of the trend-stationary DGP of the first kind perform better than the Naíve benchmark in terms of RMSE, but otherwise the ranking remains the same as in the previous table.

Forecasting the levels or log-levels of this series with the current group of models is not easy, which is well understood in the literature. However, as we now illustrate, when the series is differenced the results become very different in terms of predictability. In Table 4.19 we have the results for the case of the first differences, a rolling window of length 60 observations and a moving average of length 6 observations. Most models dominate the Naíve benchmark and the top performers across all statistics are the trend-stationary DGP θ-forecasts of the first kind.

In fact, we can note something interesting here in that the TS1-BC2-forecast, which accounts for the presence of the bias in the forecast but not in estimation of the θ-parameter has the lowest RMSE and MAE statistics and also the highest SSR among all models in the table. Also, note that even the trend-stationary DGP forecasts of the second kind, which do not perform at all well in terms of their RMSE and MAE statistics have SSR values that are on par with all the benchmark models.

Table 4.18 UNRATE-1-90-24.

	RMSE	MAE	U1	U2	SSR
Naíve	1.000	1.000	1.000	1.000	0.268
UR1	0.972	0.998	0.977	0.972	0.402
UR2	1.428	1.478	1.403	1.428	0.321
TS1	0.929	0.982	0.975	0.929	0.304
TS1-BC1	0.975	1.052	0.998	0.975	0.339
TS1-BC2	0.975	1.051	0.997	0.975	0.339
TS2	50.072	11.377	37.140	50.072	0.295
TS2-BC1	50.094	11.463	37.156	50.094	0.339
TS2-BC2	54.416	12.088	40.261	54.416	0.339
TS-DBL	1.046	1.088	1.033	1.046	0.348
AR(1)	1.004	1.055	0.987	1.004	0.375
SES	1.000	1.000	1.000	1.000	0.330
HB	1.028	1.066	1.015	1.028	0.312
ARIMA $(1,1,0)$	0.871	0.940	0.867	0.871	0.491
Auto-ARIMA	0.974	1.001	0.979	0.974	0.402

Table 4.19 UNRATE-3-60-6.

	RMSE	MAE	U1	U2	SSR
Naíve	1.000	1.000		1.000	0.063
UR1	0.842	0.849		0.842	0.620
UR2	1.305	1.323		1.305	0.627
TS1	0.686	0.722		0.686	0.768
TS1-BC1	0.688	0.723		0.688	0.768
TS1-BC2	0.686	0.722		0.686	0.775
TS2	4.623	1.422		4.623	0.725
TS2-BC1	4.621	1.423		4.621	0.725
TS2-BC2	4.502	1.407		4.502	0.732
TS-DBL	1.001	1.002		1.001	0.415
AR(1)	0.781	0.769		0.781	0.711
SES	0.710	0.739	0.757	0.710	0.754
HB	0.715	0.746	0.764	0.715	0.739
ARIMA $(1,1,0)$	0.750	0.767	0.833	0.750	0.725
Auto-ARIMA	0.840	0.850	0.838	0.840	0.627

Table 4.20 UNRATE-3-90-6.

	RMSE	MAE	U1	U2	SSR
Naíve	1.000	1.000		1.000	0.071
UR1	0.855	0.882		0.855	0.634
UR2	1.342	1.401		1.342	0.652
TS1	0.721	0.772		0.721	0.750
TS1-BC1	0.722	0.774	0.818	0.722	0.732
TS1-BC2	0.721	0.771	0.815	0.721	0.732
TS2	6.866	1.834		6.866	0.652
TS2-BC1	6.867	1.836	4.976	6.867	0.634
TS2-BC2	6.994	1.853	5.065	6.994	0.643
TS-DBL	1.000	1.001	1.000	1.000	0.429
AR(1)	0.827	0.834		0.827	0.696
SES	0.735	0.787	0.785	0.735	0.732
HB	0.741	0.792	0.791	0.741	0.732
ARIMA $(1, 1, 0)$	0.756	0.816	0.811	0.756	0.723
Auto-ARIMA	0.855	0.884	0.870	0.855	0.616

The results are similar when we increase the window length to 90 observations, as can be seen in Table 4.20. Note the slight deterioration in the evaluation statistics, but the previous θ-forecasts continue to be ranked at the top across all forecasts in the table. On the other hand, in the even larger window length of 120 observations in Table 4.21 the RMSE and MAE statistics improve compared to previous tables and we can now see that the trend-stationary DGP θ-forecasts of the second kind become top performers as well and are also ranked at the top.

Clearly, the length of the sample is used to compute the bias corrections matters and we can see here how this is reflected in our results. Note that most θ-forecasts dominate again with the exception that their SSR are second best when compared to the SES and HB-forecasts, but by less than 2%.

Finally, we take a look at one combination for the case of the seasonally differenced series, the annual percent change in the UNRATE series. The results are given in Table 4.22. We can easily see that the trend-stationary DGP θ-forecasts of both the first and the second kind completely dominate the other forecasts and they are the only ones better than the Naíve benchmark, in terms of all their statistics. In this table, we have a rolling window of 120 observations, as

Table 4.21 UNRATE-3-120-6.

	RMSE	MAE	U1	U2	SSR
Naíve	1.000	1.000		1.000	0.098
UR1	0.854	0.856		0.854	0.622
UR2	1.398	1.430		1.398	0.634
TS1	0.657	0.690		0.657	0.744
TS1-BC1	0.658	0.691	0.681	0.658	0.720
TS1-BC2	0.657	0.690	0.679	0.657	0.720
TS2	0.657	0.690		0.657	0.744
TS2-BC1	0.658	0.691	0.681	0.658	0.720
TS2-BC2	0.657	0.690	0.679	0.657	0.720
TS-DBL	1.000	1.001	1.000	1.000	0.390
AR(1)	0.724	0.720		0.724	0.720
SES	0.689	0.714	0.695	0.689	0.756
HB	0.689	0.714	0.695	0.689	0.756
ARIMA $(1,1,0)$	0.702	0.739	0.708	0.702	0.695
Auto-ARIMA	0.854	0.858	0.833	0.854	0.610

Table 4.22 UNRATE-4-120-4.

	RMSE	MAE	U1	U2	SSR
Naíve	1.000	1.000	1.000	1.000	0.061
UR1	1.009	1.005	1.006	1.009	0.500
UR2	1.297	1.269	1.292	1.297	0.512
TS1	0.941	0.958	0.920	0.941	0.500
TS1-BC1	0.941	0.956	0.917	0.941	0.561
TS1-BC2	0.941	0.956	0.918	0.941	0.561
TS2	0.941	0.958	0.920	0.941	0.500
TS2-BC1	0.941	0.956	0.917	0.941	0.561
TS2-BC2	0.941	0.956	0.918	0.941	0.561
TS-DBL	1.000	0.998	0.995	1.000	0.488
AR(1)	0.997	1.004	1.011	0.997	0.427
SES	1.000	1.001	1.000	1.000	0.512
HB	1.001	1.001	0.985	1.001	0.451
ARIMA $(1,1,0)$	1.049	1.069	1.055	1.049	0.244
Auto-ARIMA	1.008	1.003	1.004	1.008	0.488

large as before when the trend-stationary DGP θ-forecasts of the second kind used to become useful, and a moving average of length 4 observations.

The UNRATE series being difficult to forecast with simple(r) methods is worthwhile being examined further with the bivariate Θ approach by possibly accounting for other economic drivers in U.S. unemployment. This is something that we do not pursue further here, just closing by noting that even for this series the θ-forecasts are always on the top or the top performers.

4.4 Series EXPIMP

The next series which we work with is the EXPIMP series; see Figure 4.3 for the time series plots. The related descriptive statistics are given in Tables 4.23–4.25. The reader will immediately see that the series contains smaller local trends and a few "spikes" in its evolution which are different in nature from a structural break.

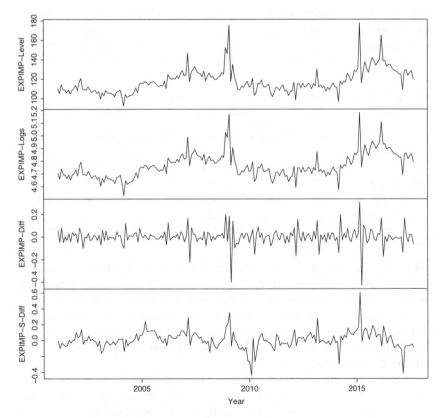

Figure 4.3 Time series plots of series EXPIMP.

Table 4.23 Full sample statistics, 2000–2017, series EXPIMP.

	Mean	Standard Deviation	Minimum	Maximum	Skewness	Kurtosis
EXPIMP-Level	117.721	12.428	92.470	178.110	1.610	7.723
EXPIMP-Logs	4.763	0.099	4.527	5.182	1.083	5.369
EXPIMP-Diff	0.001	0.078	−0.431	0.306	−1.136	11.812
EXPIMP-S-Diff	0.007	0.111	−0.441	0.609	0.304	9.123

Table 4.24 Subsample statistics, 2000–2005, series EXPIMP.

	Mean	Standard Deviation	Minimum	Maximum	Skewness	Kurtosis
EXPIMP-Level	109.014	5.335	92.470	120.880	−0.153	3.137
EXPIMP-Logs	4.690	0.049	4.527	4.795	−0.323	3.493
EXPIMP-Diff	0.001	0.042	−0.100	0.120	0.111	3.479
EXPIMP-S-Diff	0.007	0.074	−0.159	0.240	0.459	3.571

Table 4.25 Subsample statistics, 2006–2017, series EXPIMP.

	Mean	Standard Deviation	Minimum	Maximum	Skewness	Kurtosis
EXPIMP-Level	121.452	12.740	96.880	178.110	1.531	7.324
EXPIMP-Logs	4.794	0.099	4.573	5.182	1.007	5.271
EXPIMP-Diff	0.000	0.089	−0.431	0.306	−1.083	9.772
EXPIMP-S-Diff	0.007	0.123	−0.441	0.609	0.271	8.244

Starting with Table 4.26, where the series is at its level, the rolling window length is 60 observations and the moving average length is 3 observations, we can see that the benchmark AR(1)-forecast does not perform better than the benchmark, in series that does exhibit mean reversion but has the aforementioned "spikes." On the other hand, the smoothing-based forecasts all perform well and better than both the ARIMA(1, 1, 0)-forecast and the Auto-ARIMA-forecast.

The top performing forecast is the one coming from the trend-stationary DGP θ-forecast of the second kind with bias correction; the other trend-stationary DGP θ-forecasts follow closely as do the SES-forecast and the HB-forecast. We note that there are several forecasts that attain maximum

Table 4.26 EXPIMP-1-60-3.

	RMSE	MAE	U1	U2	SSR
Naïve	1.000	1.000	1.000	1.000	0.000
UR1	0.933	1.009	0.988	0.933	0.657
UR2	1.445	1.444	1.660	1.445	0.657
TS1	0.867	0.963	0.916	0.867	0.650
TS1-BC1	0.874	0.974	0.923	0.874	0.657
TS1-BC2	0.866	0.961	0.914	0.866	0.650
TS2	0.855	0.911	0.896	0.855	0.643
TS2-BC1	0.859	0.920	0.900	0.859	0.650
TS2-BC2	0.853	0.910	0.894	0.853	0.643
TS-DBL	1.000	1.003	1.001	1.000	0.514
AR(1)	1.016	1.015	1.014	1.016	0.464
SES	0.874	0.924	0.897	0.874	0.643
HB	0.877	0.934	0.900	0.877	0.657
ARIMA $(1, 1, 0)$	0.928	1.005	0.957	0.928	0.636
Auto-ARIMA	0.936	1.014	0.995	0.936	0.650

SSR and one of them is the unit root DGP θ-forecast, even if it is not a top performer in terms of the other statistics.

The results in Table 4.27, where the rolling window is increased to 90 observations and the moving average length stays at 3 observations, are basically the same where the same ranking of the different forecasts of Table 4.26 is maintained. The results for the series in its logarithms are essentially the same and thus omitted.

Turning to Table 4.28, where the series is not expressed in its first differences, the rolling window is of size 60 observations and the moving average length is 24 observations, we can see that the top forecast comes from the AR(1) model, but its performance is very closely followed by the trend-stationary DGP θ-forecasts of both kinds, the one from the first kind with bias correction being the closest to the AR(1)-forecast.

The performance of these θ-forecasts is better than that of the rest of their competing models. We also note that the highest SSR for this exercise comes from the SES-forecast at 83.6%, with the second best coming from the AR(1) model at 82.1% and third best at 81.4% coming from various θ-forecasts.

The results markedly improve in favor of the θ-forecasts in Table 4.29, where the rolling window is increased to 90 observations. While the AR(1) model is still ranked at the top, the trend-stationary θ-forecasts are again very close to it and their performance distance from all other models is increased.

Table 4.27 EXPIMP-1-90-3.

	RMSE	MAE	U1	U2	SSR
Naíve	1.000	1.000	1.000	1.000	0.000
UR1	0.896	0.990	0.947	0.896	0.636
UR2	1.403	1.477	1.620	1.403	0.627
TS1	0.864	0.973	0.912	0.864	0.618
TS1-BC1	0.867	0.977	0.915	0.867	0.627
TS1-BC2	0.864	0.972	0.911	0.864	0.618
TS2	0.829	0.905	0.865	0.829	0.618
TS2-BC1	0.832	0.909	0.868	0.832	0.627
TS2-BC2	0.829	0.906	0.865	0.829	0.618
TS-DBL	1.000	1.000	1.000	1.000	0.555
AR(1)	1.009	1.009	1.010	1.009	0.482
SES	0.865	0.930	0.891	0.865	0.627
HB	0.869	0.938	0.896	0.869	0.618
ARIMA $(1, 1, 0)$	0.906	1.011	0.952	0.906	0.609
Auto-ARIMA	0.897	0.991	0.950	0.897	0.636

Table 4.28 EXPIMP-3-60-24.

	RMSE	MAE	U1	U2	SSR
Naíve	1.000	1.000	1.000	1.000	0.000
UR1	0.745	0.773	3.260	0.745	0.757
UR2	1.304	1.321	6.339	1.304	0.757
TS1	0.523	0.569	1.131	0.523	0.814
TS1-BC1	0.525	0.570	1.136	0.525	0.807
TS1-BC2	0.522	0.568	1.127	0.522	0.814
TS2	0.547	0.609	1.096	0.547	0.814
TS2-BC1	0.549	0.611	1.102	0.549	0.807
TS2-BC2	0.547	0.609	1.090	0.547	0.814
TS-DBL	1.002	1.001	1.006	1.002	0.450
AR(1)	0.512	0.549	1.012	0.512	0.821
SES	0.577	0.567	0.989	0.577	0.836
HB	0.594	0.588	1.099	0.594	0.814
ARIMA $(1, 1, 0)$	0.593	0.663	1.692	0.593	0.807
Auto-ARIMA	0.745	0.775	3.299	0.745	0.757

Table 4.29 EXPIMP-3-90-24.

	RMSE	MAE	U1	U2	SSR
Naíve	1.000	1.000	1.000	1.000	0.000
UR1	0.726	0.771	3.205	0.726	0.755
UR2	1.290	1.330	6.295	1.290	0.755
TS1	0.521	0.567	1.142	0.521	0.782
TS1-BC1	0.521	0.568	1.145	0.521	0.782
TS1-BC2	0.521	0.567	1.142	0.521	0.782
TS2	0.539	0.597	1.143	0.539	0.782
TS2-BC1	0.539	0.597	1.145	0.539	0.782
TS2-BC2	0.538	0.596	1.142	0.538	0.782
TS-DBL	1.000	1.000	1.002	1.000	0.509
AR(1)	0.505	0.549	1.013	0.505	0.791
SES	0.578	0.568	1.018	0.578	0.800
HB	0.588	0.582	1.021	0.588	0.791
ARIMA (1, 1, 0)	0.585	0.670	1.766	0.585	0.773
Auto-ARIMA	0.727	0.772	3.234	0.727	0.755

It is also interesting to note that the SSR performance of the unit root DGP θ-forecasts, both in this and in the previous table, is quite high and comparable (albeit smaller) with the rest of the top performing forecasts.

When we look at the results of the series expressed in their seasonal differences, in Table 4.30, where the length of the rolling window is 60 observations and the length of the moving average is 4 observations, we can see that the top performing forecasts across all statistics is the trend-stationary θ-forecast of the first kind with bias correction.

This performance is followed by the SES and HB-forecasts and note that, as we have seen before, the θ-based forecasts exhibit top performance as far as their SSR statistic is concerned. It is interesting to note that the unit root DGP θ-forecast also exhibits consistently one of the top SSR values across the results we have seen so far.

Finally, when we look at Table 4.31 where the rolling window length is increased to 90 observations, we can note that both kinds of the trend-stationary DGP θ-forecasts are top performers and, in particular, we have a clear winner in terms of the SSR, the trend-stationary DGP θ-forecast of the second kind with bias correction. As in the previous tables that we have seen, the performance of the θ-forecasts is either on par with or above all benchmarks and their SSR values keep consistently appearing in the top positions in the ranking among all forecasts considered.

Table 4.30 EXPIMP-4-60-4.

	RMSE	MAE	U1	U2	SSR
Naíve	1.000	1.000	1.000	1.000	0.000
UR1	0.891	0.960	2.955	0.891	0.607
UR2	1.370	1.452	6.552	1.370	0.600
TS1	0.824	0.938	4.373	0.824	0.607
TS1-BC1	0.830	0.945	4.451	0.830	0.607
TS1-BC2	0.823	0.937	4.372	0.823	0.607
TS2	1.132	1.024	4.372	1.132	0.593
TS2-BC1	1.135	1.029	4.450	1.135	0.593
TS2-BC2	1.126	1.023	4.371	1.126	0.593
TS-DBL	1.001	1.002	1.119	1.001	0.443
AR(1)	0.869	0.929	1.003	0.869	0.607
SES	0.839	0.907	3.134	0.839	0.586
HB	0.841	0.911	3.115	0.841	0.593
ARIMA (1, 1, 0)	0.846	0.923	3.083	0.846	0.607
Auto-ARIMA	0.890	0.965	2.984	0.890	0.600

Table 4.31 EXPIMP-4-90-3.

	RMSE	MAE	U1	U2	SSR
Naíve	1.000	1.000	1.000	1.000	0.000
UR1	0.873	0.948	2.860	0.873	0.582
UR2	1.359	1.477	6.418	1.359	0.582
TS1	0.847	0.962	1.429	0.847	0.609
TS1-BC1	0.849	0.965	1.397	0.849	0.618
TS1-BC2	0.846	0.962	1.434	0.846	0.609
TS2	0.832	0.894	1.304	0.832	0.609
TS2-BC1	0.834	0.896	1.271	0.834	0.627
TS2-BC2	0.832	0.894	1.298	0.832	0.609
TS-DBL	1.000	1.000	1.014	1.000	0.491
AR(1)	0.855	0.916	1.002	0.855	0.600
SES	0.835	0.909	3.185	0.835	0.573
HB	0.837	0.913	3.214	0.837	0.564
ARIMA (1, 1, 0)	0.854	0.931	3.158	0.854	0.573
Auto-ARIMA	0.874	0.949	2.907	0.874	0.573

4.5   Series TRADE

The next series we look at is the TRADE series, the data being presented in Figure 4.4. We can see that the series displays some interesting characteristics which made it a possibly difficult candidate to work with. For the levels of the series, we can see two pronounced periods of changes, the post-reunification drop after 1990 and the 2008 crisis drop. Note the effects of scaling in the plot and also the fact that the post-reunification period with the marked structural change might affect the estimation results in the inclusive rolling window.

In the presented analysis, we have omitted the results from the levels of the series, which are similar to the ones for the logarithms of the series – but available as well. The descriptive statistics for the full sample and the two subsamples are given in Tables 4.32–4.34, and we can see the impact of the large changes in the two aforementioned periods to be reflected in the large sample kurtosis across all three tables. The increases in the average level and growth rate of the series can also be seen in the tables.

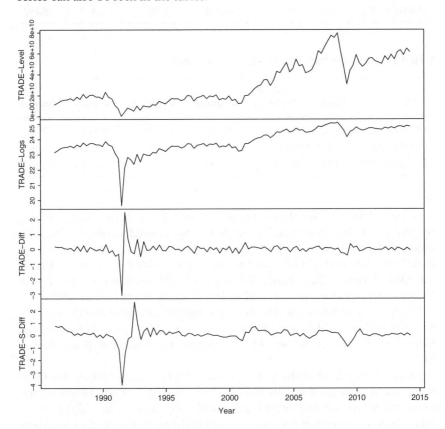

Figure 4.4 Time series plots of series TRADE.

Table 4.32 Full sample statistics, 1985–2014, series TRADE.

	Mean	Standard Deviation	Minimum	Maximum	Skewness	Kurtosis
TRADE-Logs	23.909	0.796	19.645	25.099	−1.354	8.434
TRADE-Diff	0.017	0.424	−3.110	2.483	−1.768	36.610
TRADE-S-Diff	0.078	0.569	−3.991	2.725	−2.551	28.189

Table 4.33 Subsample statistics, 1985–2000, series TRADE.

	Mean	Standard Deviation	Minimum	Maximum	Skewness	Kurtosis
TRADE-Logs	23.321	0.603	19.645	23.867	−3.978	23.569
TRADE-Diff	0.005	0.566	−3.110	2.483	−1.333	21.459
TRADE-S-Diff	0.047	0.736	−3.991	2.725	−2.067	18.492

Table 4.34 Subsample statistics, 2001–2014, series TRADE.

	Mean	Standard Deviation	Minimum	Maximum	Skewness	Kurtosis
TRADE-Logs	24.574	0.324	23.711	25.099	−0.894	3.351
TRADE-Diff	0.030	0.149	−0.423	0.443	−0.288	4.146
TRADE-S-Diff	0.112	0.283	−0.894	0.727	−0.913	5.240

In Table 4.35, we have the results for the logarithm of the series, a rolling window of 30 observations and a moving average of length 3 observations. No model or forecast can beat the Naíve benchmark with two interesting exceptions in the case of the MAE-statistic, that of the double θ-forecast and that of the AR(1)-forecast which have MAE values of 0.97 and 0.984 – the unit root DGP θ-forecast has a nominal MAE of less than one but as high as 0.997.

The AR(1) model forecast does have the highest SSR value at 59%, which is also matched by the SES-forecast and the unit root DGP forecast of the second kind; the SSR value of the best MAE performing forecast, the double θ, is at 57.8%.

So, for the log-level of the series TRADE and the current parameter combinations, we can see that only the double θ-forecast is of any additional use to the Naíve forecast and the only reasonable alternative to the AR(1) benchmark. This is also verified if we were to look at the next table, Table 4.36, where

Table 4.35 TRADE-2-30-3.

	RMSE	MAE	U1	U2	SSR
Naíve	1.000	1.000	1.000	1.000	0.000
UR1	1.040	0.997	1.038	1.040	0.566
UR2	1.501	1.448	1.500	1.501	0.590
TS1	1.105	1.095	1.101	1.105	0.542
TS1-BC1	1.112	1.087	1.108	1.112	0.578
TS1-BC2	1.101	1.086	1.096	1.101	0.554
TS2	1.104	1.092	1.099	1.104	0.542
TS2-BC1	1.110	1.084	1.106	1.110	0.566
TS2-BC2	1.102	1.085	1.097	1.102	0.554
TS-DBL	1.002	0.970	1.001	1.002	0.578
AR(1)	1.024	0.984	1.024	1.024	0.590
SES	1.020	1.028	1.021	1.020	0.590
HB	1.053	1.048	1.055	1.053	0.554
ARIMA (1, 1, 0)	1.046	1.050	1.046	1.046	0.253
Auto-ARIMA	1.051	1.012	1.050	1.051	0.530

Table 4.36 TRADE-2-60-3.

	RMSE	MAE	U1	U2	SSR
Naíve	1.000	1.000	1.000	1.000	0.000
UR1	1.065	1.033	1.065	1.065	0.509
UR2	1.619	1.529	1.616	1.619	0.472
TS1	1.209	1.185	1.207	1.209	0.472
TS1-BC1	1.201	1.166	1.198	1.201	0.528
TS1-BC2	1.210	1.185	1.207	1.210	0.509
TS2	1.206	1.182	1.204	1.206	0.472
TS2-BC1	1.198	1.164	1.195	1.198	0.528
TS2-BC2	1.206	1.181	1.204	1.206	0.509
TS-DBL	1.003	0.977	1.002	1.003	0.604
AR(1)	1.010	0.983	1.009	1.010	0.566
SES	1.116	1.158	1.117	1.116	0.472
HB	1.102	1.131	1.101	1.102	0.472
ARIMA (1, 1, 0)	1.162	1.174	1.161	1.162	0.302
Auto-ARIMA	1.071	1.043	1.071	1.071	0.491

the length of the rolling window is increased to 60 observations and the moving average length stays the same. Here the double θ-forecast completely dominates all other forecasts with the smallest MAE value and the largest SSR value.

The impact on the choice of length of the moving average in obtaining different θ-forecasts can next be seen in Table 4.37, where we maintain the same rolling window of 60 observations but we increase the length of the moving average to 12 observations. The results are reinforcing the ones of the previous table. The double θ-forecast has all metrics better than the Naíve benchmark, including the RMSE and U1 and U2 statistics and an even higher (the highest from all tables so far for this series) value of the SSR statistic.

It is interesting to note that the values of the SSR for the other θ-based forecasts appear to be more sensitive to the choices made for the moving average, which should not come as a surprise: the way that the trend is modeled in a trending time series, of course, will make a difference in the success of the forecast in predicting direction.

We next turn to the results where the TRADE series is expressed in its first differences in Table 4.38, where the length of the rolling window is set to 30 observations and the length of the moving average is set to 6 observations. The transformation to stationarity gives, as expected, a headway to model-based

Table 4.37 TRADE-2-60-12.

	RMSE	MAE	U1	U2	SSR
Naíve	1.000	1.000	1.000	1.000	0.000
UR1	1.065	1.033	1.065	1.065	0.509
UR2	1.619	1.529	1.616	1.619	0.472
TS1	1.200	1.230	1.200	1.200	0.491
TS1-BC1	1.186	1.192	1.185	1.186	0.509
TS1-BC2	1.189	1.197	1.188	1.189	0.509
TS2	1.042	1.059	1.041	1.042	0.491
TS2-BC1	1.028	1.023	1.026	1.028	0.509
TS2-BC2	1.029	1.025	1.027	1.029	0.509
TS-DBL	0.984	0.970	0.984	0.984	0.642
AR(1)	1.010	0.983	1.009	1.010	0.566
SES	1.116	1.158	1.117	1.116	0.472
HB	1.102	1.131	1.101	1.102	0.472
ARIMA (1, 1, 0)	1.162	1.174	1.161	1.162	0.302
Auto-ARIMA	1.071	1.043	1.071	1.071	0.491

Table 4.38 TRADE-3-30-6.

	RMSE	MAE	U1	U2	SSR
Naíve	1.000	1.000	1.000	1.000	0.000
UR1	0.872	0.863	1.277	0.872	0.735
UR2	1.398	1.309	2.465	1.398	0.711
TS1	0.720	0.680	1.350	0.720	0.723
TS1-BC1	0.716	0.682	1.366	0.716	0.723
TS1-BC2	0.725	0.688	1.346	0.725	0.723
TS2	0.766	0.738	1.353	0.766	0.735
TS2-BC1	0.758	0.734	1.367	0.758	0.735
TS2-BC2	0.764	0.737	1.347	0.764	0.723
TS-DBL	0.989	0.991	1.013	0.989	0.482
AR(1)	0.685	0.660	0.954	0.685	0.783
SES	0.732	0.674	1.000	0.732	0.771
HB	0.750	0.704	1.298	0.750	0.771
ARIMA $(1,1,0)$	0.832	0.814	1.168	0.832	0.699
Auto-ARIMA	0.890	0.883	1.280	0.890	0.699

forecasts and we can see that the AR(1)-forecast is at the top under all metrics. The next best forecasts are the ones in the group of the trend-stationary DGP θ-forecasts which have the next lowest values of their RMSE, MAE, and U2 statistics but have smaller values of their SSR statistic.

Note that the top SSR value is that of the AR(1)-forecast at 78.3%, with the next highest being at 77.1% from the SES- and the HB-forecasts and then we have the SSR values of the trend-stationary DGP θ-forecasts at 72.3–73.5%. In the next table, Table 4.39, we increase the moving average length to 24 observations to examine the impact that this has on forecasting performance. We can see that the statistics for the θ-forecasts become higher, but at the same time we can see that their SSR values improve compared to the previous table. For example, the trend-stationary DGP θ-forecasts of the first and second kinds with bias correction have their SSR values rise to 79.5%

Table 4.40 has results of the seasonal differences of the series, a rolling window of length 30 and a moving average length of 12 observations. A first look at these results shows that as before the top performing forecast comes from the AR(1) model across all metrics, but there is a result of the trend-stationary DGP θ-forecasts of the first kind that makes them interesting. We can see that the

Table 4.39 TRADE-3-30-24.

	RMSE	MAE	U1	U2	SSR
Naíve	1.000	1.000	1.000	1.000	0.000
UR1	0.872	0.863	1.277	0.872	0.735
UR2	1.398	1.309	2.465	1.398	0.711
TS1	0.793	0.732	1.005	0.793	0.771
TS1-BC1	0.786	0.726	1.011	0.786	0.795
TS1-BC2	0.801	0.738	1.008	0.801	0.771
TS2	0.814	0.735	1.005	0.814	0.771
TS2-BC1	0.803	0.725	1.010	0.803	0.795
TS2-BC2	0.813	0.734	1.005	0.813	0.783
TS-DBL	0.993	0.994	1.001	0.993	0.482
AR(1)	0.685	0.660	0.954	0.685	0.783
SES	0.732	0.674	1.000	0.732	0.771
HB	0.750	0.704	1.298	0.750	0.771
ARIMA $(1,1,0)$	0.832	0.814	1.168	0.832	0.699
Auto-ARIMA	0.890	0.883	1.280	0.890	0.699

Table 4.40 TRADE-4-30-12.

	RMSE	MAE	U1	U2	SSR
Naíve	1.000	1.000	1.000	1.000	0.000
UR1	0.989	1.036	1.346	0.989	0.506
UR2	1.314	1.359	2.428	1.314	0.566
TS1	0.954	0.939	0.880	0.954	0.627
TS1-BC1	0.970	0.965	1.293	0.970	0.614
TS1-BC2	0.960	0.947	0.991	0.960	0.627
TS2	3.246	1.605	1.544	3.246	0.518
TS2-BC1	3.250	1.629	1.807	3.250	0.506
TS2-BC2	2.831	1.544	1.491	2.831	0.518
TS-DBL	1.000	1.012	1.120	1.000	0.482
AR(1)	0.886	0.914	0.990	0.886	0.663
SES	0.971	1.005	1.012	0.971	0.614
HB	0.958	0.967	0.936	0.958	0.614
ARIMA $(1,1,0)$	1.008	1.047	1.005	1.008	0.048
Auto-ARIMA	0.993	1.032	1.144	0.993	0.578

Table 4.41 TRADE-4-60-12.

	RMSE	MAE	U1	U2	SSR
Naíve	1.000	1.000	1.000	1.000	0.000
UR1	1.037	1.022	0.991	1.037	0.509
UR2	1.554	1.511	1.300	1.554	0.585
TS1	0.968	0.908	0.871	0.968	0.698
TS1-BC1	0.982	0.919	0.872	0.982	0.698
TS1-BC2	0.975	0.910	0.870	0.975	0.698
TS2	1.152	1.069	0.946	1.152	0.604
TS2-BC1	1.160	1.076	0.947	1.160	0.604
TS2-BC2	1.142	1.064	0.944	1.142	0.604
TS-DBL	1.004	0.998	0.989	1.004	0.453
AR(1)	0.965	0.983	0.998	0.965	0.660
SES	1.033	1.039	0.926	1.033	0.660
HB	1.040	1.039	0.937	1.040	0.642
ARIMA $(1,1,0)$	1.071	1.079	1.075	1.071	0.057
Auto-ARIMA	1.044	1.039	0.991	1.044	0.472

first of the three forecasts in that group has the second lowest value in the MAE statistic at 0.939 (compared to the 0.914 of the AR(1)-forecast) and is the only forecast with a considerably less than one value on the U1 statistic; this forecast also has the second best SSR value across all forecasts, at 62.7% compared to 66.3% of the AR(1)-forecast.

Increasing the length of the rolling window to 60 observations, and maintaining the moving average length to 12 observations, we can see from the results of Table 4.41 that the θ-forecasts of the trend-stationary DGP of the first kind dominate again as top performers. Specifically, see that while the statistics for the RMSE, MAE, and U1 and U2 in general become higher, the three θ-forecasts of the trend-stationary DGP converge in performance, considerably decrease their MAE values, and increase their SSR values to practically 70% – also see that they continue to be the only forecasts with substantially lower than one U1 statistics. Finally, note that most other forecasts (including the AR(1)-forecast) deteriorate in performance.

4.6 Series JOBS

We turn next to the first bivariate example of the series JOBS. Here, we present the results of the forecasting performance of various models and forecasts for

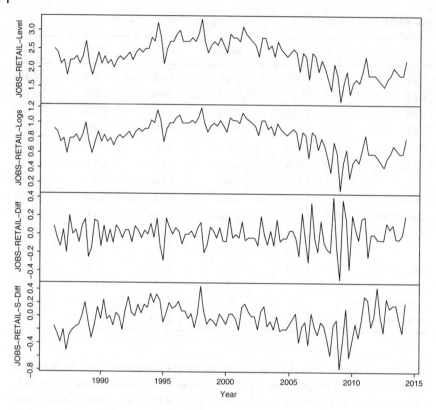

Figure 4.5 Time series plots of series JOBS-1.

the first of the two series, JOBS-1, that correspond to the rate of job openings for retail trade. In this example, we have two series that do exhibit co-movement, as we can see from Figures 4.5 and 4.6, and we have chosen to present the result of the first series as it is the more "noisy" of the two, and presumably more difficult to forecast.

The corresponding tables with the descriptive statistics on the full sample and subsamples appear in Tables 4.42–4.44, where we can see the differences in the relevant magnitudes between the two series. The results of the forecasting performance start in Table 4.45.

In this table, we have results of the JOBS-1 series in its level, with a rolling window of 60 observations and a moving average length of 3 observations. The top model across all statistics, save the SSR, is the trend-stationary DGP θ-forecast of the second kind with and without bias correction (the two forecasts tie). Their values are better than the second best performer, the SES-forecast, the latter having the second higher SSR at 56.9%. Note that

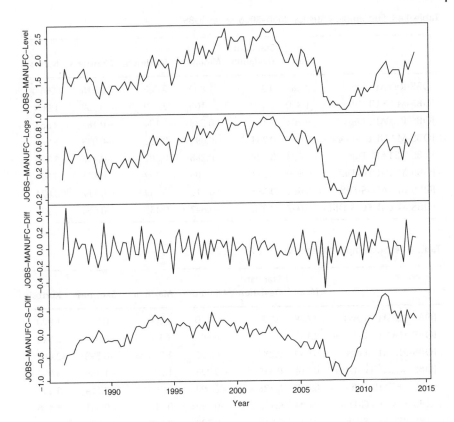

Figure 4.6 Time series plots of series JOBS-2.

Table 4.42 Full sample statistics, 2000–2017, series JOBS.

	Mean	Standard Deviation	Minimum	Maximum	Skewness	Kurtosis
JOBS-RETAIL-Level	2.623	0.633	1.100	4.000	0.321	2.496
JOBS-MANUFC-Level	2.031	0.549	0.800	3.400	−0.081	2.581
JOBS-RETAIL-Logs	0.935	0.247	0.095	1.386	−0.286	2.978
JOBS-MANUFC-Logs	0.667	0.299	−0.223	1.224	−0.786	3.274
JOBS-RETAIL-Diff	0.003	0.122	−0.492	0.405	−0.220	4.910
JOBS-MANUFC-Diff	0.006	0.129	−0.492	0.492	0.010	4.351
JOBS-RETAIL-S-Diff	0.021	0.202	−0.780	0.547	−0.631	4.222
JOBS-MANUFC-S-Diff	0.028	0.282	−0.965	0.811	−0.855	4.903

Table 4.43 Subsample statistics, 2000–2006, series JOBS.

	Mean	Standard Deviation	Minimum	Maximum	Skewness	Kurtosis
JOBS-RETAIL-Level	2.483	0.322	1.800	3.300	0.118	2.567
JOBS-MANUFC-Level	1.810	0.419	1.100	2.700	0.253	1.968
JOBS-RETAIL-Logs	0.901	0.131	0.588	1.194	−0.187	2.565
JOBS-MANUFC-Logs	0.567	0.234	0.095	0.993	−0.083	1.969
JOBS-RETAIL-Diff	0.003	0.109	−0.288	0.201	−0.436	2.776
JOBS-MANUFC-Diff	0.010	0.144	−0.305	0.492	0.471	3.803
JOBS-RETAIL-S-Diff	−0.001	0.185	−0.511	0.452	−0.117	3.074
JOBS-MANUFC-S-Diff	0.047	0.228	−0.647	0.452	−0.694	3.137

Table 4.44 Subsample statistics, 2007–2017, series JOBS.

	Mean	Standard Deviation	Minimum	Maximum	Skewness	Kurtosis
JOBS-RETAIL-Level	2.688	0.726	1.100	4.000	0.096	1.970
JOBS-MANUFC-Level	2.132	0.573	0.800	3.400	−0.378	2.845
JOBS-RETAIL-Logs	0.950	0.284	0.095	1.386	−0.393	2.484
JOBS-MANUFC-Logs	0.714	0.315	−0.223	1.224	−1.156	3.992
JOBS-RETAIL-Diff	0.002	0.128	−0.492	0.405	−0.154	5.253
JOBS-MANUFC-Diff	0.004	0.122	−0.492	0.314	−0.357	4.466
JOBS-RETAIL-S-Diff	0.031	0.210	−0.780	0.547	−0.823	4.584
JOBS-MANUFC-S-Diff	0.019	0.304	−0.965	0.811	−0.825	4.776

Table 4.45 JOBS-1-60-3.

	RMSE	MAE	U1	U2	SSR
Naíve	1.000	1.000	1.000	1.000	0.115
UR1	0.956	0.955	0.942	0.956	0.531
UR2	1.358	1.353	1.307	1.358	0.554
TS1	0.910	0.925	0.845	0.910	0.554
TS1-BC1	0.911	0.924	0.849	0.911	0.554
TS1-BC2	0.909	0.925	0.844	0.909	0.562
TS2	0.893	0.904	0.824	0.893	0.554
TS2-BC1	0.895	0.905	0.829	0.895	0.554
TS2-BC2	0.893	0.904	0.824	0.893	0.554
TS-DBL	0.996	1.004	1.000	0.996	0.462
BUR-L	0.990	1.020	1.015	0.990	0.446

Table 4.45 (Continued)

	RMSE	MAE	U1	U2	SSR
BUR-RR	0.998	1.029	1.025	0.998	0.462
BUR-D	0.971	0.966	0.959	0.971	0.546
BCT	0.994	1.007	1.009	0.994	0.415
BMA	0.915	0.926	0.846	0.915	0.577
BMA-BC	0.917	0.926	0.851	0.917	0.546
AR(1)	1.009	1.014	1.013	1.009	0.469
SES	0.898	0.877	0.837	0.898	0.569
HB	0.901	0.881	0.843	0.901	0.538
ARIMA $(1,1,0)$	0.937	0.935	0.861	0.937	0.554
Auto-ARIMA	0.959	0.958	0.946	0.959	0.538
VAR	0.977	1.002	0.909	0.977	0.485

Table 4.46 JOBS-1-90-3.

	RMSE	MAE	U1	U2	SSR
Naíve	1.000	1.000	1.000	1.000	0.140
UR1	0.962	0.952	0.949	0.962	0.550
UR2	1.426	1.419	1.456	1.426	0.540
TS1	0.959	0.978	0.900	0.959	0.540
TS1-BC1	0.963	0.979	0.904	0.963	0.540
TS1-BC2	0.958	0.978	0.900	0.958	0.560
TS2	0.940	0.956	0.879	0.940	0.550
TS2-BC1	0.944	0.958	0.883	0.944	0.540
TS2-BC2	0.940	0.956	0.879	0.940	0.540
TS-DBL	1.001	1.006	1.002	1.001	0.420
BUR-L	1.004	1.030	1.018	1.004	0.420
BUR-RR	1.005	1.030	1.021	1.005	0.430
BUR-D	0.966	0.952	0.955	0.966	0.550
BCT	1.002	1.030	1.009	1.002	0.360
BMA	0.953	0.971	0.894	0.953	0.570
BMA-BC	0.957	0.972	0.898	0.957	0.560
AR(1)	1.012	1.021	1.014	1.012	0.370
SES	0.923	0.911	0.880	0.923	0.530
HB	0.928	0.914	0.889	0.928	0.510
ARIMA $(1,1,0)$	0.940	0.955	0.890	0.940	0.540
Auto-ARIMA	0.962	0.954	0.950	0.962	0.530
VAR	1.043	1.079	0.990	1.043	0.480

the highest SSR at 57.7% is obtained by the bivariate trend-stationary DGP Θ-forecast, which has competitive statistics to the top performing forecasts.

Increasing the size of the rolling window to 90 observations and maintaining the same length of the moving average at 3 observations, as in Table 4.46, we can see that the statistics of the previously top univariate θ-forecasts deteriorate but not so the statistics of the bivariate Θ-forecast which, although not as good as the ones of the SES and HB-forecasts, are very close to them and the bivariate Θ-forecast is now the top performer in the SSR statistic by a wider margin. We can clearly see that the trade-off between forecast uncertainty and forecast direction is much less in the bivariate Θ-forecast.

Table 4.47, has the results where the series is in its logarithms, the rolling window is of length 30 observations and the moving average is of length 3 observations. The logarithmic transformation here produced even better results in favor of the θ and Θ-forecasts. Specifically, the top performing

Table 4.47 JOBS-2-60-3.

	RMSE	MAE	U1	U2	SSR
Naíve	1.000	1.000	1.000	1.000	0.115
UR1	0.963	0.959	0.746	0.963	0.554
UR2	1.375	1.363	0.877	1.375	0.554
TS1	0.869	0.908	0.443	0.869	0.569
TS1-BC1	0.872	0.907	0.440	0.872	0.562
TS1-BC2	0.868	0.906	0.443	0.868	0.569
TS2	0.844	0.880	0.417	0.844	0.569
TS2-BC1	0.846	0.883	0.426	0.846	0.562
TS2-BC2	0.844	0.880	0.418	0.844	0.569
TS-DBL	0.996	1.003	1.006	0.996	0.469
BUR-L	0.997	1.021	1.084	0.997	0.446
BUR-RR	1.003	1.031	1.106	1.003	0.446
BUR-D	0.984	0.981	0.790	0.984	0.531
BCT	0.992	1.006	1.059	0.992	0.415
BMA	0.879	0.921	0.437	0.879	0.577
BMA-BC	0.882	0.921	0.435	0.882	0.554
AR(1)	1.007	1.019	1.008	1.007	0.462
SES	0.875	0.856	0.422	0.875	0.562
HB	0.880	0.865	0.432	0.880	0.538
ARIMA $(1,1,0)$	0.880	0.888	0.423	0.880	0.608
Auto-ARIMA	0.966	0.963	0.749	0.966	0.546
VAR	0.965	1.024	0.454	0.965	0.515

forecasts are in the trend-stationary DGP θ-forecast of the second kind, without and with bias correction, with the overall lowest values in all statistics, save their SSR where they have the third best values. These are closely followed by the corresponding forecasts of the first kind.

Furthermore, we can see that the bivariate trend-stationary Θ-forecast is again a very solid performer, offering the second best SSR value, at 57.7%, compared to the top SSR performing forecast which is the ARIMA(1, 1, 0)-forecast at 60.8%. Note that the bivariate VAR(1)-forecast has not perform well so far, with the series expressed in levels and logarithms.

When we take the first differences of the series, the forecast rankings change and the parametric-model-based forecasts become better performers, but not by far and with the θ and Θ-forecasts still being at the top in terms of the ability to predict direction. The results are given in Table 4.48, with a rolling window of 60 observations and a moving average of 4 observations. We can

Table 4.48 JOBS-3-60-4.

	RMSE	MAE	U1	U2	SSR
Naíve	1.000	1.000		1.000	0.015
UR1	0.880	0.836	1.037	0.880	0.692
UR2	1.319	1.292	1.708	1.319	0.715
TS1	0.649	0.657	0.860	0.649	0.762
TS1-BC1	0.649	0.657	0.858	0.649	0.769
TS1-BC2	0.649	0.657	0.861	0.649	0.762
TS2	0.649	0.657	0.860	0.649	0.762
TS2-BC1	0.649	0.657	0.858	0.649	0.769
TS2-BC2	0.649	0.657	0.861	0.649	0.762
TS-DBL	0.998	0.997	0.996	0.998	0.569
BUR-L	0.929	0.941	1.089	0.929	0.608
BUR-RR	0.945	0.935	1.011	0.945	0.600
BUR-D	0.901	0.857	1.113	0.901	0.677
BCT	0.815	0.891	1.240	0.815	0.577
BMA	0.661	0.666	0.898	0.661	0.738
BMA-BC	0.661	0.666	0.896	0.661	0.746
AR(1)	0.582	0.584		0.582	0.731
SES	0.616	0.626	0.831	0.616	0.762
HB	0.628	0.630	0.812	0.628	0.762
ARIMA (1, 1, 0)	0.581	0.636	0.894	0.581	0.692
Auto-ARIMA	0.884	0.835	1.047	0.884	0.723
VAR	0.618	0.621	0.845	0.618	0.754

see that the trend-stationary DGP θ and Θ-forecasts have essentially the same performance, but they slightly underperform their parametric competitors, specifically the AR(1) and the ARIMA(1, 1, 0)-forecasts.

This is a point in our discussion where we can clearly indicate what we meant when we claimed in the previous chapter that the AR(1) model forecast is a θ-forecast. Over the next two tables, Tables 4.49 and 4.50, we illustrate what happens to the performance of the trend-stationary DGP, univariate and bivariate, θ and Θ-forecasts as we increase the length of the moving average and thus approach the case of the full sample mean.

The reader will notice that the θ- and Θ-forecasts approach the performance of the AR(1)-forecast and they maintain their superior position in terms of their SSR values and when the moving average length becomes 24 observations (in a rolling window of 60 observations), the univariate trend-stationary DGP

Table 4.49 JOBS-3-60-12.

	RMSE	MAE	U1	U2	SSR
Naíve	1.000	1.000		1.000	0.015
UR1	0.880	0.836	1.037	0.880	0.692
UR2	1.319	1.292	1.708	1.319	0.715
TS1	0.630	0.634	0.839	0.630	0.746
TS1-BC1	0.629	0.633	0.837	0.629	0.762
TS1-BC2	0.630	0.634	0.840	0.630	0.746
TS2	0.641	0.650	0.855	0.641	0.723
TS2-BC1	0.641	0.649	0.853	0.641	0.746
TS2-BC2	0.641	0.650	0.856	0.641	0.738
TS-DBL	0.997	0.997	0.996	0.997	0.569
BUR-L	0.929	0.941	1.089	0.929	0.608
BUR-RR	0.945	0.935	1.011	0.945	0.600
BUR-D	0.901	0.857	1.113	0.901	0.677
BCT	0.815	0.891	1.240	0.815	0.577
BMA	0.643	0.649	0.879	0.643	0.738
BMA-BC	0.643	0.648	0.877	0.643	0.746
AR(1)	0.582	0.584		0.582	0.731
SES	0.616	0.626	0.831	0.616	0.762
HB	0.628	0.630	0.812	0.628	0.762
ARIMA (1, 1, 0)	0.581	0.636	0.894	0.581	0.692
Auto-ARIMA	0.884	0.835	1.047	0.884	0.723
VAR	0.618	0.621	0.845	0.618	0.754

Table 4.50 JOBS-3-60-24.

	RMSE	MAE	U1	U2	SSR
Naíve	1.000	1.000		1.000	0.015
UR1	0.880	0.836	1.037	0.880	0.692
UR2	1.319	1.292	1.708	1.319	0.715
TS1	0.595	0.601	0.812	0.595	0.777
TS1-BC1	0.594	0.600	0.809	0.594	0.777
TS1-BC2	0.595	0.601	0.813	0.595	0.777
TS2	1.176	0.793	1.240	1.176	0.708
TS2-BC1	1.175	0.791	1.239	1.175	0.708
TS2-BC2	1.181	0.794	1.247	1.181	0.708
TS-DBL	0.998	0.997	0.996	0.998	0.577
BUR-L	0.929	0.941	1.089	0.929	0.608
BUR-RR	0.945	0.935	1.011	0.945	0.600
BUR-D	0.901	0.857	1.113	0.901	0.677
BCT	0.815	0.891	1.240	0.815	0.577
BMA	0.615	0.621	0.878	0.615	0.769
BMA-BC	0.614	0.620	0.874	0.614	0.769
AR(1)	0.582	0.584		0.582	0.731
SES	0.616	0.626	0.831	0.616	0.762
HB	0.628	0.630	0.812	0.628	0.762
ARIMA $(1,1,0)$	0.581	0.636	0.894	0.581	0.692
Auto-ARIMA	0.884	0.835	1.047	0.884	0.723
VAR	0.618	0.621	0.845	0.618	0.754

θ-forecasts of the first kind become fully competitive to the AR(1)-forecast and have the highest value in their SSR statistic; notice also the improvement in the bivariate trend-stationary DGP Θ-forecasts.

If we increase the rolling window width to 120 observations, and correspondingly increase the length of the moving average to 36 observations, as in Table 4.51, we see the same phenomenon even more clearly. In this table, the θ and Θ-forecasts are essentially the best performers in all statistics.

We finally turn our attention to the case where the series are expressed in their seasonal differences, the results being presented in Tables 4.52–4.54, and are for three different combinations of the rolling window length and the moving average length. In Table 4.52, we have the case of 60 observations for the rolling window and a moving average of length 4 observations.

Table 4.51 JOBS-3-120-36.

	RMSE	MAE	U1	U2	SSR
Naíve	1.000	1.000		1.000	0.014
UR1	0.786	0.743	0.890	0.786	0.743
UR2	1.135	1.142	1.411	1.135	0.743
TS1	0.573	0.560	0.689	0.573	0.843
TS1-BC1	0.572	0.559	0.685	0.572	0.843
TS1-BC2	0.574	0.561	0.690	0.574	0.843
TS2	1.019	0.699	2.311	1.019	0.814
TS2-BC1	1.018	0.697	2.309	1.018	0.814
TS2-BC2	1.012	0.698	2.289	1.012	0.814
TS-DBL	1.000	1.000	0.997	1.000	0.486
BUR-L	1.064	1.045	1.063	1.064	0.500
BUR-RR	0.894	0.824	0.840	0.894	0.643
BUR-D	0.794	0.759	0.915	0.794	0.743
BCT	0.912	0.938	1.265	0.912	0.571
BMA	0.575	0.564	0.698	0.575	0.829
BMA-BC	0.574	0.562	0.694	0.574	0.843
AR(1)	0.572	0.550		0.572	0.786
SES	0.610	0.599	0.756	0.610	0.843
HB	0.617	0.606	0.738	0.617	0.843
ARIMA $(1,1,0)$	0.634	0.652	0.808	0.634	0.729
Auto-ARIMA	0.786	0.745	0.894	0.786	0.729
VAR	0.589	0.580	0.709	0.589	0.843

Table 4.52 JOBS-4-60-6.

	RMSE	MAE	U1	U2	SSR
Naíve	1.000	1.000		1.000	0.046
UR1	0.963	0.961	0.982	0.963	0.585
UR2	1.394	1.396	1.292	1.394	0.577
TS1	0.852	0.876	0.936	0.852	0.615
TS1-BC1	0.853	0.876	0.934	0.853	0.623
TS1-BC2	0.851	0.875	0.935	0.851	0.623
TS2	0.889	0.906	0.990	0.889	0.600
TS2-BC1	0.891	0.907	0.989	0.891	0.600
TS2-BC2	0.890	0.907	0.992	0.890	0.592
TS-DBL	0.996	0.997	0.991	0.996	0.492
BUR-L	0.976	0.997	0.924	0.976	0.523

Table 4.52 (Continued)

	RMSE	MAE	U1	U2	SSR
BUR-RR	0.985	1.007	0.921	0.985	0.515
BUR-D	0.981	0.979	0.957	0.981	0.600
BCT	0.954	0.958	0.919	0.954	0.554
BMA	0.867	0.884	0.922	0.867	0.631
BMA-BC	0.868	0.882	0.920	0.868	0.638
AR(1)	0.872	0.862		0.872	0.615
SES	0.846	0.868	0.945	0.846	0.631
HB	0.853	0.869	0.951	0.853	0.623
ARIMA $(1, 1, 0)$	0.818	0.866	0.917	0.818	0.608
Auto-ARIMA	0.968	0.964	0.987	0.968	0.600
VAR	0.903	0.933	0.965	0.903	0.623

Table 4.53 JOBS-4-90-24.

	RMSE	MAE	U1	U2	SSR
Naíve	1.000	1.000		1.000	0.050
UR1	0.977	0.963	1.004	0.977	0.550
UR2	1.462	1.484	1.278	1.462	0.560
TS1	0.889	0.883	0.956	0.889	0.610
TS1-BC1	0.892	0.888	0.958	0.892	0.640
TS1-BC2	0.890	0.885	0.956	0.890	0.610
TS2	1.085	1.038	1.052	1.085	0.560
TS2-BC1	1.086	1.041	1.053	1.086	0.560
TS2-BC2	1.071	1.035	1.052	1.071	0.550
TS-DBL	1.001	1.001	0.997	1.001	0.480
BUR-L	1.058	1.100	1.092	1.058	0.440
BUR-RR	1.060	1.100	1.095	1.060	0.450
BUR-D	0.979	0.967	0.975	0.979	0.570
BCT	0.945	0.964	0.912	0.945	0.530
BMA	0.882	0.929	0.890	0.882	0.610
BMA-BC	0.885	0.932	0.892	0.885	0.620
AR(1)	0.875	0.864		0.875	0.610
SES	0.871	0.906	0.979	0.871	0.590
HB	0.879	0.910	0.983	0.879	0.590
ARIMA $(1, 1, 0)$	0.886	0.938	0.984	0.886	0.570
Auto-ARIMA	0.978	0.963	1.008	0.978	0.560
VAR	0.930	0.996	0.900	0.930	0.580

Table 4.54 JOBS-4-120-24.

	RMSE	MAE	U1	U2	SSR
Naíve	1.000	1.000		1.000	0.071
UR1	0.976	0.977	0.963	0.976	0.586
UR2	1.447	1.474	1.314	1.447	0.586
TS1	0.871	0.852	0.854	0.871	0.586
TS1-BC1	0.870	0.851	0.854	0.870	0.586
TS1-BC2	0.871	0.852	0.854	0.871	0.586
TS2	0.983	1.022	1.072	0.983	0.529
TS2-BC1	0.983	1.022	1.068	0.983	0.557
TS2-BC2	0.982	1.021	1.065	0.982	0.557
TS-DBL	1.000	0.999	0.996	1.000	0.457
BUR-L	1.063	1.044	1.047	1.063	0.557
BUR-RR	1.064	1.041	1.052	1.064	0.571
BUR-D	0.969	0.970	0.949	0.969	0.571
BCT	0.974	0.974	0.999	0.974	0.543
BMA	0.976	0.930	0.963	0.976	0.543
BMA-BC	0.974	0.927	0.964	0.974	0.571
AR(1)	0.952	0.906		0.952	0.600
SES	0.972	0.962	0.992	0.972	0.571
HB	0.974	0.966	0.990	0.974	0.586
ARIMA (1, 1, 0)	1.089	1.095	1.153	1.089	0.529
Auto-ARIMA	0.975	0.976	0.963	0.975	0.557
VAR	1.104	1.116	1.024	1.104	0.557

The univariate trend-stationary DGP θ-forecasts of the first kind are the best overall performers and tie with the HB-forecast.

What is more interesting here is that the top SSR value is given by the bivariate trend-stationary DGP Θ-forecast with bias correction at 63.8%, the second best value being 62.3% of the previously mentioned univariate forecasts.

In Table 4.53, we increase the rolling window length to 90 observations and the moving average to 24 observations and the top performers, in terms of their RMSE, MAE, and U2 statistics, are the AR(1), SES, and HB-forecasts. However, these are closely tracked by the bivariate trend-stationary DGP Θ-forecasts, the latter having a higher SSR statistic than the top contenders.

Also see that the bivariate forecasts have lower values of the $U1$ statistic than the univariate ones in general. Furthermore, note that the highest value of the SSR statistic for this table is given by the bias-corrected, univariate, trend-stationary DGP θ-forecast.

We close the analysis of these series with Table 4.54, where the rolling window is of length 120 observations and the moving average is of length 24 observations. The results here are all in favor of the θ and Θ-forecasts. The univariate trend-stationary DGP θ-forecasts of the first kind have the top performance in all statistics, save a close second best for the SSR statistic, and they are quite apart from the second best which is the AR(1)-forecast; to get the relevant numbers, note that, for example, the RMSE for the θ-forecasts is 0.871 and for the AR(1)-forecast is 0.952; their corresponding SSR values are 58.6% vs. 60%, a close call.

Furthermore, note that the bivariate trend-stationary DGP Θ-forecasts and the bivariate unit root DGP in differences Θ-forecast do outperform the Naíve benchmark, something that the parametric VAR(1)-forecast is not able to do.

4.7   Series FINANCE

We close this section with the second bivariate example of the series FINANCE. As in the previous section, we present results of the forecasting performance of various models and forecasts for the first of the two series, FINANCE-1, that corresponds to the foreign exchange rate series for United States/United Kingdom, the US dollar vs. the British pound. The two series, whose plots are given in Figures 4.7 and 4.8, do exhibit a certain degree of co-movement – as it is to be expected since both are affected by similar economic factors and have a common reference, the US dollar. Our interest mainly lies with the British pound, for which we present results; but similar results were found on the second series of the US/EU rate that are also available.

The main statistics of the two series, for their full and two subsamples, are given in Tables 4.55–4.58, for the levels, logarithms, first differences, and seasonal differences. The results that we provide in the discussion that follows are for the levels, differences, and seasonal differences; the results for the logarithms are very similar to that of the levels and are thus omitted.

It is well understood that series such as the exchange rates contain stochastic trends that make them difficult to forecast, but also that they contain within them the effects of longer-term economic policies and thus over such periods one can possibly construct forecasting models that account for economic fundamentals. Such models, containing, for example, interest rate differentials as explanatory variables, sometimes provide additional forecasting improvements over simpler time series models. Here, however, we concentrate on the use of the models we have been examining so far, and the implications of using

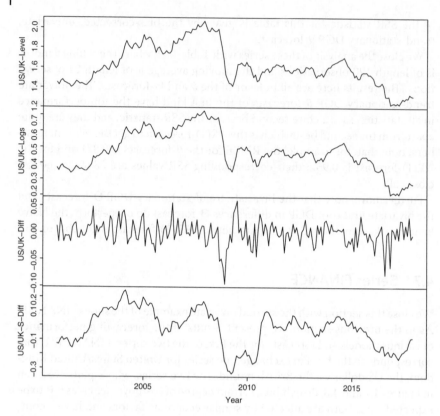

Figure 4.7 Time series plots of series FINANCE-1.

economic variables in a bivariate forecasting model for the Θ-approach are not discussed.

We start off our discussion with the results in Tables 4.59–4.61, where the series is at its level, the rolling window is of length 60 observations, and the moving average length is 3 observations. Only three forecasts are slightly better than the benchmark, the unit root DGP θ-forecasts, the (broadly equivalent) ARIMA(1, 1, 0)-forecast, and the Auto-ARIMA-forecast, the latter having the top performance but by far to the θ-forecast.

It is interesting to note two things here: (i) while the ARIMA(1, 1, 0)-forecast has values for its statistics similar to those of the unit root DGP θ-forecast, its SSR value is considerably smaller; (ii) the SSR value of the bivariate unit root DGP Θ-forecast in differences is also ranked at the top, while this forecast cannot outperform in terms of the other statistics the Naïve benchmark.

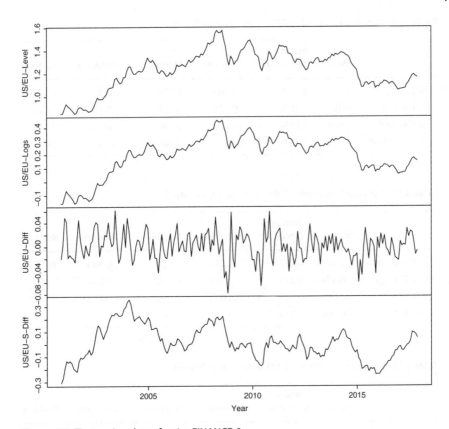

Figure 4.8 Time series plots of series FINANCE-2.

Table 4.55 Full sample statistics, 1999–2017, series FINANCE-1.

	Mean	Standard Deviation	Minimum	Maximum	Skewness	Kurtosis
US/UK-Level	1.623	0.196	1.233	2.070	0.312	2.513
US/UK-Logs	0.477	0.120	0.209	0.728	0.040	2.566
US/UK-Diff	−0.000	0.022	−0.095	0.060	−0.647	5.173
US/UK-S-Diff	−0.019	0.126	−0.338	0.246	−0.357	2.440

Table 4.56 Subsample statistics, 2000–2005, series FINANCE-1.

	Mean	Standard Deviation	Minimum	Maximum	Skewness	Kurtosis
US/UK-Level	1.631	0.172	1.402	1.929	0.208	1.472
US/UK-Logs	0.484	0.105	0.338	0.657	0.136	1.444
US/UK-Diff	0.004	0.019	−0.038	0.048	0.217	2.338
US/UK-S-Diff	0.052	0.118	−0.158	0.246	−0.377	1.683

Table 4.57 Subsample statistics, 2006–2017, series FINANCE-1.

	Mean	Standard Deviation	Minimum	Maximum	Skewness	Kurtosis
US/UK-Level	1.620	0.205	1.233	2.070	0.346	2.650
US/UK-Logs	0.474	0.126	0.209	0.728	0.037	2.689
US/UK-Diff	−0.002	0.023	−0.095	0.060	−0.793	5.367
US/UK-S-Diff	−0.049	0.118	−0.338	0.169	−0.532	2.362

Table 4.58 Full sample statistics, 1999–2017, series FINANCE-2.

	Mean	Standard Deviation	Minimum	Maximum	Skewness	Kurtosis
US/EU-Level	1.228	0.168	0.853	1.576	−0.473	2.669
US/EU-Logs	0.195	0.144	−0.160	0.455	−0.778	2.992
US/EU-Diff	0.001	0.023	−0.078	0.062	−0.148	3.443
US/EU-S-Diff	0.010	0.133	−0.307	0.355	0.214	2.598

Table 4.59 Subsample statistics, 2000–2005, series FINANCE-2.

	Mean	Standard Deviation	Minimum	Maximum	Skewness	Kurtosis
US/EU-Level	1.076	0.161	0.853	1.341	0.001	1.407
US/EU-Logs	0.062	0.151	−0.160	0.293	−0.095	1.390
US/EU-Diff	0.006	0.024	−0.044	0.062	0.355	2.307
US/EU-S-Diff	0.075	0.171	−0.307	0.355	−0.435	1.999

Table 4.60 Subsample statistics, 2006–2017, series FINANCE-2.

	Mean	Standard Deviation	Minimum	Maximum	Skewness	Kurtosis
US/EU-Level	1.290	0.126	1.054	1.576	−0.073	2.360
US/EU-Logs	0.250	0.099	0.053	0.455	−0.263	2.286
US/EU-Diff	−0.000	0.023	−0.078	0.059	−0.383	3.692
US/EU-S-Diff	−0.016	0.103	−0.242	0.222	0.051	2.908

Table 4.61 FINANCE-1-60-3.

	RMSE	MAE	U1	U2	SSR
Naíve	1.000	1.000	1.000	1.000	0.000
UR1	0.976	1.041	0.981	0.976	0.555
UR2	1.411	1.402	1.407	1.411	0.493
TS1	1.173	1.143	1.169	1.173	0.493
TS1-BC1	1.180	1.139	1.176	1.180	0.493
TS1-BC2	1.175	1.141	1.171	1.175	0.486
TS2	1.173	1.143	1.169	1.173	0.493
TS2-BC1	1.180	1.139	1.176	1.180	0.493
TS2-BC2	1.175	1.141	1.171	1.175	0.486
TS-DBL	1.012	1.005	1.014	1.012	0.527
BUR-L	1.014	1.012	1.014	1.014	0.527
BUR-RR	1.031	1.044	1.031	1.031	0.541
BUR-D	1.010	1.090	1.014	1.010	0.562
BCT	1.010	1.020	1.009	1.010	0.534
BMA	1.197	1.173	1.192	1.197	0.514
BMA-BC	1.210	1.175	1.203	1.210	0.459
AR(1)	1.008	1.017	1.008	1.008	0.541
SES	1.000	1.000	1.000	1.000	0.486
HB	1.005	1.009	1.006	1.005	0.500
ARIMA $(1, 1, 0)$	0.983	1.049	0.987	0.983	0.370
Auto-ARIMA	0.974	1.040	0.979	0.974	0.562
VAR	1.108	1.123	1.114	1.108	0.459

Table 4.62 FINANCE-3-60-3.

	RMSE	MAE	U1	U2	SSR
Naíve	1.000	1.000	1.000	1.000	0.000
UR1	0.935	0.954	0.968	0.935	0.637
UR2	1.323	1.306	1.971	1.323	0.644
TS1	0.869	0.901	0.986	0.869	0.699
TS1-BC1	0.873	0.906	0.991	0.873	0.712
TS1-BC2	0.869	0.901	0.987	0.869	0.699
TS2	0.868	0.900	0.986	0.868	0.699
TS2-BC1	0.871	0.905	0.991	0.871	0.712
TS2-BC2	0.868	0.900	0.987	0.868	0.699
TS-DBL	1.001	1.001	0.971	1.001	0.486
BUR-L	1.037	1.051	0.968	1.037	0.486
BUR-RR	1.038	1.047	1.063	1.038	0.507
BUR-D	0.950	0.966	1.547	0.950	0.630
BCT	0.948	0.966	1.270	0.948	0.596
BMA	0.876	0.900	1.451	0.876	0.692
BMA-BC	0.880	0.904	1.455	0.880	0.699
AR(1)	0.815	0.797	1.002	0.815	0.740
SES	0.872	0.853	1.127	0.872	0.733
HB	0.880	0.867	1.050	0.880	0.692
ARIMA (1, 1, 0)	0.916	0.906	0.777	0.916	0.534
Auto-ARIMA	0.933	0.952	0.973	0.933	0.637
VAR	0.869	0.878	1.310	0.869	0.664

The levels of the series, in different combinations of the rolling window width and the length of the moving average, did not produce results that were either better or considerably different and, therefore, we turn our attention to the series of returns. In Table 4.62, we have the first set of results for the monthly returns, with a rolling window of 60 observations and a moving average length of 3 observations. As before, we examine the pattern of the results as we change the length of the moving average.

The top performer here is the AR(1)-forecast across all statistics. The second best, overall, performance is obtained by the trend-stationary DGP θ-forecast of both the first and second kind with bias correction and by the SES-forecast. Note that the VAR-forecast also performs well in terms of its statistics, save its relatively lower value for its SSR, while the bivariate trend-stationary DGP Θ-forecast performs reasonably well, close to the VAR-forecast but with higher SSR value.

Table 4.63 FINANCE-3-60-36.

	RMSE	MAE	U1	U2	SSR
Naíve	1.000	1.000	1.000	1.000	0.000
UR1	0.935	0.954	0.968	0.935	0.637
UR2	1.323	1.306	1.971	1.323	0.644
TS1	0.833	0.808	1.007	0.833	0.753
TS1-BC1	0.832	0.809	0.990	0.832	0.753
TS1-BC2	0.833	0.808	1.005	0.833	0.753
TS2	1.376	0.986	1.007	1.376	0.658
TS2-BC1	1.378	0.987	0.990	1.378	0.664
TS2-BC2	1.383	0.988	1.004	1.383	0.664
TS-DBL	1.000	1.000	0.984	1.000	0.507
BUR-L	1.037	1.051	0.968	1.037	0.486
BUR-RR	1.038	1.047	1.063	1.038	0.507
BUR-D	0.950	0.966	1.547	0.950	0.630
BCT	0.948	0.966	1.270	0.948	0.596
BMA	0.859	0.832	1.143	0.859	0.740
BMA-BC	0.858	0.830	1.132	0.858	0.747
AR(1)	0.815	0.797	1.002	0.815	0.740
SES	0.872	0.853	1.127	0.872	0.733
HB	0.880	0.867	1.050	0.880	0.692
ARIMA $(1, 1, 0)$	0.916	0.906	0.777	0.916	0.534
Auto-ARIMA	0.933	0.952	0.973	0.933	0.637
VAR	0.869	0.878	1.310	0.869	0.664

Increasing the moving average length to 36 observations, as in Table 4.63, we can see that the performance improvements of the θ and Θ-forecasts can be attributed to better estimation of the mean of the series. Specifically, note that the trend-stationary DGP θ-forecast of the first kind now has almost identical RMSE, MAE, U1, and U2 statistics with the AR(1)-forecast but slightly higher SSR value, at 75.3% vs. 74%. Also note the SSR improvement for the bivariate trend-stationary DGP Θ-forecast as well.

In the next four tables, Tables 4.64–4.67, we present the results of the differenced series when we increase the rolling window length to 90 and then to 120 observations and for the two values of 3 and 36 observations for the moving average. We can see in these tables the changes, i.e. improvements, in forecasting performance by the increase in the moving average length and, in particular, the increase in the SSR- of the θ- and Θ-forecasts.

Table 4.64 FINANCE-3-90-3.

	RMSE	MAE	U1	U2	SSR
Naíve	1.000	1.000	1.000	1.000	0.000
UR1	0.920	0.944	0.951	0.920	0.664
UR2	1.303	1.234	2.059	1.303	0.664
TS1	0.867	0.895	0.699	0.867	0.664
TS1-BC1	0.869	0.896	0.697	0.869	0.672
TS1-BC2	0.867	0.895	0.699	0.867	0.664
TS2	0.870	0.904	0.656	0.870	0.664
TS2-BC1	0.873	0.905	0.654	0.873	0.672
TS2-BC2	0.870	0.904	0.656	0.870	0.664
TS-DBL	1.000	0.999	0.983	1.000	0.534
BUR-L	0.978	0.976	0.733	0.978	0.578
BUR-RR	0.979	0.967	0.838	0.979	0.603
BUR-D	0.927	0.939	1.064	0.927	0.647
BCT	0.941	0.965	1.211	0.941	0.569
BMA	0.879	0.898	0.718	0.879	0.698
BMA-BC	0.881	0.899	0.716	0.881	0.698
AR(1)	0.821	0.798	1.001	0.821	0.724
SES	0.910	0.890	0.771	0.910	0.690
HB	0.906	0.888	0.771	0.906	0.681
ARIMA $(1,1,0)$	0.864	0.850	0.757	0.864	0.672
Auto-ARIMA	0.921	0.944	0.963	0.921	0.664
VAR	0.864	0.860	1.091	0.864	0.698

Table 4.65 FINANCE-3-90-36.

	RMSE	MAE	U1	U2	SSR
Naíve	1.000	1.000	1.000	1.000	0.000
UR1	0.920	0.944	0.951	0.920	0.664
UR2	1.303	1.234	2.059	1.303	0.664
TS1	0.851	0.835	0.998	0.851	0.733
TS1-BC1	0.851	0.835	0.991	0.851	0.733
TS1-BC2	0.851	0.835	0.996	0.851	0.733
TS2	0.903	0.892	0.995	0.903	0.724
TS2-BC1	0.904	0.892	0.988	0.904	0.716
TS2-BC2	0.904	0.892	0.994	0.904	0.716
TS-DBL	0.999	0.998	0.994	0.999	0.534
BUR-L	0.978	0.976	0.733	0.978	0.578

Table 4.65 (Continued)

	RMSE	MAE	U1	U2	SSR
BUR-RR	0.979	0.967	0.838	0.979	0.603
BUR-D	0.927	0.939	1.064	0.927	0.647
BCT	0.941	0.965	1.211	0.941	0.569
BMA	0.871	0.880	1.039	0.871	0.698
BMA-BC	0.870	0.879	1.032	0.870	0.707
AR(1)	0.821	0.798	1.001	0.821	0.724
SES	0.910	0.890	0.771	0.910	0.690
HB	0.906	0.888	0.771	0.906	0.681
ARIMA $(1, 1, 0)$	0.864	0.850	0.757	0.864	0.672
Auto-ARIMA	0.921	0.944	0.963	0.921	0.664
VAR	0.864	0.860	1.091	0.864	0.698

Table 4.66 FINANCE-3-120-3.

	RMSE	MAE	U1	U2	SSR
Naíve	1.000	1.000	1.000	1.000	0.000
UR1	0.906	0.932	0.970	0.906	0.674
UR2	1.285	1.178	1.891	1.285	0.674
TS1	0.800	0.814	0.623	0.800	0.674
TS1-BC1	0.802	0.818	0.627	0.802	0.686
TS1-BC2	0.800	0.814	0.623	0.800	0.674
TS2	1.484	1.287	0.631	1.484	0.523
TS2-BC1	1.486	1.290	0.635	1.486	0.535
TS2-BC2	1.490	1.291	0.631	1.490	0.523
TS-DBL	1.001	1.002	1.007	1.001	0.430
BUR-L	1.046	1.076	1.559	1.046	0.512
BUR-RR	1.031	1.049	1.755	1.031	0.477
BUR-D	0.936	0.944	1.179	0.936	0.593
BCT	0.960	0.974	1.250	0.960	0.558
BMA	0.816	0.826	0.603	0.816	0.709
BMA-BC	0.818	0.830	0.608	0.818	0.709
AR(1)	0.766	0.751	1.001	0.766	0.744
SES	0.792	0.805	0.757	0.792	0.686
HB	0.793	0.806	0.761	0.793	0.686
ARIMA $(1, 1, 0)$	0.792	0.803	0.703	0.792	0.709
Auto-ARIMA	0.905	0.930	0.974	0.905	0.674
VAR	0.788	0.791	1.206	0.788	0.698

Table 4.67 FINANCE-3-120-36.

	RMSE	MAE	U1	U2	SSR
Naíve	1.000	1.000	1.000	1.000	0.000
UR1	0.906	0.932	0.970	0.906	0.674
UR2	1.285	1.178	1.891	1.285	0.674
TS1	0.770	0.747	0.997	0.770	0.721
TS1-BC1	0.771	0.749	1.011	0.771	0.709
TS1-BC2	0.770	0.748	1.003	0.770	0.709
TS2	1.451	1.030	1.002	1.451	0.640
TS2-BC1	1.452	1.031	1.016	1.452	0.628
TS2-BC2	1.455	1.031	1.011	1.455	0.628
TS-DBL	1.001	1.001	1.014	1.001	0.512
BUR-L	1.046	1.076	1.559	1.046	0.512
BUR-RR	1.031	1.049	1.755	1.031	0.477
BUR-D	0.936	0.944	1.179	0.936	0.593
BCT	0.960	0.974	1.250	0.960	0.558
BMA	0.781	0.768	1.063	0.781	0.709
BMA-BC	0.782	0.770	1.077	0.782	0.698
AR(1)	0.766	0.751	1.001	0.766	0.744
SES	0.792	0.805	0.757	0.792	0.686
HB	0.793	0.806	0.761	0.793	0.686
ARIMA $(1,1,0)$	0.792	0.803	0.703	0.792	0.709
Auto-ARIMA	0.905	0.930	0.974	0.905	0.674
VAR	0.788	0.791	1.206	0.788	0.698

In Table 4.64, where the rolling window length is 90 observations and the moving average length is 3 observations, we can see a similar ranking as in the case where the rolling window length was 60 observations, but note the slight deterioration in the statistics for the SES-forecast. The θ- and Θ-forecasts are closely trailing the ARIMA$(1,1,0)$-forecast and the VAR-forecast. Note that the highest SSR values, after the top, that is, to the AR(1)-forecast, are for the bivariate trend-stationary DGP Θ-forecasts and the VAR-forecast.

Increasing the moving average length, as in Table 4.65, results in improvements in the univariate and bivariate θ- and Θ-forecasts, respectively, but more so in the univariate ones. Now the univariate trend-stationary DGP θ-forecasts of the first kind have performance almost equivalent to the AR(1)-forecast in terms of the RMSE, MAE, U1, and U2 statistics, but have higher values of the SSR statistics at 73.3% vs. 72.4%.

In the next two tables, we increase the size of the rolling window length to 120 observations. In Table 4.66, the moving average length is three observations and we can see that many forecasts are on par with one another and all under the performance of the AR(1)-forecast.

When we increase the size of the moving average to 36 observations, as in Table 4.67, we can see that, as before, the trend-stationary DGP θ-forecasts of the first kind perform almost on par with the AR(1)-forecast and are ranked second best overall. The performance of the bivariate trend-stationary Θ-forecasts continues to be robust and are just slightly ahead of the VAR-forecast.

Turning next to the results where we examine the annual returns of the series, i.e. the series expressed in their seasonal differences, we can see that this transformation is not easy to forecast. In particular, in Table 4.68, with a rolling window length of 60 observations and a moving average of 3 observations,

Table 4.68 FINANCE-4-60-3.

	RMSE	MAE	U1	U2	SSR
Naíve	1.000	1.000	1.000	1.000	0.000
UR1	0.969	1.033	1.497	0.969	0.514
UR2	1.398	1.376	0.443	1.398	0.411
TS1	1.166	1.126	1.222	1.166	0.473
TS1-BC1	1.173	1.126	1.200	1.173	0.452
TS1-BC2	1.170	1.125	1.206	1.170	0.466
TS2	1.166	1.126	1.222	1.166	0.473
TS2-BC1	1.173	1.126	1.200	1.173	0.452
TS2-BC2	1.170	1.125	1.206	1.170	0.466
TS-DBL	1.015	1.011	1.011	1.015	0.500
BUR-L	1.043	1.018	0.559	1.043	0.486
BUR-RR	1.053	1.031	0.571	1.053	0.500
BUR-D	0.994	1.045	1.679	0.994	0.541
BCT	1.006	1.004	0.986	1.006	0.521
BMA	1.196	1.154	1.502	1.196	0.473
BMA-BC	1.204	1.156	1.480	1.204	0.452
AR(1)	1.020	1.025	1.000	1.020	0.521
SES	1.001	1.004	1.000	1.001	0.418
HB	1.008	1.011	0.863	1.008	0.466
ARIMA $(1, 1, 0)$	0.971	1.028	1.507	0.971	0.425
Auto-ARIMA	0.968	1.031	1.505	0.968	0.521
VAR	1.084	1.092	1.145	1.084	0.493

only 3 forecasts are better than the Naíve benchmark, the unit root DGP θ-forecast, the ARIMA(1, 1, 0)-forecast, and the Auto-ARIMA-forecast.

They are very close in their statistics, save for the ARIMA(1, 1, 0)-forecast that has a considerably lower SSR value. This is of practical interest, as we have explained the equivalence between the unit root DGP θ-forecast and the ARIMA(1, 1, 0)-forecast, so we can see that this equivalence will not always hold but only when the underlying true DGP conforms to the conditions for it.

Increasing the moving average length to 36 observations, as in Table 4.69, provides us with one considerable improvement and that is on the bivariate trend-stationary Θ-forecasts. Their RMSE, U1, and U2 statistics improve and their SSR values are ranked at the top, clearly ahead of the ARIMA(1, 1, 0)- and the Auto-ARIMA-forecasts.

This is again of some practical interest, as it shows the potential of the bivariate models that we have examined so far and, especially, in a difficult context

Table 4.69 FINANCE-4-60-36.

	RMSE	MAE	U1	U2	SSR
Naíve	1.000	1.000	1.000	1.000	0.000
UR1	0.969	1.033	1.497	0.969	0.514
UR2	1.398	1.376	0.443	1.398	0.411
TS1	1.015	0.997	0.186	1.015	0.555
TS1-BC1	1.024	1.002	0.216	1.024	0.548
TS1-BC2	1.024	1.003	0.205	1.024	0.568
TS2	5.211	3.345	0.338	5.211	0.507
TS2-BC1	5.221	3.360	0.355	5.221	0.514
TS2-BC2	5.162	3.352	0.342	5.162	0.527
TS-DBL	0.999	0.990	0.752	0.999	0.534
BUR-L	1.043	1.018	0.559	1.043	0.486
BUR-RR	1.053	1.031	0.571	1.053	0.500
BUR-D	0.994	1.045	1.679	0.994	0.541
BCT	1.006	1.004	0.986	1.006	0.521
BMA	0.981	1.033	0.529	0.981	0.555
BMA-BC	0.976	1.024	0.335	0.976	0.534
AR(1)	1.020	1.025	1.000	1.020	0.521
SES	1.001	1.004	1.000	1.001	0.418
HB	1.008	1.011	0.863	1.008	0.466
ARIMA (1, 1, 0)	0.971	1.028	1.507	0.971	0.425
Auto-ARIMA	0.968	1.031	1.505	0.968	0.521
VAR	1.084	1.092	1.145	1.084	0.493

such as in the series we are examining here which shows little evidence of predictability with this group of time series forecasting models.

In the section that follows, we collect the results that we have presented for all six series so far and provide the reader with some empirical guidelines for the use of the proposed θ- and Θ-forecasts and, in particular, about the choice of forecasting method and choice of trend function.

4.8   Summary of Empirical Findings

The results presented in the previous section provide us not only with an evaluation about the efficacy of the methods proposed earlier – they are after all conditional on the datasets being used – but also with some practical guidelines on the implementation of the θ- and Θ-forecasts in different forms of time series.

The overall conclusion that comes from the empirical exercises is that θ- and Θ-forecasts are not just competitive to benchmarks but consistently rank at the top three forecasting methods/models and much more show in their ability to provide more accurate directional forecasts. The differences in the statistics considered are not always large and, admittedly, might not necessarily be statistically significant if we were to subject them to any of the statistical tests on the matter. However, the simplicity of the methods proposed recommend them not only as competitors to the existing benchmarks but also as the new benchmarks themselves. This is what our analysis, and previously published research, suggests and this is what our results could possibly be interpreted as. For if we consider the staple AR(1)-forecast as being a θ-forecast (which we already illustrated the connection), then most series and irrespective of their transformation can be successfully forecasted using one of the θ-methods. It is not just computationally simple to obtain the θ- and Θ-forecasts, but they can easily be programmed into one go along with all other benchmarks. A second conclusion that is also prevalent in our results is that the θ-forecasts that do work are robust to perturbations of the rolling window size, and will produce approximately the same performance rankings across different rolling window sizes. The adaptability of the θ-forecasts is an important practical aspect of them.

The individual θ- and Θ-forecasts, be that of the univariate unit root or trend-stationary DGP or the bivariate ones, perform differently on different series and depending on their transformations. From what we have seen, the unit root DGP θ-forecasts and the double θ-forecasts appear to work better in the levels or log-levels of a series and for such series where it is difficult to beat the Naíve benchmark. In these series, the specification of the moving average length for the trend-stationary DGP θ-forecasts is important and one might obviously envision the use of different trend functions that could be tried to improve forecasting performance. The trend-stationary DGP θ-forecasts, which are of two kinds depending on how we treat the bias in the estimation of $\widehat{\theta}^*$, appear to work well under different conditions. The first kind works well in most occasions, while the second kind does not always work as well as the first. The proposed common trend θ-forecast, which is bivariate, has been seen to perform better than the Naíve benchmark, but it is not a top performer overall.

The length of the moving average is an important factor in the performance of these forecasts and the forecasts of the second kind are more sensitive to it. We note that the trend-stationary DGP θ-forecasts work in both levels and differences of the time series and a natural rule for the length of the moving average used emerges: the more stationary the series, the longer the length of the moving average. At the limit, where the length of the moving average is the sample size itself, the trend-stationary DGP θ-forecast collapses to the AR(1)-forecast. This result supports our earlier argument about the use of θ and Θ-forecasts as benchmarks, as they nest a number of other models.

In closing, we stress the directional forecasting performance of the θ- and Θ-forecasts which is always on top. This is a result that is new compared to our past published research where we concentrated on traditional measures of forecast evaluation. The success in making good directional forecasts has merits that go beyond the RMSE and MAE measures, merits that can be purely practical. Directional forecasts have a number of uses in decision making, when signs and not magnitudes are concerned, such as whether an asset return will be positive, whether an economy will grow or whether sales might increase. Such sign predictions are useful in designing decision-making systems and have obvious implications related to allocation of resources. This ability to generate good directional forecasts certainly warrants further investigation into the way that the currently proposed methods under the θ approach can be expanded and improved.

5

Applications in Health Care

By Kostas I. Nikolopoulos and Dimitrios D. Thomakos

5.1 Forecasting the Number of Dispensed Units of Branded and Generic Pharmaceuticals

In this chapter, we use the variations of Theta method along with the aforementioned established benchmarks in order to forecast pharmaceutical life cycles, specifically around the time of patent expiry when the generic form of the product is introduced to the market, while the branded form is still available for prescription. Assessing the number of dispensed units of branded and generic forms of pharmaceuticals is increasingly important due to their relatively large market value globally and the limited number of new "blockbuster" branded drugs. As a result, pharmaceutical companies make every effort to extend the commercial life of their branded products and forecast their sales in the future, while public health institutes seek insights for effective governance as the use of a branded drug, when a generic form is available. In essence, this chapter presents an application of the method in the border of two disciplines: healthcare management and marketing. Marketers have always been encouraged to become more socially relevant and to broaden their viewpoints and extend their research into areas not traditionally associated with marketing (Andreasen 1978). Forecasting plays a major role in increasing marketing relevance, as it is included in more than 98% of companies' marketing plans and should be taught in business schools as a vital marketing tool (Armstrong et al. 1987). Despite its importance, managers do not appear to use the technique effectively. This was evident when a survey of marketing managers found that self-reported forecast accuracy did not exceed 47% for new category entrants, and 40% for products that were new to the world (Kahn 2002). The introduction of products in a given period changes the existing industry, as it adapts so as to include them (Darroch and Miles 2011), and affects how forecast managers perform because many companies cite

Forecasting with the Theta Method: Theory and Applications, First Edition.
Kostas I. Nikolopoulos and Dimitrios D. Thomakos.
© 2019 John Wiley & Sons Ltd. Published 2019 by John Wiley & Sons Ltd.

forecasting of genuinely new products as one of the most difficult forecasting problems they face, considering that new product forecasting is a leap into the unknown with little or no historical information to tell us which way to leap, which can require substantial time from the sales forecasting team, hurt its credibility through poor new product forecasting accuracy, and can also reduce its morale (Mentzer and Moon 2005). Previous studies by Cox (1967) and Easingwood (1987) modeled pharmaceutical life cycles but did not incorporate the forecasting element.

The chapter describes an approach for forecasting branded and generic pharmaceutical life cycles in which the sales of branded drugs decline and prescriptions for generic alternatives increase when the patents of the branded drugs expire. Many models are used to predict new product sales, but they were limited to consumer goods and did not address pharmaceuticals (Wind et al. 1981). Models that specifically consider pharmaceutical drugs (Lilien et al. 1981) were proposed which were then changed and their predictability were tested using pharmaceutical data (Rao and Yamada 1988). However, it was posited that the traditional (Bass 1969) model, like other methods used to predict consumer goods, cannot be applied to pharmaceutical products. The application and predictability of diffusion models have received limited empirical testing with mixed results; however, complicated forecasting techniques do not always generate the most accurate results, and in some situations, simpler approaches can be more effective.

An extensive study in the exact pharmaceutical context has been made in 2015 with annual branded and generic dispenses data, published in the International Journal of Forecasting from Nikolopoulos, Buxton, Khammash, and Stern including as benchmarks the Bass Diffusion Model (Bass 1969), the Repeat Purchase Diffusion Model (Lilien et al. 1981), Adaptation Models (Rao and Yamada 1988) and Benchmark Models including Moving Average, Exponential Smoothing and Naïve Models. Naïve models performed very well, with the Naïve with drift showing promising results for 1–5 years ahead of forecasts. The dominance of the Naïve model indicates the difficulty of forecasting such data and this is why we decided to employ the Theta method for the task.

5.2 The Data

The data are part of the JIGSAW database, a commercially operated panel of general practitioners (GPs) and was donated by Synovate for the purposes of academic research. The database was established by ISIS research in 1985. The time series associated with the current research are taken from a much larger database that contains 2 570 000 prescription records from 1506 GPs all over the United Kingdom. The time series run from 1987 to 2008. From this database, seven chemical substances were selected and it is the same data that

Table 5.1 Basic information on the seven most-prescribed substances in the database.

Branded	Generic	Use	Company	In market	Patent expiry (extension)	
Lustral	Sertraline	Anti-depressant	Pfizer	1981	2000	2005
Mobic	Meloxican	Analgesic/ Anti-inflammatory	Boehringer Ingelheim	1979	1998	2003
Naprosyn	Naproxen	Anti-inflammatory	Syntex	1972	1988	NA
Tagamet	Cimetidine	Acid reflux	SmithKline & French	1971	1992	NA
Tenormin	Atenolol	Hypertension	ICI	1972	1990	NA
Tritace	Ramipril	Hypertension	Hoechst AG	1983	2002	2004
Zantac	Ranitidine	Peptic ulcer disease	Allen & Hanburys	1980	1997	NA

Source: MPA Services, Espacenet and Patent Archives.

have been used for the aforementioned Nikolopoulos et al. study Nikolopoulos et al. (2016) as well as in the Phd thesis of Dr. Samantha Buxton – now an Assistant Professor of Business Analytics in Swansea University, the United Kingdom. Those chemical substances were initially circulated as branded drugs; but once the patents expired, both a branded and a generic version of each substance was available in the market. Those seven substances that were selected had over 10 000 prescriptions recorded (in either their branded or generic forms) between 1987 and 2008 (see Table 5.1), so are the ones with the most dispensed units in the respective database. All these drugs exhibited a branded-generic crossover; sales of the branded version first increased before reaching its peak, and then began to decline. Upon patent expiry, the number of generic prescriptions increased, peaked and then, more often than not, also began to decline as new prescription medicines are always being released. These drugs may be more beneficial and have fewer side effects for the patient. If this is the case, then GPs may switch the patient to the newer medicine. This is the primary life-cycle pattern exhibited by the branded and generic versions of the same pharmaceutical drug (Kvesic 2008).

5.2.1 Prescribed vs. Dispensed

The dataset records the drugs that were actually prescribed by GPs. If the drug is protected by a patent, then the brand name must be dispensed regardless of whether a GP writes a branded or a generic name on the prescription (Stern 1994). Therefore, if a GP prescribed generically before patent expiry, then the branded version would have to be dispensed. However, after patent expiry, the generic version would have to be dispensed in that case instead, while the branded version would only be dispensed if a GP prescribed it explicitly. Table 5.1 depicts the differences between the drugs that were initially prescribed by the GPs and the drugs that were actually dispensed by the pharmacists.

5.2.2   The Dataset

For the full monthly dataset of the 14 branded and generic drugs, you may either contact the authors at kostas@fortank.com or directly from the original JIGSAW database through recompiling the monthly data for the respective substances. For the sake of experimentation and replicability of our analysis for the reader, as well as ease of access, we do provide hereafter in the Appendix of the chapter Table 5.A.1 containing the data for the first two duets of generic-branded drugs: (Atenolol/Tenormin and Ramipril/Tritace) (Figure 5.1).

For all the empirical analysis that is about to be presented, we follow the same notation for the tables' captions as in previous chapter: "SERIES NAME-Transformation Type-Rolling Window-Length of Moving Average" where:

- Transformation type = 1, so all data are on levels where in this specific instance stands for units dispatched.

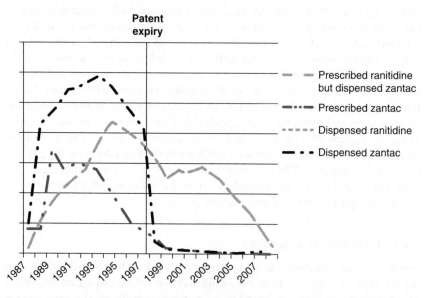

Figure 5.1 The figure presents the differences between the number of prescriptions written and dispensed for Zantac/ranitidine. The number of dispensed prescriptions for Zantac is higher because although some GPs prescribed ranitidine, the prescriptions were dispensed as Zantac until 1997, when the patent expired.

- Rolling window = ranging from 51 to 119, depending on time series length.
- Length of moving average = ranging from 3 to 24, again depending on time series length.

5.3 Results for Branded

Tables 5.2–5.6 present the empirical evaluation for the forecasts for the branded drug Tenormin with a rolling window of 119 and length of moving average, respectively 3, 4, 6, 12, and 24. This is yet another difficult-to-forecast series with Naíve proved unbeatable; only AR(1) is marginally close – but still worse on average – than Naíve, while from the Theta models (see Table 4.1 for the definitions) TS-DBL is the best across all (but for SSR) metrics and for all lengths of moving average, where when the latter becomes large (12 or 24) the performance of TS-DBL is almost on par with Naíve and AR(1).

When it comes to SSR and the very important accuracy of the sign and direction of the forecast: for moving average equal to 3 we observe that TS1 and TS2 achieve the highest score of 60%; for moving average equal to 4 we observe that TS1, TS2, and SES achieve the highest score of 56.7%; for moving averages equal to 6, 12, and 24, SES achieves the highest score of 56.7%.

Table 5.2 Tenormin..B.-1-119-3.

	RMSE	MAE	U1	U2	SSR
Naíve	1.000	1.000		1.000	0.192
UR1	1.071	1.247	1.492	1.071	0.450
UR2	1.714	2.035	3.278	1.714	0.483
TS1	1.210	1.352		1.210	0.600
TS1-BC1	1.214	1.409	1.673	1.214	0.508
TS1-BC2	1.210	1.358	1.557	1.210	0.550
TS2	1.203	1.331		1.203	0.600
TS2-BC1	1.207	1.388	1.673	1.207	0.508
TS2-BC2	1.203	1.337	1.557	1.203	0.550
TS-DBL	1.006	1.053	1.241	1.006	0.433
AR(1)	1.001	1.004		1.001	0.483
SES	1.221	1.375	1.715	1.221	0.567
HB	1.225	1.406	1.801	1.225	0.442
ARIMA(1, 1, 0)	1.148	1.403		1.148	0.500
Auto-ARIMA	1.074	1.251	1.494	1.074	0.450

Table 5.3 Tenormin..B.-1-119-4.

	RMSE	MAE	U1	U2	SSR
Naíve	1.000	1.000		1.000	0.192
UR1	1.071	1.247	1.492	1.071	0.450
UR2	1.714	2.035	3.278	1.714	0.483
TS1	1.240	1.442		1.240	0.567
TS1-BC1	1.244	1.491	1.829	1.244	0.458
TS1-BC2	1.240	1.455	1.735	1.240	0.475
TS2	1.239	1.441		1.239	0.567
TS2-BC1	1.244	1.489	1.829	1.244	0.458
TS2-BC2	1.240	1.453	1.735	1.240	0.475
TS-DBL	1.005	1.055	1.240	1.005	0.425
AR(1)	1.001	1.004		1.001	0.483
SES	1.221	1.375	1.715	1.221	0.567
HB	1.225	1.406	1.801	1.225	0.442
ARIMA(1, 1, 0)	1.148	1.403		1.148	0.500
Auto-ARIMA	1.074	1.251	1.494	1.074	0.450

Table 5.4 Tenormin..B.-1-119-6.

	RMSE	MAE	U1	U2	SSR
Naíve	1.000	1.000		1.000	0.192
UR1	1.071	1.247	1.492	1.071	0.450
UR2	1.714	2.035	3.278	1.714	0.483
TS1	1.239	1.570		1.239	0.558
TS1-BC1	1.243	1.618	1.867	1.243	0.450
TS1-BC2	1.240	1.595	1.797	1.240	0.458
TS2	1.239	1.570		1.239	0.558
TS2-BC1	1.243	1.618	1.867	1.243	0.450
TS2-BC2	1.240	1.595	1.797	1.240	0.458
TS-DBL	1.004	1.055	1.238	1.004	0.425
AR(1)	1.001	1.004		1.001	0.483
SES	1.221	1.375	1.715	1.221	0.567
HB	1.225	1.406	1.801	1.225	0.442
ARIMA(1, 1, 0)	1.148	1.403		1.148	0.500
Auto-ARIMA	1.074	1.251	1.494	1.074	0.450

Table 5.5 Tenormin..B.-1-119-12.

	RMSE	MAE	U1	U2	SSR
Naíve	1.000	1.000		1.000	0.192
UR1	1.071	1.247	1.492	1.071	0.450
UR2	1.714	2.035	3.278	1.714	0.483
TS1	1.196	1.734	1.807	1.196	0.517
TS1-BC1	1.200	1.786	1.934	1.200	0.417
TS1-BC2	1.198	1.772	1.890	1.198	0.425
TS2	4.523	4.355	104.074	4.523	0.517
TS2-BC1	4.526	4.406	104.185	4.526	0.408
TS2-BC2	5.157	4.677	122.659	5.157	0.425
TS-DBL	1.001	1.056	1.235	1.001	0.400
AR(1)	1.001	1.004		1.001	0.483
SES	1.221	1.375	1.715	1.221	0.567
HB	1.225	1.406	1.801	1.225	0.442
ARIMA(1, 1, 0)	1.148	1.403		1.148	0.500
Auto-ARIMA	1.074	1.251	1.494	1.074	0.450

Table 5.6 Tenormin..B.-1-119-24.

	RMSE	MAE	U1	U2	SSR
Naíve	1.000	1.000		1.000	0.192
UR1	1.071	1.247	1.492	1.071	0.450
UR2	1.714	2.035	3.278	1.714	0.483
TS1	1.145	1.857	1.586	1.145	0.517
TS1-BC1	1.148	1.905	1.661	1.148	0.383
TS1-BC2	1.147	1.897	1.638	1.147	0.383
TS2	2.186	2.684	3.295	2.186	0.450
TS2-BC1	2.184	2.733	3.388	2.184	0.383
TS2-BC2	2.231	2.843	4.718	2.231	0.392
TS-DBL	1.000	1.055	1.175	1.000	0.383
AR(1)	1.001	1.004		1.001	0.483
SES	1.221	1.375	1.715	1.221	0.567
HB	1.225	1.406	1.801	1.225	0.442
ARIMA(1, 1, 0)	1.148	1.403		1.148	0.500
Auto-ARIMA	1.074	1.251	1.494	1.074	0.450

Table 5.7 Tritace..B.-1-119-3.

	RMSE	MAE	U1	U2	SSR
Naíve	1.000	1.000		1.000	0.217
UR1	0.933	0.901	6.042	0.933	0.500
UR2	1.439	1.399	16.809	1.439	0.517
TS1	0.945	0.904		0.945	0.592
TS1-BC1	0.947	0.908	14.466	0.947	0.533
TS1-BC2	0.945	0.904	14.377	0.945	0.558
TS2	0.906	0.875		0.906	0.592
TS2-BC1	0.908	0.878	13.304	0.908	0.525
TS2-BC2	0.906	0.875	13.223	0.906	0.533
TS-DBL	0.999	1.003	1.054	0.999	0.417
AR(1)	1.008	1.013		1.008	0.517
SES	0.914	0.892	11.292	0.914	0.558
HB	0.920	0.912	11.717	0.920	0.525
ARIMA(1, 1, 0)	0.932	0.925	11.122	0.932	0.567
Auto-ARIMA	0.934	0.903	6.109	0.934	0.500

Tables 5.7–5.11 present the empirical evaluation for the forecasts for the branded drug Tritace with a rolling window of 119 and length of moving average, respectively, 3, 4, 6, 12, and 24.

For the length of moving average equal to 3 (Table 5.7), the TS2 and TS2-BC2 show the best performance with RMSE of 0.906 and MAE of 0.875, respectively. For the SSR, we see that the TS1 and TS2 illustrate the best accuracy at 59.2%.

For the length of moving average equal to 4 (Table 5.8), the ARIMA(1, 1, 0) is the winner for RMSE, while for the MAE we find that the UR1, TS2, and TS2-BC2 are the joint winners. For the SSR, we find that the ARIMA(1, 1, 0) presents the best performance at 56.7%.

Finally, for the other lengths of the moving averages, 6, 12, and 24, (in Tables 5.9–5.11), the SES presents the best performance for RMSE and MAE. For the SSR in these tables, we still have that the ARIMA(1, 1, 0) presents the best performance at 56.7%.

Tables 5.12–5.17 present the empirical evaluation for the forecasts for the branded drug Zantac with a rolling window of 119 and length of moving average, respectively, 3, 4, 6, 12, and 24.

For the length of the moving average equal to 3 (Table 5.12), the SES is the most accurate for RMSE, with TS1 and TS2 coming a close second; while for

Table 5.8 Tritace..B.-1-119-4.

	RMSE	MAE	U1	U2	SSR
Naíve	1.000	1.000		1.000	0.217
UR1	0.933	0.901	6.042	0.933	0.500
UR2	1.439	1.399	16.809	1.439	0.517
TS1	0.967	0.921		0.967	0.550
TS1-BC1	0.969	0.923	16.314	0.969	0.533
TS1-BC2	0.967	0.921	16.205	0.967	0.550
TS2	0.949	0.901		0.949	0.550
TS2-BC1	0.951	0.904	16.133	0.951	0.533
TS2-BC2	0.949	0.901	16.025	0.949	0.550
TS-DBL	0.999	1.002	1.073	0.999	0.417
AR(1)	1.008	1.013		1.008	0.517
SES	0.914	0.892	11.292	0.914	0.558
HB	0.920	0.912	11.717	0.920	0.525
ARIMA(1, 1, 0)	0.932	0.925	11.122	0.932	0.567
Auto-ARIMA	0.934	0.903	6.109	0.934	0.500

Table 5.9 Tritace..B.-1-119-6.

	RMSE	MAE	U1	U2	SSR
Naíve	1.000	1.000		1.000	0.217
UR1	0.933	0.901	6.042	0.933	0.500
UR2	1.439	1.399	16.809	1.439	0.517
TS1	0.982	0.985	18.266	0.982	0.533
TS1-BC1	0.984	0.989	18.428	0.984	0.525
TS1-BC2	0.983	0.984	18.302	0.983	0.525
TS2	0.970	0.973	18.266	0.970	0.533
TS2-BC1	0.972	0.977	18.428	0.972	0.525
TS2-BC2	0.970	0.973	18.302	0.970	0.525
TS-DBL	0.998	1.000	1.110	0.998	0.417
AR(1)	1.008	1.013		1.008	0.517
SES	0.914	0.892	11.292	0.914	0.558
HB	0.920	0.912	11.717	0.920	0.525
ARIMA(1, 1, 0)	0.932	0.925	11.122	0.932	0.567
Auto-ARIMA	0.934	0.903	6.109	0.934	0.500

Table 5.10 Tritace..B.-1-119-12.

	RMSE	MAE	U1	U2	SSR
Naíve	1.000	1.000		1.000	0.217
UR1	0.933	0.901	6.042	0.933	0.500
UR2	1.439	1.399	16.809	1.439	0.517
TS1	1.030	1.127	19.365	1.030	0.525
TS1-BC1	1.031	1.130	19.625	1.031	0.500
TS1-BC2	1.031	1.130	19.496	1.031	0.525
TS2	1.030	1.127	19.365	1.030	0.525
TS2-BC1	1.031	1.130	19.625	1.031	0.500
TS2-BC2	1.031	1.130	19.496	1.031	0.525
TS-DBL	0.998	1.001	1.218	0.998	0.433
AR(1)	1.008	1.013		1.008	0.517
SES	0.914	0.892	11.292	0.914	0.558
HB	0.920	0.912	11.717	0.920	0.525
ARIMA(1, 1, 0)	0.932	0.925	11.122	0.932	0.567
Auto-ARIMA	0.934	0.903	6.109	0.934	0.500

Table 5.11 Tritace..B.-1-119-24.

	RMSE	MAE	U1	U2	SSR
Naíve	1.000	1.000		1.000	0.217
UR1	0.933	0.901	6.042	0.933	0.500
UR2	1.439	1.399	16.809	1.439	0.517
TS1	1.060	1.194	15.790	1.060	0.442
TS1-BC1	1.060	1.201	16.250	1.060	0.442
TS1-BC2	1.061	1.199	16.140	1.061	0.433
TS2	1.060	1.194	15.790	1.060	0.442
TS2-BC1	1.060	1.201	16.250	1.060	0.442
TS2-BC2	1.061	1.199	16.140	1.061	0.433
TS-DBL	1.001	1.008	1.520	1.001	0.483
AR(1)	1.008	1.013		1.008	0.517
SES	0.914	0.892	11.292	0.914	0.558
HB	0.920	0.912	11.717	0.920	0.525
ARIMA(1, 1, 0)	0.932	0.925	11.122	0.932	0.567
Auto-ARIMA	0.934	0.903	6.109	0.934	0.500

Table 5.12 Zantac..B.-1-119-3.

	RMSE	MAE	U1	U2	SSR
Naíve	1.000	1.000	1.000	1.000	0.158
UR1	1.274	1.454	1.497	1.274	0.433
UR2	2.030	2.366	1.991	2.030	0.442
TS1	0.947	0.907	0.897	0.947	0.608
TS1-BC1	1.123	1.216	1.245	1.123	0.492
TS1-BC2	0.952	0.927	0.926	0.952	0.567
TS2	0.947	0.907	0.897	0.947	0.608
TS2-BC1	1.123	1.217	1.245	1.123	0.492
TS2-BC2	0.952	0.927	0.926	0.952	0.567
TS-DBL	1.167	1.260	1.410	1.167	0.408
AR(1)	0.980	0.989	1.005	0.980	0.408
SES	0.923	0.923	0.913	0.923	0.533
HB	1.064	1.138	1.232	1.064	0.458
ARIMA(1, 1, 0)	1.054	1.119	1.153	1.054	0.408
Auto-ARIMA	1.273	1.449	1.458	1.273	0.433

Table 5.13 Zantac..B.-1-119-4.

	RMSE	MAE	U1	U2	SSR
Naíve	1.000	1.000	1.000	1.000	0.158
UR1	1.274	1.454	1.497	1.274	0.433
UR2	2.030	2.366	1.991	2.030	0.442
TS1	0.912	0.901	0.910	0.912	0.575
TS1-BC1	1.088	1.197	1.252	1.088	0.450
TS1-BC2	0.928	0.939	0.982	0.928	0.575
TS2	0.912	0.901	0.910	0.912	0.575
TS2-BC1	1.088	1.197	1.252	1.088	0.450
TS2-BC2	0.928	0.939	0.982	0.928	0.575
TS-DBL	1.169	1.265	1.413	1.169	0.408
AR(1)	0.980	0.989	1.005	0.980	0.408
SES	0.923	0.923	0.913	0.923	0.533
HB	1.064	1.138	1.232	1.064	0.458
ARIMA(1, 1, 0)	1.054	1.119	1.153	1.054	0.408
Auto-ARIMA	1.273	1.449	1.458	1.273	0.433

Table 5.14 Zantac..B.-1-119-6.

	RMSE	MAE	U1	U2	SSR
Naíve	1.000	1.000	1.000	1.000	0.158
UR1	1.274	1.454	1.497	1.274	0.433
UR2	2.030	2.366	1.991	2.030	0.442
TS1	0.900	0.899	0.893	0.900	0.592
TS1-BC1	1.067	1.196	1.238	1.067	0.475
TS1-BC2	0.942	0.979	1.036	0.942	0.517
TS2	0.900	0.899	0.893	0.900	0.592
TS2-BC1	1.067	1.196	1.238	1.067	0.475
TS2-BC2	0.942	0.979	1.036	0.942	0.517
TS-DBL	1.169	1.266	1.413	1.169	0.408
AR(1)	0.980	0.989	1.005	0.980	0.408
SES	0.923	0.923	0.913	0.923	0.533
HB	1.064	1.138	1.232	1.064	0.458
ARIMA(1, 1, 0)	1.054	1.119	1.153	1.054	0.408
Auto-ARIMA	1.273	1.449	1.458	1.273	0.433

Table 5.15 Zantac..B.-1-119-12.

	RMSE	MAE	U1	U2	SSR
Naíve	1.000	1.000	1.000	1.000	0.158
UR1	1.274	1.454	1.497	1.274	0.433
UR2	2.030	2.366	1.991	2.030	0.442
TS1	0.902	0.905	0.901	0.902	0.583
TS1-BC1	1.046	1.154	1.265	1.046	0.442
TS1-BC2	0.974	1.041	1.142	0.974	0.458
TS2	0.902	0.905	0.901	0.902	0.583
TS2-BC1	1.046	1.154	1.265	1.046	0.442
TS2-BC2	0.974	1.041	1.142	0.974	0.458
TS-DBL	1.166	1.261	1.410	1.166	0.408
AR(1)	0.980	0.989	1.005	0.980	0.408
SES	0.923	0.923	0.913	0.923	0.533
HB	1.064	1.138	1.232	1.064	0.458
ARIMA(1, 1, 0)	1.054	1.119	1.153	1.054	0.408
Auto-ARIMA	1.273	1.449	1.458	1.273	0.433

Table 5.16 Zantac..B.-1-119-24.

	RMSE	MAE	U1	U2	SSR
Naíve	1.000	1.000	1.000	1.000	0.158
UR1	1.274	1.454	1.497	1.274	0.433
UR2	2.030	2.366	1.991	2.030	0.442
TS1	0.973	0.969	0.919	0.973	0.558
TS1-BC1	1.070	1.163	1.306	1.070	0.475
TS1-BC2	1.039	1.113	1.237	1.039	0.475
TS2	46.884	8.059	10.013	46.884	0.542
TS2-BC1	46.939	8.278	10.069	46.939	0.458
TS2-BC2	48.584	8.473	10.406	48.584	0.458
TS-DBL	1.154	1.242	1.403	1.154	0.408
AR(1)	0.980	0.989	1.005	0.980	0.408
SES	0.923	0.923	0.913	0.923	0.533
HB	1.064	1.138	1.232	1.064	0.458
ARIMA(1, 1, 0)	1.054	1.119	1.153	1.054	0.408
Auto-ARIMA	1.273	1.449	1.458	1.273	0.433

Table 5.17 Tagament..B.-1-104-3.

	RMSE	MAE	U1	U2	SSR
Naíve	1.000	1.000		1.000	0.356
UR1	1.343	1.330	1.679	1.343	0.337
UR2	2.150	2.217	2.211	2.150	0.385
TS1	0.821	0.886		0.821	0.615
TS1-BC1	1.188	1.180	1.441	1.188	0.365
TS1-BC2	0.857	0.906	0.947	0.857	0.452
TS2	0.820	0.884		0.820	0.615
TS2-BC1	1.187	1.178	1.439	1.187	0.365
TS2-BC2	0.856	0.903	0.943	0.856	0.433
TS-DBL	1.300	1.311	1.672	1.300	0.327
AR(1)	0.969	0.972		0.969	0.577
SES	0.904	0.948	0.895	0.904	0.519
HB	1.051	1.059	1.220	1.051	0.365
ARIMA(1, 1, 0)	1.409	1.300		1.409	0.356
Auto-ARIMA	1.341	1.323	1.669	1.341	0.337

MAE the picture is reversed with TS1 and TS2 giving the best performance and SES being a close second. For the SSR, we see that the TS1 and TS2 illustrate the best accuracy at 60.8%.

For the length of moving average equal to 4 (Table 5.13), TS1 and TS2 are the winners for all metrics. For the SSR, we see that TS1, TS1-BC2, TS2, and TS2-BC2 show the best performance at 57.5%.

For the length of moving average equal to 6 (Table 5.14), TS1 and TS2 are the winners for all metrics, including the SSR, with performance on the latter being at 59.2%.

For the length of moving average equal to 12 (Table 5.15), the situation is similar, with TS1 and TS2 being the winners for all metrics including the SSR, with performance on the latter being at 58.3%.

For the maximum length of moving average at 24 (Table 5.16), we see that the SES is the top performer. For the SSR, we find that the TS1, which was the second best in the accuracy metrics, presents the best performance at forecasting the direction of the forecast with a ratio of 55.8%.

Tables 5.17–5.21 present the empirical evaluation for the forecasts for the branded drug Tagamet with a rolling window of 104 and length of moving average, respectively, 3, 4, 6, 12, and 24.

For the length of the moving average equal to 3 (Table 5.17), TS2 is the most accurate for RMSE and MAE, with TS1 a close second. For the SSR, TS1 and TS2 illustrate the best accuracy at 61.5%.

Table 5.18 Tagament..B.-1-104-4.

	RMSE	MAE	U1	U2	SSR
Naíve	1.000	1.000		1.000	0.356
UR1	1.343	1.330	1.679	1.343	0.337
UR2	2.150	2.217	2.211	2.150	0.385
TS1	0.812	0.880		0.812	0.587
TS1-BC1	1.173	1.171	1.473	1.173	0.356
TS1-BC2	0.885	0.927	1.035	0.885	0.413
TS2	0.811	0.876		0.811	0.587
TS2-BC1	1.172	1.168	1.472	1.172	0.356
TS2-BC2	0.884	0.923	1.034	0.884	0.404
TS-DBL	1.302	1.312	1.681	1.302	0.327
AR(1)	0.969	0.972		0.969	0.577
SES	0.904	0.948	0.895	0.904	0.519
HB	1.051	1.059	1.220	1.051	0.365
ARIMA(1, 1, 0)	1.409	1.300		1.409	0.356
Auto-ARIMA	1.341	1.323	1.669	1.341	0.337

Table 5.19 Tagament..B.-1-104-6.

	RMSE	MAE	U1	U2	SSR
Naíve	1.000	1.000		1.000	0.356
UR1	1.343	1.330	1.679	1.343	0.337
UR2	2.150	2.217	2.211	2.150	0.385
TS1	0.822	0.872		0.822	0.577
TS1-BC1	1.161	1.162	1.521	1.161	0.375
TS1-BC2	0.937	0.975	1.173	0.937	0.394
TS2	0.821	0.870		0.821	0.577
TS2-BC1	1.160	1.160	1.520	1.160	0.375
TS2-BC2	0.937	0.972	1.171	0.937	0.394
TS-DBL	1.303	1.312	1.679	1.303	0.327
AR(1)	0.969	0.972		0.969	0.577
SES	0.904	0.948	0.895	0.904	0.519
HB	1.051	1.059	1.220	1.051	0.365
ARIMA(1, 1, 0)	1.409	1.300		1.409	0.356
Auto-ARIMA	1.341	1.323	1.669	1.341	0.337

Table 5.20 Tagament..B.-1-104-12.

	RMSE	MAE	U1	U2	SSR
Naíve	1.000	1.000		1.000	0.356
UR1	1.343	1.330	1.679	1.343	0.337
UR2	2.150	2.217	2.211	2.150	0.385
TS1	0.882	0.917	0.856	0.882	0.538
TS1-BC1	1.179	1.175	1.542	1.179	0.375
TS1-BC2	1.033	1.060	1.297	1.033	0.433
TS2	0.881	0.916	0.855	0.881	0.538
TS2-BC1	1.179	1.174	1.541	1.179	0.375
TS2-BC2	1.033	1.059	1.296	1.033	0.433
TS-DBL	1.295	1.304	1.667	1.295	0.327
AR(1)	0.969	0.972		0.969	0.577
SES	0.904	0.948	0.895	0.904	0.519
HB	1.051	1.059	1.220	1.051	0.365
ARIMA(1, 1, 0)	1.409	1.300		1.409	0.356
Auto-ARIMA	1.341	1.323	1.669	1.341	0.337

Table 5.21 Tagament..B.-1-104-24.

	RMSE	MAE	U1	U2	SSR
Naíve	1.000	1.000		1.000	0.356
UR1	1.343	1.330	1.679	1.343	0.337
UR2	2.150	2.217	2.211	2.150	0.385
TS1	0.933	0.978	0.904	0.933	0.490
TS1-BC1	1.201	1.200	1.566	1.201	0.385
TS1-BC2	1.127	1.147	1.452	1.127	0.394
TS2	0.933	0.978	0.904	0.933	0.490
TS2-BC1	1.201	1.200	1.566	1.201	0.385
TS2-BC2	1.127	1.147	1.452	1.127	0.394
TS-DBL	1.281	1.291	1.649	1.281	0.327
AR(1)	0.969	0.972		0.969	0.577
SES	0.904	0.948	0.895	0.904	0.519
HB	1.051	1.059	1.220	1.051	0.365
ARIMA(1, 1, 0)	1.409	1.300		1.409	0.356
Auto-ARIMA	1.341	1.323	1.669	1.341	0.337

For the length of moving average equal to 4 (Table 5.18), TS2 is the most accurate for RMSE and MAE, with TS1 being a close second. For the SSR, TS1 and TS2 illustrate the best accuracy at 58.7%.

For the length of moving average equal to 6 (Table 5.19), TS2 is the most accurate for RMSE and MAE, with TS1 again a close second. For SSR, TS1 and TS2 illustrate the best accuracy at 57.7%.

For the length of moving average equal to 12 (Table 5.20), the situation is similar, with TS2 and TS1 being the winners for all metrics including SSR, with the performance on the latter being at 53.8%.

For the maximum length of moving average equal to 24 (Table 5.21), we find that SES is the top performer across all metrics including SSR with a ratio of 51.9%.

Tables 5.22–5.26 present the empirical evaluation for the forecasts for the branded drug Naprosyn with a rolling window of 119 and length of moving average, respectively, 3, 4, 6, 12, and 24.

For the length of moving average equal to 3 (Table 5.22), HB is the most accurate for RMSE and MAE, with SES and UR1 being quite close. For the SSR, HB still illustrates the best accuracy at 64.2%, with many θ-models very close at 63.3%.

Table 5.22 Naprosyn..B.-1-119-3.

	RMSE	MAE	U1	U2	SSR
Naíve	1.000	1.000	1.000	1.000	0.058
UR1	0.909	0.913	0.926	0.909	0.617
UR2	1.282	1.301	1.010	1.282	0.592
TS1	0.917	0.903	0.725	0.917	0.625
TS1-BC1	0.913	0.886	0.785	0.913	0.633
TS1-BC2	0.917	0.904	0.723	0.917	0.633
TS2	0.914	0.902	0.730	0.914	0.625
TS2-BC1	0.910	0.887	0.796	0.910	0.633
TS2-BC2	0.913	0.901	0.730	0.913	0.633
TS-DBL	1.001	0.989	1.107	1.001	0.542
AR(1)	0.982	0.969	1.011	0.982	0.542
SES	0.893	0.907	0.771	0.893	0.608
HB	0.873	0.871	0.850	0.873	0.642
ARIMA(1, 1, 0)	0.915	0.936	0.989	0.915	0.592
Auto-ARIMA	0.906	0.910	0.913	0.906	0.625

Table 5.23 Naprosyn..B.-1-119-4.

	RMSE	MAE	U1	U2	SSR
Naíve	1.000	1.000	1.000	1.000	0.058
UR1	0.909	0.913	0.926	0.909	0.617
UR2	1.282	1.301	1.010	1.282	0.592
TS1	0.918	0.919	0.773	0.918	0.642
TS1-BC1	0.911	0.897	0.832	0.911	0.608
TS1-BC2	0.917	0.916	0.778	0.917	0.650
TS2	0.918	0.919	0.773	0.918	0.642
TS2-BC1	0.911	0.897	0.832	0.911	0.608
TS2-BC2	0.917	0.916	0.778	0.917	0.650
TS-DBL	1.000	0.989	1.107	1.000	0.542
AR(1)	0.982	0.969	1.011	0.982	0.542
SES	0.893	0.907	0.771	0.893	0.608
HB	0.873	0.871	0.850	0.873	0.642
ARIMA(1, 1, 0)	0.915	0.936	0.989	0.915	0.592
Auto-ARIMA	0.906	0.910	0.913	0.906	0.625

Table 5.24 Naprosyn..B.-1-119-6.

	RMSE	MAE	U1	U2	SSR
Naíve	1.000	1.000	1.000	1.000	0.058
UR1	0.909	0.913	0.926	0.909	0.617
UR2	1.282	1.301	1.010	1.282	0.592
TS1	0.916	0.926	0.787	0.916	0.642
TS1-BC1	0.905	0.906	0.851	0.905	0.642
TS1-BC2	0.914	0.922	0.799	0.914	0.658
TS2	0.916	0.926	0.787	0.916	0.642
TS2-BC1	0.905	0.906	0.851	0.905	0.642
TS2-BC2	0.914	0.922	0.799	0.914	0.658
TS-DBL	0.998	0.987	1.105	0.998	0.542
AR(1)	0.982	0.969	1.011	0.982	0.542
SES	0.893	0.907	0.771	0.893	0.608
HB	0.873	0.871	0.850	0.873	0.642
ARIMA(1, 1, 0)	0.915	0.936	0.989	0.915	0.592
Auto-ARIMA	0.906	0.910	0.913	0.906	0.625

Table 5.25 Naprosyn..B.-1-119-12.

	RMSE	MAE	U1	U2	SSR
Naíve	1.000	1.000	1.000	1.000	0.058
UR1	0.909	0.913	0.926	0.909	0.617
UR2	1.282	1.301	1.010	1.282	0.592
TS1	0.925	0.937	0.814	0.925	0.617
TS1-BC1	0.904	0.905	0.867	0.904	0.625
TS1-BC2	0.918	0.924	0.832	0.918	0.608
TS2	0.925	0.937	0.814	0.925	0.617
TS2-BC1	0.904	0.905	0.867	0.904	0.625
TS2-BC2	0.918	0.924	0.832	0.918	0.608
TS-DBL	0.996	0.986	1.099	0.996	0.542
AR(1)	0.982	0.969	1.011	0.982	0.542
SES	0.893	0.907	0.771	0.893	0.608
HB	0.873	0.871	0.850	0.873	0.642
ARIMA(1, 1, 0)	0.915	0.936	0.989	0.915	0.592
Auto-ARIMA	0.906	0.910	0.913	0.906	0.625

Table 5.26 Naprosyn..B.-1-119-24.

	RMSE	MAE	U1	U2	SSR
Naíve	1.000	1.000	1.000	1.000	0.058
UR1	0.909	0.913	0.926	0.909	0.617
UR2	1.282	1.301	1.010	1.282	0.592
TS1	0.971	1.025	0.821	0.971	0.575
TS1-BC1	0.938	0.976	0.870	0.938	0.592
TS1-BC2	0.953	0.997	0.844	0.953	0.608
TS2	0.971	1.025	0.821	0.971	0.575
TS2-BC1	0.938	0.976	0.870	0.938	0.592
TS2-BC2	0.953	0.997	0.844	0.953	0.608
TS-DBL	0.996	0.990	1.093	0.996	0.542
AR(1)	0.982	0.969	1.011	0.982	0.542
SES	0.893	0.907	0.771	0.893	0.608
HB	0.873	0.871	0.850	0.873	0.642
ARIMA(1, 1, 0)	0.915	0.936	0.989	0.915	0.592
Auto-ARIMA	0.906	0.910	0.913	0.906	0.625

For the length of moving average equal to 4 (Table 5.23), HB remains the most accurate for RMSE and MAE; but for the SSR, we find that the TS1, TS1-BC1, and TS2-BC2 illustrate the best accuracy at 65.0%.

For the length of moving average equal to 6 (Table 5.24), HB is the most accurate for RMSE and MAE, with SES and UR1 being quite close. For the SSR, HB still illustrates the best accuracy at 64.2%, this time jointly first with TS1, TS1-BC1, TS2, and TS2-BC2.

For the length of moving average equal to 12 (Table 5.25), HB is the most accurate for RMSE and MAE, with SES and TS2-BC2 being quite close. For the SSR, HB still illustrates the best accuracy at 64.2%.

For the maximum length of moving average equal to 24 (Table 5.26), HB is the most accurate for RMSE at 0.873 and MAE at 0.872, with SES and UR1 again being quite close. For the SSR, HB still illustrates clearly the best accuracy at 64.2%.

Tables 5.27–5.31 present the empirical evaluation for the forecasts for the branded drug Mobic with a rolling window of 111 and length of moving average, respectively, 3, 4, 6, 12, and 24.

For the length of moving average equal to 3 (Table 5.22), TS2 is the most accurate for RMSE and MAE, with TS1 and TS2-BC2 being almost identical in performance. For the SSR, TS1-BC1, TS2-BC2, and SES illustrate the best accuracy at 65.2%, with many other θ-models very close at 64.3%.

Table 5.27 Mobic..B.-1-111-3.

	RMSE	MAE	U1	U2	SSR
Naíve	1.000	1.000	1.000	1.000	0.027
UR1	0.932	0.945	1.098	0.932	0.616
UR2	1.148	1.165	1.438	1.148	0.625
TS1	0.830	0.855	0.906	0.830	0.643
TS1-BC1	0.836	0.859	0.979	0.836	0.652
TS1-BC2	0.831	0.855	0.896	0.831	0.643
TS2	0.829	0.853	0.899	0.829	0.643
TS2-BC1	0.836	0.858	0.982	0.836	0.652
TS2-BC2	0.830	0.853	0.900	0.830	0.643
TS-DBL	1.004	1.005	1.109	1.004	0.446
AR(1)	0.997	0.986	1.009	0.997	0.562
SES	0.908	0.926	0.884	0.908	0.652
HB	0.914	0.934	0.977	0.914	0.589
ARIMA(1, 1, 0)	0.958	0.935	0.921	0.958	0.598
Auto-ARIMA	0.932	0.946	1.097	0.932	0.616

Table 5.28 Mobic..B.-1-111-4.

	RMSE	MAE	U1	U2	SSR
Naíve	1.000	1.000	1.000	1.000	0.027
UR1	0.932	0.945	1.098	0.932	0.616
UR2	1.148	1.165	1.438	1.148	0.625
TS1	0.847	0.881	0.899	0.847	0.634
TS1-BC1	0.853	0.887	0.962	0.853	0.634
TS1-BC2	0.848	0.882	0.896	0.848	0.652
TS2	0.846	0.880	0.895	0.846	0.634
TS2-BC1	0.853	0.886	0.962	0.853	0.634
TS2-BC2	0.848	0.881	0.895	0.848	0.652
TS-DBL	1.004	1.005	1.107	1.004	0.446
AR(1)	0.997	0.986	1.009	0.997	0.562
SES	0.908	0.926	0.884	0.908	0.652
HB	0.914	0.934	0.977	0.914	0.589
ARIMA(1, 1, 0)	0.958	0.935	0.921	0.958	0.598
Auto-ARIMA	0.932	0.946	1.097	0.932	0.616

Table 5.29 Mobic..B.-1-111-6.

	RMSE	MAE	U1	U2	SSR
Naíve	1.000	1.000	1.000	1.000	0.027
UR1	0.932	0.945	1.098	0.932	0.616
UR2	1.148	1.165	1.438	1.148	0.625
TS1	0.885	0.936	0.924	0.885	0.670
TS1-BC1	0.892	0.944	0.953	0.892	0.616
TS1-BC2	0.888	0.938	0.926	0.888	0.652
TS2	0.885	0.936	0.924	0.885	0.670
TS2-BC1	0.892	0.944	0.953	0.892	0.616
TS2-BC2	0.888	0.938	0.926	0.888	0.652
TS-DBL	1.003	1.005	1.102	1.003	0.446
AR(1)	0.997	0.986	1.009	0.997	0.562
SES	0.908	0.926	0.884	0.908	0.652
HB	0.914	0.934	0.977	0.914	0.589
ARIMA(1, 1, 0)	0.958	0.935	0.921	0.958	0.598
Auto-ARIMA	0.932	0.946	1.097	0.932	0.616

Table 5.30 Mobic..B.-1-111-12.

	RMSE	MAE	U1	U2	SSR
Naíve	1.000	1.000	1.000	1.000	0.027
UR1	0.932	0.945	1.098	0.932	0.616
UR2	1.148	1.165	1.438	1.148	0.625
TS1	0.928	0.980	0.964	0.928	0.571
TS1-BC1	0.935	0.989	0.926	0.935	0.589
TS1-BC2	0.932	0.985	0.944	0.932	0.580
TS2	0.928	0.980	0.964	0.928	0.571
TS2-BC1	0.935	0.989	0.926	0.935	0.589
TS2-BC2	0.932	0.985	0.944	0.932	0.580
TS-DBL	1.003	1.006	1.084	1.003	0.446
AR(1)	0.997	0.986	1.009	0.997	0.562
SES	0.908	0.926	0.884	0.908	0.652
HB	0.914	0.934	0.977	0.914	0.589
ARIMA(1, 1, 0)	0.958	0.935	0.921	0.958	0.598
Auto-ARIMA	0.932	0.946	1.097	0.932	0.616

Table 5.31 Mobic..B.-1-111-24.

	RMSE	MAE	U1	U2	SSR
Naíve	1.000	1.000	1.000	1.000	0.027
UR1	0.932	0.945	1.098	0.932	0.616
UR2	1.148	1.165	1.438	1.148	0.625
TS1	0.952	1.010	0.857	0.952	0.562
TS1-BC1	0.958	1.019	0.873	0.958	0.554
TS1-BC2	0.957	1.017	0.866	0.957	0.554
TS2	0.952	1.010	0.857	0.952	0.562
TS2-BC1	0.958	1.019	0.873	0.958	0.554
TS2-BC2	0.957	1.017	0.866	0.957	0.554
TS-DBL	1.002	1.006	1.077	1.002	0.446
AR(1)	0.997	0.986	1.009	0.997	0.562
SES	0.908	0.926	0.884	0.908	0.652
HB	0.914	0.934	0.977	0.914	0.589
ARIMA(1, 1, 0)	0.958	0.935	0.921	0.958	0.598
Auto-ARIMA	0.932	0.946	1.097	0.932	0.616

For the length of moving average equal to 4 (Table 5.23), TS2 is the most accurate for RMSE and MAE, with TS1, TS1-BC1 and TS2-BC2 being almost identical in performance. For the SSR, we find that TS1-BC2, TS2-BC2, and SES illustrate the best accuracy at 65.2%, with many other θ-models being very close at 64.3%.

For length of moving average equal to 6 (Table 5.24), we again have that TS2 is the most accurate for RMSE and MAE as well as for the SSR, with an impressive success ratio at 67.0%.

For length of moving average equal to 12 (Table 5.25), we have that the SES is the most accurate for RMSE (and MAE) with a value of 0.908 as well as for the SSR with a ratio of 65.2%.

For the maximum length of moving average equal to 24 (Table 5.26), we have again that SES is the top performer across all metrics including the SSR with a ratio of 65.2%.

Tables 5.32–5.36 present the empirical evaluation for the forecasts for the branded drug Lustral with a rolling window of 105 and length of moving average, respectively, 3, 4, 6, 12, and 24.

Table 5.32 Lustral..B.-1-105-3.

	RMSE	MAE	U1	U2	SSR
Naíve	1.000	1.000	1.000	1.000	0.066
UR1	0.899	0.888	1.902	0.899	0.613
UR2	1.357	1.361	5.616	1.357	0.613
TS1	0.795	0.852	3.049	0.795	0.679
TS1-BC1	0.798	0.859	2.957	0.798	0.660
TS1-BC2	0.794	0.853	3.062	0.794	0.698
TS2	0.764	0.794	2.702	0.764	0.679
TS2-BC1	0.766	0.800	2.617	0.766	0.642
TS2-BC2	0.764	0.795	2.699	0.764	0.660
TS-DBL	1.000	1.004	1.118	1.000	0.434
AR(1)	0.986	0.992	1.011	0.986	0.453
SES	0.853	0.907	3.249	0.853	0.651
HB	0.857	0.912	3.029	0.857	0.651
ARIMA(1, 1, 0)	0.869	0.938	3.147	0.869	0.623
Auto-ARIMA	0.900	0.889	1.924	0.900	0.604

Table 5.33 Lustral..B.-1-105-4.

	RMSE	MAE	U1	U2	SSR
Naíve	1.000	1.000	1.000	1.000	0.066
UR1	0.899	0.888	1.902	0.899	0.613
UR2	1.357	1.361	5.616	1.357	0.613
TS1	0.824	0.888	3.049	0.824	0.670
TS1-BC1	0.826	0.891	2.924	0.826	0.679
TS1-BC2	0.824	0.888	3.048	0.824	0.679
TS2	0.779	0.826	3.047	0.779	0.689
TS2-BC1	0.781	0.828	2.922	0.781	0.698
TS2-BC2	0.779	0.825	3.046	0.779	0.698
TS-DBL	1.000	1.003	1.115	1.000	0.443
AR(1)	0.986	0.992	1.011	0.986	0.453
SES	0.853	0.907	3.249	0.853	0.651
HB	0.857	0.912	3.029	0.857	0.651
ARIMA(1, 1, 0)	0.869	0.938	3.147	0.869	0.623
Auto-ARIMA	0.900	0.889	1.924	0.900	0.604

Table 5.34 Lustral..B.-1-105-6.

	RMSE	MAE	U1	U2	SSR
Naíve	1.000	1.000	1.000	1.000	0.066
UR1	0.899	0.888	1.902	0.899	0.613
UR2	1.357	1.361	5.616	1.357	0.613
TS1	0.875	0.955	3.703	0.875	0.689
TS1-BC1	0.876	0.957	3.570	0.876	0.651
TS1-BC2	0.874	0.954	3.688	0.874	0.698
TS2	0.859	0.927	3.702	0.859	0.679
TS2-BC1	0.860	0.927	3.568	0.860	0.642
TS2-BC2	0.859	0.925	3.686	0.859	0.689
TS-DBL	0.999	1.003	1.110	0.999	0.453
AR(1)	0.986	0.992	1.011	0.986	0.453
SES	0.853	0.907	3.249	0.853	0.651
HB	0.857	0.912	3.029	0.857	0.651
ARIMA(1, 1, 0)	0.869	0.938	3.147	0.869	0.623
Auto-ARIMA	0.900	0.889	1.924	0.900	0.604

Table 5.35 Lustral..B.-1-105-12.

	RMSE	MAE	U1	U2	SSR
Naíve	1.000	1.000	1.000	1.000	0.066
UR1	0.899	0.888	1.902	0.899	0.613
UR2	1.357	1.361	5.616	1.357	0.613
TS1	0.940	1.013	3.932	0.940	0.670
TS1-BC1	0.940	1.012	3.792	0.940	0.651
TS1-BC2	0.939	1.012	3.886	0.939	0.651
TS2	0.939	1.043	3.927	0.939	0.642
TS2-BC1	0.939	1.041	3.787	0.939	0.613
TS2-BC2	0.938	1.040	3.881	0.938	0.623
TS-DBL	0.998	1.003	1.093	0.998	0.453
AR(1)	0.986	0.992	1.011	0.986	0.453
SES	0.853	0.907	3.249	0.853	0.651
HB	0.857	0.912	3.029	0.857	0.651
ARIMA(1, 1, 0)	0.869	0.938	3.147	0.869	0.623
Auto-ARIMA	0.900	0.889	1.924	0.900	0.604

Table 5.36 Lustral..B.-1-105-24.

	RMSE	MAE	U1	U2	SSR
Naíve	1.000	1.000	1.000	1.000	0.066
UR1	0.899	0.888	1.902	0.899	0.613
UR2	1.357	1.361	5.616	1.357	0.613
TS1	1.025	1.172	3.418	1.025	0.613
TS1-BC1	1.024	1.158	3.287	1.024	0.604
TS1-BC2	1.023	1.162	3.350	1.023	0.613
TS2	1.389	1.368	3.451	1.389	0.557
TS2-BC1	1.384	1.353	3.321	1.384	0.538
TS2-BC2	1.314	1.333	3.375	1.314	0.547
TS-DBL	0.998	1.001	1.079	0.998	0.462
AR(1)	0.986	0.992	1.011	0.986	0.453
SES	0.853	0.907	3.249	0.853	0.651
HB	0.857	0.912	3.029	0.857	0.651
ARIMA(1, 1, 0)	0.869	0.938	3.147	0.869	0.623
Auto-ARIMA	0.900	0.889	1.924	0.900	0.604

For the length of moving average equal to 3 (Table 5.32), TS2 and TS2-BC2 are the most accurate for RMSE (at 0.764) and MAE (at 0.794 and 0.795, respectively). For the SSR, we have that the TS1-BC2 illustrates the best accuracy at an impressive 69.8% rate, with many other Theta models being very close, most notably TS2 and TS1 at 67.9%.

For the length of moving average being equal to 4 (Table 5.33), we find that TS2 and TS2-BC2 are again the most accurate for RMSE and MAE; while for the SSR, we have now the TS1-BC2 and TS2-BC2 illustrate the best accuracy with rates at 69.8%, with TS2 following at 68.9%.

For the length of moving average equal to 6 (Table 5.34), SES is the most accurate for the RMSE and MAE, while for the SSR we find that the TS1-BC2 illustrates the best accuracy at a rate of 69.8%, with TS1 and TS2-BC2 following at 68.9%.

For the length of moving average equal to 12 (Table 5.35), the SES is the most accurate for RMSE (and MAE) with values of 0.853 as well as for the SSR with a ratio of 65.1%, this time jointly first with TS1-BC1 and TS1-BC2.

For the maximum length of moving average equal to 24 (Table 5.36), the SES is yet again the top performer across all metrics, including the SSR with a ratio of 65.1%.

5.4 Results for Generic

The generic drugs – as they are only introduced after the patent expiry – have inevitably shorter time series length and, as such for some, the empirical evaluation was impossible, while for all the rolling windows were much smaller than the paired branded ones.

Tables 5.37–5.41 present the empirical evaluation for the forecasts for the generic drug Atenolol with a rolling window of 51 and length of moving average, respectively, 3, 4, 6, 12, and 24.

For the length of moving average equal to 3 (Table 5.37), ARIMA(1, 1, 0) is the most accurate for RMSE (0.814) and MAE (0.804), with TS1-BC1 quite close. For the SSR, we find that UR1 illustrates the best accuracy at a rate of 71.2% with many θ-models being close and the UR2 second of all at a rate of 67.3%.

For the length of moving average being equal to 4 (Table 5.38), the ARIMA(1, 1, 0) is the most accurate for RMSE (0.814) and MAE (0.804), with UR1 quite close at 0.839 and 0.858, respectively. For the SSR, the UR1 illustrates the best accuracy at a rate of 71.2%, with many θ-models close and UR2 and TS1 second of all at a rate of 67.3%.

For the length of moving average being equal to 6 and 12 (Tables 5.39 and 5.40), we can see a similar overall picture with ARIMA(1, 1, 0) being the most

Table 5.37 Atenolol..G.-1-51-3.

	RMSE	MAE	U1	U2	SSR
Naíve	1.000	1.000	1.000	1.000	0.038
UR1	0.839	0.858	0.898	0.839	0.712
UR2	1.343	1.336	1.344	1.343	0.673
TS1	0.852	0.824	1.021	0.852	0.635
TS1-BC1	0.818	0.805	0.970	0.818	0.654
TS1-BC2	0.863	0.832	1.035	0.863	0.635
TS2	0.909	0.903	0.991	0.909	0.635
TS2-BC1	0.886	0.883	0.951	0.886	0.615
TS2-BC2	0.918	0.919	0.993	0.918	0.615
TS-DBL	0.985	0.985	0.999	0.985	0.538
AR(1)	0.971	0.976	0.991	0.971	0.558
SES	0.977	0.968	0.991	0.977	0.615
HB	0.875	0.858	0.924	0.875	0.615
ARIMA(1, 1, 0)	0.814	0.804	0.925	0.814	0.654
Auto-ARIMA	0.829	0.853	0.898	0.829	0.712

Table 5.38 Atenolol..G.-1-51-4.

	RMSE	MAE	U1	U2	SSR
Naíve	1.000	1.000	1.000	1.000	0.038
UR1	0.839	0.858	0.898	0.839	0.712
UR2	1.343	1.336	1.344	1.343	0.673
TS1	0.893	0.906	1.022	0.893	0.673
TS1-BC1	0.853	0.865	0.966	0.853	0.615
TS1-BC2	0.900	0.912	1.029	0.900	0.654
TS2	0.910	0.921	1.002	0.910	0.635
TS2-BC1	0.879	0.885	0.954	0.879	0.577
TS2-BC2	0.918	0.926	1.003	0.918	0.615
TS-DBL	0.982	0.983	0.995	0.982	0.538
AR(1)	0.971	0.976	0.991	0.971	0.558
SES	0.977	0.968	0.991	0.977	0.615
HB	0.875	0.858	0.924	0.875	0.615
ARIMA(1, 1, 0)	0.814	0.804	0.925	0.814	0.654
Auto-ARIMA	0.829	0.853	0.898	0.829	0.712

Table 5.39 Atenolol..G.-1-51-6.

	RMSE	MAE	U1	U2	SSR
Naíve	1.000	1.000	1.000	1.000	0.038
UR1	0.839	0.858	0.898	0.839	0.712
UR2	1.343	1.336	1.344	1.343	0.673
TS1	0.922	0.948	1.043	0.922	0.577
TS1-BC1	0.869	0.883	0.977	0.869	0.577
TS1-BC2	0.925	0.953	1.043	0.925	0.577
TS2	0.919	0.936	1.030	0.919	0.596
TS2-BC1	0.873	0.879	0.968	0.873	0.596
TS2-BC2	0.924	0.939	1.027	0.924	0.596
TS-DBL	0.983	0.982	0.993	0.983	0.519
AR(1)	0.971	0.976	0.991	0.971	0.558
SES	0.977	0.968	0.991	0.977	0.615
HB	0.875	0.858	0.924	0.875	0.615
ARIMA(1, 1, 0)	0.814	0.804	0.925	0.814	0.654
Auto-ARIMA	0.829	0.853	0.898	0.829	0.712

Table 5.40 Atenolol..G.-1-51-12.

	RMSE	MAE	U1	U2	SSR
Naíve	1.000	1.000	1.000	1.000	0.038
UR1	0.839	0.858	0.898	0.839	0.712
UR2	1.343	1.336	1.344	1.343	0.673
TS1	1.207	1.275	1.177	1.207	0.538
TS1-BC1	1.142	1.184	1.098	1.142	0.519
TS1-BC2	1.199	1.262	1.158	1.199	0.519
TS2	1.164	1.238	1.159	1.164	0.538
TS2-BC1	1.098	1.147	1.079	1.098	0.519
TS2-BC2	1.154	1.224	1.138	1.154	0.519
TS-DBL	0.988	0.986	0.997	0.988	0.519
AR(1)	0.971	0.976	0.991	0.971	0.558
SES	0.977	0.968	0.991	0.977	0.615
HB	0.875	0.858	0.924	0.875	0.615
ARIMA(1, 1, 0)	0.814	0.804	0.925	0.814	0.654
Auto-ARIMA	0.829	0.853	0.898	0.829	0.712

Table 5.41 Atenolol..G.-1-51-24.

	RMSE	MAE	U1	U2	SSR
Naíve	1.000	1.000	1.000	1.000	0.038
UR1	0.839	0.858	0.898	0.839	0.712
UR2	1.343	1.336	1.344	1.343	0.673
TS1	1.269	1.290	1.152	1.269	0.442
TS1-BC1	1.222	1.220	1.097	1.222	0.481
TS1-BC2	1.243	1.247	1.114	1.243	0.462
TS2	1.269	1.290	1.152	1.269	0.442
TS2-BC1	1.222	1.220	1.097	1.222	0.481
TS2-BC2	1.243	1.247	1.114	1.243	0.462
TS-DBL	0.996	0.991	0.999	0.996	0.596
AR(1)	0.971	0.976	0.991	0.971	0.558
SES	0.977	0.968	0.991	0.977	0.615
HB	0.875	0.858	0.924	0.875	0.615
ARIMA(1, 1, 0)	0.814	0.804	0.925	0.814	0.654
Auto-ARIMA	0.829	0.853	0.898	0.829	0.712

accurate for RMSE and for MAE and with UR1 coming a close second. For the SSR, we find that the UR1 illustrates the best accuracy at a rate of 71.2%, again with many θ-models being close and UR2 second of all at a rate of 67.3%.

For the maximum length of moving average equal to 24 (Table 5.41), still the ARIMA$(1, 1, 0)$ and UR1 dominate, respectively, the accuracy measures.

Tables 5.42–5.46 present the empirical evaluation for the forecasts for the generic drug Cimetidine with a rolling window of 119 and length of moving average, respectively, 3, 4, 6, 12, and 24.

For all moving average lengths (Tables 5.42–5.46), the SES is the most accurate for RMSE (0.917) and the HB for MAE (0.859). For the SSR, yet again HB illustrates the best accuracy at a rate of 62.5%. The only differentiation comes for moving averages of length 6 where for the SSR only the winner comes from the new family of θ-models and the TS1-BC1 at a rate of 64.2%.

Tables 5.47–5.51 present the empirical evaluation for the forecasts for the generic drug Naproxen with a rolling window of 119 and length of moving average, respectively, 3, 4, 6, 12, and 24.

For the length of moving averages being equal 3, 4, 12, and 24 (Tables 5.47, 5.48, 5.50, 5.51), we find that the SES is the most accurate for RMSE (0.816) and MAE (0.798). Similarly, for the SSR, yet again the SES illustrates the best accuracy at a rate of 73.3%.

Table 5.42 Cimetidine..G.-1-119-3.

	RMSE	MAE	U1	U2	SSR
Naíve	1.000	1.000	1.000	1.000	0.075
UR1	0.933	0.913	1.149	0.933	0.592
UR2	1.433	1.532	1.268	1.433	0.600
TS1	0.963	0.910	0.779	0.963	0.583
TS1-BC1	0.968	0.911	0.907	0.968	0.592
TS1-BC2	0.963	0.910	0.777	0.963	0.592
TS2	0.961	0.910	0.778	0.961	0.583
TS2-BC1	0.966	0.911	0.908	0.966	0.592
TS2-BC2	0.961	0.910	0.776	0.961	0.592
TS-DBL	1.002	1.003	1.234	1.002	0.483
AR(1)	0.990	0.988	1.007	0.990	0.500
SES	0.917	0.860	0.810	0.917	0.558
HB	0.919	0.859	0.982	0.919	0.625
ARIMA(1, 1, 0)	0.949	1.007	2.055	0.949	0.600
Auto-ARIMA	0.934	0.917	1.164	0.934	0.567

Table 5.43 Cimetidine..G.-1-119-4.

	RMSE	MAE	U1	U2	SSR
Naíve	1.000	1.000	1.000	1.000	0.075
UR1	0.933	0.913	1.149	0.933	0.592
UR2	1.433	1.532	1.268	1.433	0.600
TS1	0.959	0.918	0.814	0.959	0.542
TS1-BC1	0.963	0.915	0.951	0.963	0.600
TS1-BC2	0.959	0.917	0.825	0.959	0.575
TS2	0.959	0.918	0.814	0.959	0.542
TS2-BC1	0.963	0.915	0.951	0.963	0.600
TS2-BC2	0.959	0.917	0.825	0.959	0.575
TS-DBL	1.002	1.003	1.236	1.002	0.483
AR(1)	0.990	0.988	1.007	0.990	0.500
SES	0.917	0.860	0.810	0.917	0.558
HB	0.919	0.859	0.982	0.919	0.625
ARIMA(1, 1, 0)	0.949	1.007	2.055	0.949	0.600
Auto-ARIMA	0.934	0.917	1.164	0.934	0.567

Table 5.44 Cimetidine..G.-1-119-6.

	RMSE	MAE	U1	U2	SSR
Naíve	1.000	1.000	1.000	1.000	0.075
UR1	0.933	0.913	1.149	0.933	0.592
UR2	1.433	1.532	1.268	1.433	0.600
TS1	0.938	0.920	0.855	0.938	0.592
TS1-BC1	0.943	0.921	0.982	0.943	0.642
TS1-BC2	0.940	0.919	0.883	0.940	0.625
TS2	0.938	0.920	0.855	0.938	0.592
TS2-BC1	0.943	0.921	0.982	0.943	0.642
TS2-BC2	0.940	0.919	0.883	0.940	0.625
TS-DBL	1.001	1.002	1.234	1.001	0.483
AR(1)	0.990	0.988	1.007	0.990	0.500
SES	0.917	0.860	0.810	0.917	0.558
HB	0.919	0.859	0.982	0.919	0.625
ARIMA(1, 1, 0)	0.949	1.007	2.055	0.949	0.600
Auto-ARIMA	0.934	0.917	1.164	0.934	0.567

Table 5.45 Cimetidine..G.-1-119-12.

	RMSE	MAE	U1	U2	SSR
Naíve	1.000	1.000	1.000	1.000	0.075
UR1	0.933	0.913	1.149	0.933	0.592
UR2	1.433	1.532	1.268	1.433	0.600
TS1	0.918	0.945	0.803	0.918	0.542
TS1-BC1	0.921	0.922	0.901	0.921	0.617
TS1-BC2	0.920	0.935	0.829	0.920	0.592
TS2	0.918	0.945	0.803	0.918	0.542
TS2-BC1	0.921	0.922	0.901	0.921	0.617
TS2-BC2	0.920	0.935	0.829	0.920	0.592
TS-DBL	1.000	1.000	1.218	1.000	0.483
AR(1)	0.990	0.988	1.007	0.990	0.500
SES	0.917	0.860	0.810	0.917	0.558
HB	0.919	0.859	0.982	0.919	0.625
ARIMA(1, 1, 0)	0.949	1.007	2.055	0.949	0.600
Auto-ARIMA	0.934	0.917	1.164	0.934	0.567

Table 5.46 Cimetidine..G.-1-119-24.

	RMSE	MAE	U1	U2	SSR
Naíve	1.000	1.000	1.000	1.000	0.075
UR1	0.933	0.913	1.149	0.933	0.592
UR2	1.433	1.532	1.268	1.433	0.600
TS1	0.968	1.052	0.880	0.968	0.467
TS1-BC1	0.966	1.014	0.823	0.966	0.550
TS1-BC2	0.969	1.037	0.837	0.969	0.492
TS2	0.968	1.052	0.880	0.968	0.467
TS2-BC1	0.966	1.014	0.823	0.966	0.550
TS2-BC2	0.969	1.037	0.837	0.969	0.492
TS-DBL	1.000	0.999	1.185	1.000	0.483
AR(1)	0.990	0.988	1.007	0.990	0.500
SES	0.917	0.860	0.810	0.917	0.558
HB	0.919	0.859	0.982	0.919	0.625
ARIMA(1, 1, 0)	0.949	1.007	2.055	0.949	0.600
Auto-ARIMA	0.934	0.917	1.164	0.934	0.567

Table 5.47 Naproxen..G.-1-119-3.

	RMSE	MAE	U1	U2	SSR
Naíve	1.000	1.000	1.000	1.000	0.025
UR1	0.847	0.854	0.796	0.847	0.667
UR2	1.212	1.272	1.023	1.212	0.667
TS1	0.849	0.848	0.756	0.849	0.717
TS1-BC1	0.852	0.849	0.760	0.852	0.708
TS1-BC2	0.849	0.848	0.755	0.849	0.725
TS2	0.850	0.843	0.782	0.850	0.717
TS2-BC1	0.853	0.845	0.788	0.853	0.708
TS2-BC2	0.850	0.843	0.783	0.850	0.717
TS-DBL	0.999	1.002	1.004	0.999	0.467
AR(1)	0.994	1.011	1.010	0.994	0.442
SES	0.816	0.798	0.733	0.816	0.733
HB	0.824	0.804	0.746	0.824	0.683
ARIMA(1, 1, 0)	0.844	0.851	0.773	0.844	0.692
Auto-ARIMA	0.847	0.857	0.797	0.847	0.667

Table 5.48 Naproxen..G.-1-119-4.

	RMSE	MAE	U1	U2	SSR
Naíve	1.000	1.000	1.000	1.000	0.025
UR1	0.847	0.854	0.796	0.847	0.667
UR2	1.212	1.272	1.023	1.212	0.667
TS1	0.822	0.810	0.730	0.822	0.700
TS1-BC1	0.825	0.812	0.735	0.825	0.700
TS1-BC2	0.822	0.809	0.730	0.822	0.708
TS2	0.817	0.796	0.749	0.817	0.708
TS2-BC1	0.819	0.800	0.754	0.819	0.692
TS2-BC2	0.817	0.796	0.749	0.817	0.717
TS-DBL	0.999	1.002	1.003	0.999	0.450
AR(1)	0.994	1.011	1.010	0.994	0.442
SES	0.816	0.798	0.733	0.816	0.733
HB	0.824	0.804	0.746	0.824	0.683
ARIMA(1, 1, 0)	0.844	0.851	0.773	0.844	0.692
Auto-ARIMA	0.847	0.857	0.797	0.847	0.667

Table 5.49 Naproxen..G.-1-119-6.

	RMSE	MAE	U1	U2	SSR
Naíve	1.000	1.000	1.000	1.000	0.025
UR1	0.847	0.854	0.796	0.847	0.667
UR2	1.212	1.272	1.023	1.212	0.667
TS1	0.817	0.799	0.724	0.817	0.733
TS1-BC1	0.820	0.801	0.728	0.820	0.733
TS1-BC2	0.817	0.799	0.724	0.817	0.742
TS2	0.810	0.785	0.727	0.810	0.733
TS2-BC1	0.814	0.786	0.732	0.814	0.733
TS2-BC2	0.810	0.785	0.728	0.810	0.742
TS-DBL	0.999	1.002	1.003	0.999	0.458
AR(1)	0.994	1.011	1.010	0.994	0.442
SES	0.816	0.798	0.733	0.816	0.733
HB	0.824	0.804	0.746	0.824	0.683
ARIMA(1, 1, 0)	0.844	0.851	0.773	0.844	0.692
Auto-ARIMA	0.847	0.857	0.797	0.847	0.667

Table 5.50 Naproxen..G.-1-119-12.

	RMSE	MAE	U1	U2	SSR
Naíve	1.000	1.000	1.000	1.000	0.025
UR1	0.847	0.854	0.796	0.847	0.667
UR2	1.212	1.272	1.023	1.212	0.667
TS1	0.848	0.862	0.736	0.848	0.675
TS1-BC1	0.852	0.864	0.740	0.852	0.667
TS1-BC2	0.848	0.862	0.736	0.848	0.675
TS2	0.848	0.862	0.737	0.848	0.675
TS2-BC1	0.852	0.864	0.741	0.852	0.667
TS2-BC2	0.848	0.862	0.737	0.848	0.675
TS-DBL	0.999	1.002	1.002	0.999	0.458
AR(1)	0.994	1.011	1.010	0.994	0.442
SES	0.816	0.798	0.733	0.816	0.733
HB	0.824	0.804	0.746	0.824	0.683
ARIMA(1, 1, 0)	0.844	0.851	0.773	0.844	0.692
Auto-ARIMA	0.847	0.857	0.797	0.847	0.667

Table 5.51 Naproxen..G.-1-119-24.

	RMSE	MAE	U1	U2	SSR
Naíve	1.000	1.000	1.000	1.000	0.025
UR1	0.847	0.854	0.796	0.847	0.667
UR2	1.212	1.272	1.023	1.212	0.667
TS1	0.928	0.966	0.854	0.928	0.608
TS1-BC1	0.931	0.967	0.855	0.931	0.600
TS1-BC2	0.930	0.967	0.855	0.930	0.608
TS2	5.181	2.338	5.658	5.181	0.600
TS2-BC1	5.183	2.339	5.660	5.183	0.592
TS2-BC2	5.227	2.344	5.711	5.227	0.600
TS-DBL	0.999	1.003	1.002	0.999	0.483
AR(1)	0.994	1.011	1.010	0.994	0.442
SES	0.816	0.798	0.733	0.816	0.733
HB	0.824	0.804	0.746	0.824	0.683
ARIMA(1, 1, 0)	0.844	0.851	0.773	0.844	0.692
Auto-ARIMA	0.847	0.857	0.797	0.847	0.667

For the length of moving average being equal to 6 (Table 5.49), we find that the TS2 is the most accurate for the RMSE (0.810) and the MAE (0.786), with the TS2-BC1 being a close second (at 0.814 and 0.786, respectively). For the SSR, we have that the TS1-BC2 and TS2-BC2 illustrate the best accuracy at a staggering rate of 74.2%, with many other θ-models and the SES being close at a rate of 73.3%.

Tables 5.52 and 5.53 present the last empirical evaluation for generic pharmaceuticals: the forecasts for the very popular generic drug Ranitidine with a rolling window of 119 and length of moving average, respectively, 3, 4, 6, 12, and 24.

For the length of moving averages being equal to 3 (Table 5.52), TS2 and TS2-BC2 are the most accurate for the RMSE (0.820) and the MAE (0.801), with TS1 and TS1-BC2 being very close. For the SSR, we find that UR1, U2, and the Auto-ARIMA give the best performance at a rate of 74.2%.

For the length of moving averages being equal to 4 (Table 5.53), TS1 and TS1-BC2 are the most accurate for the RMSE (0.836) and the MAE (0.795 and 0.796, respectively), with the TS2 and TS2-BC2 being very close. For the SSR, we have that the TS1-BC2 and TS2-BC2 give the best performance at an impressive rate of 77.5%, with many other θ-models following closely at 76.7%.

Table 5.52 Ranitidine..G.-1-119-3.

	RMSE	MAE	U1	U2	SSR
Naíve	1.000	1.000	1.000	1.000	0.008
UR1	0.862	0.841	0.843	0.862	0.742
UR2	1.135	1.114	1.179	1.135	0.742
TS1	0.821	0.801	0.801	0.821	0.708
TS1-BC1	0.824	0.806	0.797	0.824	0.708
TS1-BC2	0.821	0.802	0.802	0.821	0.708
TS2	0.820	0.801	0.795	0.820	0.708
TS2-BC1	0.824	0.806	0.793	0.824	0.700
TS2-BC2	0.820	0.801	0.795	0.820	0.717
TS-DBL	1.002	1.001	0.996	1.002	0.500
AR(1)	0.994	0.997	1.021	0.994	0.475
SES	0.860	0.839	0.867	0.860	0.733
HB	0.859	0.837	0.853	0.859	0.725
ARIMA(1, 1, 0)	0.868	0.849	0.867	0.868	0.717
Auto-ARIMA	0.862	0.839	0.841	0.862	0.742

Table 5.53 Ranitidine..G.-1-119-4.

	RMSE	MAE	U1	U2	SSR
Naíve	1.000	1.000	1.000	1.000	0.008
UR1	0.862	0.841	0.843	0.862	0.742
UR2	1.135	1.114	1.179	1.135	0.742
TS1	0.836	0.795	0.831	0.836	0.767
TS1-BC1	0.839	0.798	0.826	0.839	0.767
TS1-BC2	0.836	0.796	0.831	0.836	0.775
TS2	0.834	0.793	0.825	0.834	0.767
TS2-BC1	0.837	0.796	0.820	0.837	0.767
TS2-BC2	0.835	0.794	0.824	0.835	0.775
TS-DBL	1.002	1.001	0.997	1.002	0.500
AR(1)	0.994	0.997	1.021	0.994	0.475
SES	0.860	0.839	0.867	0.860	0.733
HB	0.859	0.837	0.853	0.859	0.725
ARIMA(1, 1, 0)	0.868	0.849	0.867	0.868	0.717
Auto-ARIMA	0.862	0.839	0.841	0.862	0.742

5.A Appendix

Table 5.1 Monthly data for (i) atenolol and Tenormin and (ii) ramipril and tritace.

Month	Atenolol (G)	Tenormin (B)	Ramipril (G)	Tritace (B)
Jan-87		0		0
Feb-87		0		0
Mar-87		0		0
Apr-87		0		0
May-87		0		0
Jun-87		0		0
Jul-87		0		0
Aug-87		0		0
Sep-87		15		0
Oct-87		140		1
Nov-87		107		0
Dec-87		112		0
Jan-88		124		1
Feb-88		157		2
Mar-88		162		0
Apr-88		146		0
May-88		130		1
Jun-88		134		2
Jul-88		137		0
Aug-88		126		1
Sep-88		150		0
Oct-88		169		0
Nov-88		179		0
Dec-88		149		0
Jan-89		159		0
Feb-89		158		1
Mar-89		144		0
Apr-89		134		1
May-89		143		0
Jun-89		123		0
Jul-89		145		1
Aug-89		122		0
Sep-89		129		1

Table 5.1 (Continued)

Month	Atenolol (G)	Tenormin (B)	Ramipril (G)	Tritace (B)
Oct-89		162		0
Nov-89		145		0
Dec-89		98		1
Jan-90		147		0
Feb-90		160		0
Mar-90		152		0
Apr-90		127		3
May-90		150		4
Jun-90		166		1
Jul-90		142		2
Aug-90		106		2
Sep-90		170		3
Oct-90		177		0
Nov-90		176		5
Dec-90		148		4
Jan-91		180		9
Feb-91		151		4
Mar-91		168		9
Apr-91		170		13
May-91		141		32
Jun-91		140		12
Jul-91		143		12
Aug-91		105		11
Sep-91		128		14
Oct-91		159		14
Nov-91		149		17
Dec-91		134		26
Jan-92		146		21
Feb-92		130		23
Mar-92		156		27
Apr-92		141		17
May-92		132		16
Jun-92		156		18
Jul-92		133		22

(Continued)

Table 5.1 (Continued)

Month	Atenolol (G)	Tenormin (B)	Ramipril (G)	Tritace (B)
Aug-92		111		18
Sep-92		140		25
Oct-92		125		21
Nov-92		134		27
Dec-92		113		21
Jan-93		121		17
Feb-93		124		14
Mar-93		145		14
Apr-93		125		11
May-93		118		10
Jun-93		131		13
Jul-93		126		18
Aug-93		128		11
Sep-93		142		16
Oct-93		136		16
Nov-93		150		18
Dec-93		128		12
Jan-94		151		7
Feb-94		163		18
Mar-94		200		24
Apr-94		165		18
May-94		177		18
Jun-94		172		29
Jul-94		137		28
Aug-94		157		20
Sep-94		184		36
Oct-94		174		33
Nov-94		191		29
Dec-94		152		31
Jan-95		182		23
Feb-95		185		22
Mar-95		251		30
Apr-95		154		13
May-95		171		44
Jun-95		159		43

Table 5.1 (Continued)

Month	Atenolol (G)	Tenormin (B)	Ramipril (G)	Tritace (B)
Jul-95		146		24
Aug-95		124		20
Sep-95		160		29
Oct-95		160		38
Nov-95		190		42
Dec-95		143		38
Jan-96		212		35
Feb-96		192		39
Mar-96		214		29
Apr-96		196		37
May-96		198		39
Jun-96		197		32
Jul-96		200		40
Aug-96		162		26
Sep-96		170		40
Oct-96		194		23
Nov-96		207		38
Dec-96		184		50
Jan-97		205		45
Feb-97		214		44
Mar-97		223		57
Apr-97		224		62
May-97		230		67
Jun-97		238		57
Jul-97		211		67
Aug-97		154		43
Sep-97		227		73
Oct-97		221		69
Nov-97		228		72
Dec-97		203		73
Jan-98		195		79
Feb-98		222		49
Mar-98		277		84
Apr-98		224		87

(Continued)

Table 5.1 (Continued)

Month	Atenolol (G)	Tenormin (B)	Ramipril (G)	Tritace (B)
May-98		221		51
Jun-98		274		81
Jul-98		193		76
Aug-98		184		75
Sep-98		259		96
Oct-98		270		72
Nov-98		291		8
Dec-98		286		83
Jan-99	16	306		79
Feb-99	42	337		95
Mar-99	37	384		134
Apr-99	17	303		99
May-99	16	330		77
Jun-99	197	12		56
Jul-99	237	10		84
Aug-99	213	17		85
Sep-99	286	16		126
Oct-99	268	5		92
Nov-99	366	13		125
Dec-99	267	10		121
Jan-00	296	8		101
Feb-00	374	7		129
Mar-00	405	15		172
Apr-00	290	9		130
May-00	307	12		160
Jun-00	261	12		148
Jul-00	283	13		131
Aug-00	221	3		99
Sep-00	272	11		148
Oct-00	329	8		152
Nov-00	153	1		90
Dec-00	409	11		265
Jan-01	323	7		207
Feb-01	310	6		181
Mar-01	349	8		228

Table 5.1 (Continued)

Month	Atenolol (G)	Tenormin (B)	Ramipril (G)	Tritace (B)
Apr-01	300	1		181
May-01	268	4		207
Jun-01	247	3		199
Jul-01	244	8		166
Aug-01	212	9		180
Sep-01	248	6		209
Oct-01	322	7		215
Nov-01	278	10		216
Dec-01	236	5		179
Jan-02	293	5		237
Feb-02	262	10		213
Mar-02	275	3		245
Apr-02	280	7		310
May-02	290	7		286
Jun-02	225	4		200
Jul-02	254	8		267
Aug-02	200	7		172
Sep-02	272	5		245
Oct-02	242	9		222
Nov-02	260	7		240
Dec-02	226	5		193
Jan-03	281	7		204
Feb-03	236	11		172
Mar-03	293	8		199
Apr-03	242	5		186
May-03	217	1		191
Jun-03	247	3		165
Jul-03	227	2		163
Aug-03	184	4		155
Sep-03	236	6		166
Oct-03	233	6		156
Nov-03	232	4		158
Dec-03	231	2		169
Jan-04	223	3	169	3

(Continued)

Table 5.1 (Continued)

Month	Atenolol (G)	Tenormin (B)	Ramipril (G)	Tritace (B)
Feb-04	204	4	142	1
Mar-04	262	3	204	0
Apr-04	215	0	193	2
May-04	204	1	186	2
Jun-04	244	0	179	1
Jul-04	179	1	167	1
Aug-04	209	5	162	1
Sep-04	191	1	161	1
Oct-04	187	2	164	2
Nov-04	197	0	176	0
Dec-04	152	1	148	0
Jan-05	164	1	156	0
Feb-05	134	0	181	0
Mar-05	175	1	140	1
Apr-05	164	1	181	2
May-05	168	1	128	1
Jun-05	128	2	128	2
Jul-05	117	2	123	0
Aug-05	143	3	131	1
Sep-05	126	1	137	0
Oct-05	134	1	139	3
Nov-05	109	1	157	5
Dec-05	115	2	151	3
Jan-06	124	0	135	1
Feb-06	115	2	166	1
Mar-06	137	2	220	3
Apr-06	96	0	159	3
May-06	92	1	192	3
Jun-06	106	1	192	0
Jul-06	117	0	247	2
Aug-06	104	1	251	1
Sep-06	110	0	279	1
Oct-06	116	2	293	0
Nov-06	101	1	308	0
Dec-06	69	0	249	0

Table 5.1 (Continued)

Month	Atenolol (G)	Tenormin (B)	Ramipril (G)	Tritace (B)
Jan-07	87	2	305	0
Feb-07	83	0	293	1
Mar-07	82	1	286	0
Apr-07	73	0	267	0
May-07	72	0	245	0
Jun-07	85	0	206	1
Jul-07	69	0	252	0
Aug-07	69	0	246	0
Sep-07	65	0	210	0
Oct-07	65	0	284	0
Nov-07	78	1	315	0
Dec-07	46	1	245	1
Jan-08	71	0	314	1
Feb-08	72	0	270	0
Mar-08	56	0	268	0
Apr-08	81	0	288	0
May-08	53	1	257	0
Jun-08	46	0	267	0
Jul-08	9	0	36	0
Aug-08	0	0	0	0
Sep-08	0	0	0	0
Oct-08	0	0	0	0
Nov-08	0	0	0	0
Dec-08	0	0	0	0

Part III

The Future of the θ-method

6

θ-Reflections from the Next Generation of Forecasters
By Fotios Petropoulos

The Theta method, as it was applied by Assimakopoulos and Nikolopoulos (2000) to produce forecasts for the M3 competition (Makridakis and Hibon 2000), involved several ad hoc decisions and simplifications, such as the following:

- Adjust the data for seasonality using multiplicative classical decomposition;
- Decompose the seasonally adjusted data into exactly two theta lines, with theta coefficients equal to 0 and 2 corresponding to the simple linear regression line on time and a line with double the curvatures of the seasonally adjusted data respectively;
- Extrapolate the theta line 0 as usual, using the regression model fitted on that line assuming a linear trend;
- Extrapolate the theta line 2 using the simplest form of exponential smoothing models, simple (or single) exponential smoothing (SES);
- Combine the forecasts produced for theta lines 0 and 2 using equal weights.

We further on refer to the Theta method based on the aforementioned settings as the *standard Theta method*. The standard Theta method can be extended by considering several deviations from the standard setup, such as the following:

- Alternative seasonal adjustments,
- Different values for the theta parameters,
- Multiple theta lines,
- Alternative extrapolation methods,
- Unequal combination weights.

This chapter reports some results in the literature as well as some new results that show the potential of extending the standard Theta method. In doing so, the next section describes the data used to produce the results as well as how performance is measured. The last section reviews the available open source

Forecasting with the Theta Method: Theory and Applications, First Edition.
Kostas I. Nikolopoulos and Dimitrios D. Thomakos.
© 2019 John Wiley & Sons Ltd. Published 2019 by John Wiley & Sons Ltd.

packages and functions for the R statistical software that can be used to apply the Theta method in practice.

6.1 Design

The results reported in this chapter have been produced using the monthly subset of the M3 competition data set (Makridakis and Hibon 2000). This consists of 1428 real monthly time series with varying in-sample lengths, from 48 (4 years) to 126 periods (10.5 years). The length of the out-of-sample period is 18 months for all time series. In other words, forecasts for the next 18 periods are produced and tested for their accuracy. The monthly series of the M3 competition originate from various fields, such as demographic, finance, industry, macro, micro, and others.

Forecasting performance is measured by means of the symmetric mean absolute percentage error (sMAPE). While this error measure has some drawbacks (Goodwin and Lawton 1999), we opt to use this measure instead of other alternatives as to be directly comparable to the original accuracy results published by Makridakis and Hibon (2000). The sMAPE for one time series is calculated as follows:

$$\text{sMAPE} = \frac{200}{H} \sum_{h=1}^{H} \frac{|y_{n+h} - f_{n+h|n}|}{|y_{n+h}| + |f_{n+h|n}|} \tag{6.1}$$

where n is the number of observations in the in-sample, y_{n+h} is the actual value at period $n + h$, $f_{n+h|n}$ is the corresponding forecast as produced at origin n, and H is the maximum forecast horizon (18 months). Given that this error measure is scale independent, the values of sMAPE can be summarized across several series.

6.2 Seasonal Adjustment

In the original implementation, Assimakopoulos and Nikolopoulos (2000) considered seasonal adjustment based on multiplicative classical decomposition. Moreover, they performed a prior autocorrelation test to determine if the data are seasonal, where the significance level was set to 90%. In this section, we provide some results where we consider the following:

- Varying the significance level for identifying a series as seasonal (80%, 90%, 95%),
- Both additive and multiplicative forms of classical decomposition for seasonal adjustment.

The results are presented in Table 6.1. It is apparent that at least for the M3 competition monthly series, a multiplicative seasonal adjustment offers by far

Table 6.1 Forecasting performance of the Theta method for various seasonal adjustments.

Significance level	Seasonal form	sMAPE (%)
90%	Multiplicative	13.85[a]
80%	Multiplicative	13.91
90%	Multiplicative	13.87
95%	Multiplicative	13.89
80%	Additive	15.04
90%	Additive	14.96
95%	Additive	14.61

a) Published result in Makridakis and Hibon (2000).

better results compared to an additive seasonal form. Moreover, we would expect that when dealing with real data, multiplicative seasonal forms occur more naturally. A second observation comes from comparing the various significance levels. While the 80% level is worse than 90% and 95% for both seasonal forms (multiplicative and additive), the performance of 90% and 95% significance levels depend on the seasonal form. In any case, a 90% significance level coupled with a multiplicative seasonal form provides the best results. Lastly, note that our results slightly deviate from the originally published results (sMAPE of 13.85%). We advocate any differences on the implementation of the method using different software and, consequently, different optimization techniques.

Further extensions with regard to the prior seasonal adjustment of the data could involve an optimal identification of the seasonal form (additive or multiplicative) so that such a decision is not imposed in an aggregate manner (across all time series) but set for each series individually. To the best of our knowledge, such a test does not exist; however, several heuristics could be applied. Furthermore, one could consider applying several approaches to robustify the estimation of the seasonal component. For example, Petropoulos and Nikolopoulos (2013), following the results of Miller and Williams (2003), considered possible shrinkage of the seasonal indices. The distribution of the seasonal indices (symmetric or skewed) as well as the value of the James–Stein shrinkage estimator are used to decide between the seasonal indices directly provided by classical decomposition or shrinking these indices by applying the James–Stein or the Lemon–Krutchkoff shrinkage estimators. Petropoulos and Nikolopoulos (2013) report a small improvement in the value of sMAPE (13.78%) if seasonal shrinkage is considered.

6.3 Optimizing the Theta Lines

Two recent studies have considered optimization of the second theta line, the line that focuses on the extrapolation of the short-term behavior.

Fiorucci et al. (2015) determined the optimal value of this theta line by measuring the performance of the Theta method with different lines using a cross-validation exercise. In more detail, they proposed a generalized rolling origin evaluation (GROE), defined as

$$l(\theta) = \sum_{i=1}^{p} \sum_{h=1}^{\min(H, n-t)} g(y_{t+h}, f_{t+h|t}) \tag{6.2}$$

where y_{t+h} is the actual at period $t + h$, $f_{t+h|t}$ is the h-step-ahead forecast as calculated at period t, H is the number of forecasts produced at each origin, and p denotes how many times the origin is updated. If we assume that m is the step movement for each origin update, with $m \in \mathbb{N}*$, then

$$p = 1 + \left\| \frac{n - n_1}{m} \right\| \tag{6.3}$$

where n_1 is the first origin and $||x||$ is a function returning the largest integer so that $||x|| < x$.

Fiorucci et al. (2015) note that the proposed GROE can be used to construct evaluation schemes with overlapping, semi-overlapping or nonoverlapping validation blocks. Also, fixed-origin evaluation and rolling-origin evaluation, as discussed by Tashman (2000), are special cases of the GROE, as follows:

- GROE falls to fixed-origin evaluation when $m = H = n - n_1$, which also suggests that $p = 1$.
- GROE falls to rolling-origin evaluation when $m = 1$ and $H \geq n - n_1$. Also, the number of origins evaluated can be adjusted by appropriately setting the value of n_1.

Fiorucci et al. (2015) examined several setups of their GROE to select between theta models with different θ values so that $\theta \in 1, 1.5, \ldots, 4.5, 5$. The θ value of the other theta line was fixed at zero. Fiorucci et al. (2015) referred to this approach as the optimized Theta method (OTM); however, in this chapter we refer to it as OTM-GROE.

In an extension of this study, Fiorucci et al. (2016) proposed the following state space (SS) model for the theta method:

$$y_t = \mu_t + \varepsilon_t \tag{6.4}$$

$$\mu_t = \ell_{t-1} + \left(1 - \frac{1}{\theta}\right) \left\{ (1-\alpha)^{t-1} A_n + \left[\frac{1 - (1-\alpha)^t}{\alpha}\right] B_n \right\} \tag{6.5}$$

$$\ell_t = \alpha y_t + (1 - \alpha)\ell_{t-1} \tag{6.6}$$

where A_n and B_n are the intercept and slope of the linear regression line as calculated for all observations in the in-sample data and ℓ_0, α and θ are the parameters of the model, which are estimated by minimizing the sum of squared errors. For ℓ_0 and α, the usual constraints of SES apply ($\ell_0 \in \mathbb{R}$ and $\alpha \in (0, 1)$), whereas the constraint for the third parameter is $\theta \geq 1$. Fiorucci et al. (2016) referred to this model as the OTM; we hereafter refer to this model as OTM-SS. Note that if $\theta = 2$, then OTM is equivalent to the standard Theta method. However, a state space formulation allows for computation of the conditional variance and the corresponding prediction intervals.

Fiorucci et al. (2016) also proposed a dynamic version of this state space model, so that the coefficients for the intercept and the slope are updated dynamically, along with the other states of the model. The dynamic optimized theta model (DOTM) is expressed as follows:

$$y_t = \mu_t + \varepsilon_t \tag{6.7}$$

$$\mu_t = \ell_{t-1} + \left(1 - \frac{1}{\theta}\right)\left[(1 - \alpha)^{t-1}A_{t-1} + \left(\frac{1 - (1 - \alpha)^t}{\alpha}\right)B_{t-1}\right] \tag{6.8}$$

$$\ell_t = \alpha y_t + (1 - \alpha)\ell_{t-1} \tag{6.9}$$

$$A_t = \bar{y}_t - \frac{t+1}{2}B_t \tag{6.10}$$

$$B_t = \frac{1}{t+1}\left[(t - 2)B_{t-1} + \frac{6}{t}(y_t - \bar{y}_{t-1})\right] \tag{6.11}$$

$$\bar{y}_t = \frac{1}{t}[(t - 1)\bar{y}_{t-1} + y_t] \tag{6.12}$$

All methods and models in this section, OTM-GROE, OTM-SS, and DOTM, implicitly or explicitly consider a linear combination of the actuals and the forecasts of the two theta lines so that the original signal is reconstructed, or:

$$y_t = \omega L_t(\theta_1) + (1 - \omega)L_t(\theta_2) \tag{6.13}$$

Given that $\theta_1 = 0$ and $\theta_2 = \theta$, Fiorucci et al. (2015, 2016) show that $\omega = 1 - \frac{1}{\theta}$, which corresponds to the factor multiplied by the linear trend estimation in Eqs. (6.5) and (6.8).

Table 6.2 presents the performance of Theta methods and models that consider an optimal θ value for the theta line for the short-term behavior. More specifically, with regard to the OTM-GROE, two different versions that correspond to the fixed-origin and the rolling-origin evaluations, respectively, are reported.

The results in Table 6.2 suggest that optimizing the theta line that corresponds to the short-term behavior (amplified local curvatures) can lead to improved forecasting performance. GROE gives slightly better performance; however, the state space model provides the basis for calculating prediction intervals as well. Also, rolling-origin evaluation (cross-validation) does a better job in identifying an optimal θ value compared to fixed-origin evaluation

Table 6.2 Forecasting performance of the Theta method when the θ value of the short-term behavior theta line is optimized.

Method/Model	Settings	sMAPE
Standard theta method		13.85[a]
OTM-GROE	$p = 1, m = H, n_1 = n - H$	13.78[b]
OTM-GROE	$p = H, m = 1, n_1 = n - H$	13.66[b]
OTM-SS		14.11[c]
DOTM		13.74[c]

a) Published result in Makridakis and Hibon (2000).
b) Published result in Fiorucci et al. (2015), sMAPE as cost function.
c) Published result in Fiorucci et al. (2016).

(validation). This was expected, as the former does not overfocus on a single validation window. Moreover, Fiorucci et al. (2016) show that the percentage improvements of DOTM over a nonoptimized Theta method are greater for trended series compared to nontrended ones.

6.4 Adding a Third Theta Line

Other research has focused on the performance of the Theta method if a third line is added into the mix. For instance, Petropoulos and Nikolopoulos (2013) considered the addition of a third theta line with integer values for the theta parameter of the third theta line so that $\theta \in [-1, 3]$.

- Theta line with $\theta = 1$ corresponds to the deseasonalized series.
- Theta line with $\theta = 0$ is the linear regression on time (no curvatures).
- Theta line with $\theta = 2$ has double the curvatures of the deseasonalized series.
- Theta line with $\theta = 3$ has triple the curvatures of the deseasonalized series.
- Theta line with $\theta = -1$ exhibits curvatures that mirror the curvatures of the deseasonalized series ($\theta = 1$), with theta line with $\theta = 0$ acting as the symmetry axis.

In Petropoulos and Nikolopoulos (2013), the forecast for the third theta line is produced using SES, as is the case for the theta line with $\theta = 2$. The optimal value of the third theta line is estimated for each series individually, through maximizing the forecasting accuracy on a single validation sample. Also, Petropoulos and Nikolopoulos (2013) varied the contribution weight of this third theta line. The various combinations, together with the corresponding sMAPE values, are reported in Table 6.3 in rows 2–6.

Table 6.3 Forecasting performance of the Theta method when a third theta line is added.

Function for final forecast	sMAPE (%)
$0.5 \times L(0) + 0.5 \times L(2)$	13.85[a]
$1/3 \times L(0) + 1/3 \times L(2) + 1/3 \times L(\theta)$	14.34[b]
$0.45 \times L(0) + 0.45 \times L(2) + 0.1 \times L(\theta)$	13.71[b]
$0.475 \times L(0) + 0.475 \times L(2) + 0.05 \times L(\theta)$	13.70[b]
$0.5 \times L(0) + 0.3 \times L(2) + 0.2 \times L(\theta)$	13.74[b]
$0.5 \times L(0) + 0.4 \times L(2) + 0.1 \times L(\theta)$	13.68[b]
$1/3 \times L(0) + 1/3 \times L(1) + 1/3 \times L(2)$	13.68

a) Published result in Makridakis and Hibon (2000).
b) Published result in Petropoulos and Nikolopoulos (2013).

We observe that in most of the cases, the addition of a third theta line leads to decreases in the value of sMAPE. The best performance is recorded for the case where the weights for lines with $\theta = 0, 2$ and θ are 50%, 40%, and 10% respectively. The accuracy improvement is, on average, 1.2% compared to the standard Theta method.

The last row of Table 6.3 reports a new set of results, based on the equal-weight combination of the forecasts of three theta lines with $\theta = 0, 1$, and 2. In this last case, the extrapolation of the additional theta line ($\theta = 1$) is performed using the damped exponential smoothing (DES) method. DES has been proved to be a good benchmark method in several empirical forecasting studies when applied on the seasonally adjusted data. The performance of this simple last combination (which can also be regarded as $2/3 \times$ theta and $1/3 \times$ DES) achieves accuracy similar to the best combination of three theta lines where the θ value of the third line is optimally selected per series ($0.5 \times L(0) + 0.4 \times L(2) + 0.1 \times L(\theta)$).

In any case, more than three theta lines might be also produced and calculated separately. Theta lines with θ values lower than unity are better for estimating the long-term component, while theta lines with θ values higher than unity focus on the short-term curvatures.

6.5 Adding a Short-term Linear Trend Line

The standard theta line considers a single linear trend that is calculated using all data points of the seasonally adjusted series. However, as is often in practice, the trend of a time series changes over time, so that the long-term and short-term trends may exhibit different directions. In such cases, a Theta method that is

Table 6.4 Forecasting performance of the Theta method when a short-term linear trend line is added.

Short-term trend estimation window (k)	sMAPE (%)
—	13.85[a]
m	14.49
H	13.68
$2 \times m$	13.99
$2 \times H$	14.40

a) Published result in Makridakis and Hibon (2000).

simply based on the long-term trend might be an over- or underestimation of the short-term reality.

We suggest that the Theta method be expanded so that a second linear trend line is added. This second linear trend line should focus on the short-term trend component. In other words, a linear trend is fitted on the last k data points of the seasonally adjusted data. There are several options for specifying the value of k; however, two simple alternatives can be linked with the problem and data in hand:

- $k = H$, where H is the required forecasting horizon and $H < n$,
- $k = m$, where m is the periodicity of the data ($m = 12$ for monthly data) and $m < n$.

Table 6.4 presents the performance of the Theta method when a short-term linear trend line is added. It appears that for the specific case of the monthly M3 competition data, the sMAPE is a U-shaped function of k and that a minimum exists for $k = H$, where the value of sMAPE is 13.68%. We conclude that the addition of a linear line that focuses on the short-term trend can add value to the Theta method.

6.6 Extrapolating Theta Lines

Originally, Assimakopoulos and Nikolopoulos (2000) suggested that the theta line with $\theta = 0$, corresponding to the linear regression line, should be extrapolated as usual assuming a linear trend for the future values. At the same time, the theta line with $\theta = 2$ should be forecasted using SES. However, alternative extrapolating methods for these two lines may be considered.

Hyndman et al. (2002) proposed a state space framework for the exponential smoothing family of models. Each model consists of three terms, the error term (which can be either additive, A, or multiplicative, M), the trend component (which can be either none, N, additive, A, or multiplicative, M), and the seasonal term (which is similar to trend and can be either none, N, additive, A, or multiplicative, M). In addition, if trend exists, this might be damped or not. Under this framework, an exponential smoothing (ETS) model form is abbreviated with these three terms. For example, ETS(M,Ad,N) is an exponential smoothing model with multiplicative errors, additive damped trend, and no seasonality. Along with this framework, Hyndman et al. (2002) proposed how automatic forecasting should be applied with the use of information criteria, which account for the goodness-of-fit of the candidate models after penalizing it to take into account the varying complexity across different models (number of parameters). The model with the minimum value for a prespecified information criterion is selected as the optimal model.

Another alternative for automatic forecasting would be to use the autoregressive integrated moving average (ARIMA) family of models. This involves the correct identification of the autoregressive order (AR, $p \in \mathbb{N}$), differencing order ($d \in \mathbb{N}$), and moving average order (MA, $q \in \mathbb{N}$). Obviously, infinite number of combinations and potential models exist; however, high-order models lead to overfitting. Hyndman and Khandakar (2008) proposed an algorithm that, after applying the appropriate number of differences as suggested by unit root tests, initially considers a set of simple ARIMA models (ARIMA(2, d, 2), ARIMA(0, d, 0), ARIMA(1, d, 0), and ARIMA(0, d, 1)) and selects the one with the lowest value on the corrected Akaikes' information criterion (AIC). Subsequently, a stepwise search is performed so that the AR and MA orders are modified by one unit (plus or minus) until a better model cannot be found. Moreover, the default implementation of this algorithm (hereafter referred to as Auto-ARIMA), which is available as the `auto.arima()` function of the `forecast` package of the R statistical software, limits the maximum number of AR and MA terms to five so that overfitting is further avoided.

Whether we consider ETS or Auto-ARIMA as automatic forecasting frameworks, it is apparent that these can be applied to produce forecasts for any of the theta lines with $\theta \neq 0$. We assume the three-line theta method that consists of the theta lines with $\theta = 0, 1$, and 2 (Section 6.4) and we apply ETS and ARIMA to either or both theta lines with $\theta = 1$ and $\theta = 2$. We benchmark against the standard two-line theta method as well as the three-line theta method where the theta lines with $\theta = 1$ and $\theta = 2$ have been extrapolated by DES and SES, respectively.

Table 6.5 presents the respective results. Interestingly, applying automatic forecasting approaches to extrapolate either of the theta lines does not lead to improvements. Simply extrapolating the theta lines with fixed and prespecified methods performs best. In any case, the performance of all combinations tested is very similar, apart from the case where Auto-ARIMA is applied to both lines with $\theta = 1$ and $\theta = 2$.

Table 6.5 Forecasting performance of the Theta method using automatic forecasting for extrapolating theta lines with $\theta \neq 0$.

$\theta = 1$	$\theta = 2$	sMAPE (%)
—	SES	13.85[a]
Damped	SES	13.68
ETS	SES	13.68
Damped	ETS	13.78
ETS	ETS	13.85
Auto-ARIMA	SES	13.87
Damped	Auto-ARIMA	13.82
Auto-ARIMA	Auto-ARIMA	14.24
ETS	Auto-ARIMA	13.90
Auto-ARIMA	ETS	13.96

a) Published result in Makridakis and Hibon (2000).

6.7 Combination Weights

The standard Theta method suggests that once the two theta lines (with $\theta = 0$ and $\theta = 2$) are extrapolated, the two sets of forecasts should be combined with equal weights. However, Petropoulos and Nikolopoulos (2013) considered optimizing these weights for each series separately, based on the out-of-sample performance on a hold-out-sample consisting of the last year of data (12 observations). In other words, they optimized, through validation, the value of ω when $y_t = \omega L_t(\theta_1) + (1 - \omega)L_t(\theta_2)$. Moreover, they examined several parametric spaces for the value of ω, so that ω deviates from 10% up to 40% from equal-weight combination (corresponding to $\omega = 0.5$).

Table 6.6 presents the respective results. Small deviations from the 50–50% combination enhance the performance of the Theta method. For $\omega \in [0.45, 0.55]$, the average value of sMAPE drops to 13.65%. Smaller improvements are recorded as the deviations from the equal weights increase, while larger deviations lead to small decrease in the performance compared to an equal-weight combination. It should be noted, however, that considering nonequal weights for combining the forecasts for theta lines with symmetric values (as is the case for theta lines with $\theta = 0$ and $\theta = 2$), results in a signal that is not a "reconstruction" of the seasonally adjusted series (theta line with $\theta = 1$).

An alternative approach to combining with unequal weights the forecasts produced through extrapolating the two theta lines derives from the nature of the theta lines itself. In the original study, Assimakopoulos and Nikolopoulos

Table 6.6 Forecasting performance of the Theta method with optimized combination weights.

Weights (range)	sMAPE (%)
Equal weights	13.85[a]
[0.45, 0.55]	13.65[b]
[0.4, 0.6]	13.70[b]
[0.35, 0.65]	13.83[b]
[0.3, 0.7]	14.00[b]

a) Published result in Makridakis and Hibon (2000).
b) Published result in Petropoulos and Nikolopoulos (2013).

(2000) suggest that when $\theta < 1$ the long-term behavior of the series is amplified. At the same time, $\theta > 1$ results in theta lines with enhanced short-term behavior of the data. Following this logic, one could consider weights that vary as the combined forecast for different horizons is computed. In more detail, a higher weight should be assigned on the theta line with $\theta = 2$ for the shorter horizons, while a lower weight should be assigned for the longer horizons.

Assuming that ω deviates within a particular range $[0.5 - d, 0.5 + d]$, we consider a linear function of ω so that $\omega(h) = (0.5 - d) + \frac{2d(h-1)}{(H-1)}$, where h is the forecast horizon and H is the maximum forecast horizon ($H = 18$ for the data used in this chapter). Table 6.7 presents the results for this approach. As is evident, simply setting the weights of the theta line forecasts to match the short- or long-term horizons does not improve the average performance of the theta method. On the contrary, as the value of d increases, the value of sMAPE increases as well.

Table 6.7 Forecasting performance of the Theta method with combination weights suggested by the forecasting horizon.

Weights (range)	sMAPE (%)
Equal weights	13.85[a]
[0.45, 0.55]	13.94
[0.4, 0.6]	14.07
[0.35, 0.65]	14.25
[0.3, 0.7]	14.47

a) Published result in Makridakis and Hibon (2000).

6.8 A Robust Theta Method

Building on the results from the previous sections, we propose a simple and robust modification of the standard Theta method that adds the following:

- A third theta line, which is extrapolated with DES (Section 6.4),
- A short-term linear trend line (Section 6.5).

Table 6.8 presents the results of the robust Theta method as applied to the monthly subset of the M3 competition data. The robust Theta method reduces the average value of sMAPE to 13.59%, which is the lowest compared to all modifications suggested in this chapter.

6.9 Applying Theta Method in R Statistical Software

There are several packages in R that provide different implementations of the Theta method (and some of its variations).

- `stheta` function of the `forecTheta` package (version 2.2) is, to the best of our knowledge, the closest open source implementation of the standard Theta method as it was applied to the M3 competition.
- `stm` and `dstm` functions of the `forecTheta` package (version 2.2) are implemented on the basis of the state space model proposed by Fiorucci et al. (2016). The main difference between `stm` and `dstm` is that the latter dynamically updates the values of the intercept and slope coefficients of the theta line with $\theta = 0$. The user can define the initialization of the parameters, the parameter search space, as well as the optimization method to be used (selection between Nelder–Mead, L-BFGS-B or SANN). The function can output prediction intervals as well, where the confidence levels can be specified by the user.
- `otm` and `dotm` functions of the `forecTheta` package (version 2.2) work similar to the functions `stm` but `dstm` with one important difference. They introduce an additional parameter, which is the θ value for the theta line

Table 6.8 Forecasting performance of the standard and robust Theta methods.

Method	sMAPE (%)
Standard theta method	13.85[a]
Robust theta method	13.59

a) Published result in Makridakis and Hibon (2000).

focusing on the short-term curvatures ($\theta > 1$). In other words, the stm and dstm are special cases of otm and dotm, if the value of θ is fixed to 2. The value for the other theta line is kept fixed, $\theta = 0$. Moreover, the combination weights for the two theta lines are calculated so that the original signal is reproduced. The respective models are described in Fiorucci et al. (2016).

- otm.arxiv function of the forecTheta package (version 2.2) allows for optimal selection of the θ value for the second theta line (similarly to the otm function). The main difference between otm and otm.arxiv is that while the former performs optimization via maximizing the likelihood of the respective state space model, the latter does not consider θ as an additional parameter within the model. Instead, it selects the optimal θ value through a cross-validation exercise. Regarding this, the user can specify the cost function, the first origin, the number of origins skipped in each step, the number of origin updates, and the forecast horizon. The respective algorithm and parameters are discussed in detail by Fiorucci et al. (2015). However, this function cannot output prediction intervals of the produced forecasts.

- thetaf function of the forecast package (version 8.2) provides forecasts from the SES with drift method (Hyndman and Billah 2003). Data are tested for seasonality and adjusted along the lines of Assimakopoulos and Nikolopoulos (2000). The function can also provide prediction intervals of desired levels, which are computed on the basis of state space model of Hyndman and Billah (2003).

- theta function of the TStools package is an implementation of the standard Theta method with some tweaks. First, the existence of trend and seasonality is done automatically, where the significance level can be specified by the user. Second, it allows for both additive and multiplicative seasonality. Third, the function supports alternative cost functions to the mean squared error for the estimation of the theta lines and the seasonal element. Lastly, it allows for exclusion of outliers for the estimation of the theta line with $\theta = 0$; however, their timings have to be specified by the user.

Petropoulos and Nikolopoulos (2017) provide a step-by-step tutorial of how the standard version of the Theta method can be applied in practice. They also show how this can be done in R statistical software using just 10 lines of code.

7

Conclusions and the Way Forward

By Dimitrios D. Thomakos and Kostas I. Nikolopoulos

From its inception, in the minds of computer engineers, to its current form, as an all-purpose, multidisciplinary, forecasting tool, the θ-method follows the time-honored path of simplicity. Once we understood how to link the original derivations to an underlying data-generating process, it became not only apparent why the method might have worked but also why it will continue to work in many different contexts: the keyword here is "adaptability" or "flexibility" across different types of time series. If we consider the trend-stationary representation of the univariate θ-method, we see that with a choice (which maybe we can make more "automatic" in the future) of the trend function, we can address both stationary and nonstationary time series representations.

The results of our analyses presented in the previous chapters provide us with a wealth of practically relevant and theoretically motivated recommendations that support our abovementioned claim. Let us review some of them. First, the θ-forecasts are good for predicting direction, most times being above the benchmarks, sometimes at par, fewer times below them. Directional performance has been found in all our example series. Second, θ- and Θ-forecasts are prime competitors when the going gets tough: for series that the Naïve benchmark is difficult to beat, then the θ-forecasts are the ones to consider. Third, give us nonstationarity and we will forecast well: the θ-forecasts are top performers when we have to consider trending time series, be that even of the unit root of the trend-stationary variety. Fourth, stationary time series θ-forecasts can be the new benchmark to beat since, as we have showed explicitly, the AR(1) model forecast is, in fact, a θ-forecast. Fifth, bias correction works in many cases and it is inexpensive to include the bias-corrected θ-forecasts in our forecasting toolbox. Sixth, the double θ-method should be the method of last resort for difficult time series, as we have found some instances where nothing else could beat the benchmark even by a small margin.

Forecasting with the Theta Method: Theory and Applications, First Edition.
Kostas I. Nikolopoulos and Dimitrios D. Thomakos.
© 2019 John Wiley & Sons Ltd. Published 2019 by John Wiley & Sons Ltd.

There are things that our analysis did not cover in their entirety, as one would expect of an on-going project. These are part of our current research and we are open to anyone who wishes to continue the work along the lines of this volume. The choice of the trend function and its implications for the resulting properties of the forecast errors and forecasting performance must be studied further. In particular, we have only used a simple moving average as the trend function of choice with an obvious qualification: for trending time series, the length of the moving average is shorter than in the stationary time series and, for time series that have a constant mean the θ-forecast is the AR(1)-forecast – when the moving average becomes the sample average. This, of course, suggests that in cases of local stationarity we would expect that the θ-forecast will beat the AR(1)-forecast, and we have seen examples in our results that might be suggestive of that. Other flexible forms of trend functions (e.g. a nonparametric kernel-based trend) will convert the existing θ-line – in the context of a model – into a semi-parametric problem whose properties are well understood and have been analyzed.

The multivariate Θ results we presented are confined to the bivariate case and an extension to larger dimensions might provide additional insights. Again, for the trend-stationary case, it is worthwhile to research further on the types of trend functions that we can use in applications and, in particular, what sort of restrictions might be applicable to them for accounting on types of co-movement. In addition, we should consider trend functions that come from unobserved components akin to those used in dynamic factor models. But, as is the case for the univariate θ-forecasts, we caution the reader about avoiding the trap of going overboard: the θ-method is a method that thrives on its simplicity and without this understanding one might fall into the trap of mental overfitting.

A natural question to ask in any time series forecasting context is "can you handle nonlinearity"? The short answer is "yes": the θ-method is a method and not a model and thus has universal applicability. We have examined its theoretical properties in the context of two data-generating processes, one of which is linear but the other can be anything by an appropriate choice of the data-generating process assumed trend function (simplest example, an exponential parametric trend). However, as it is currently structured, the θ-method is not explicitly designed to handle nonlinearities in time series – that does not mean that it cannot. The following example illustrates this point. Let a θ-line be defined as in

$$Q_t(\theta) \overset{\text{def}}{=} \theta X_t + (1 - \theta)X_t^2 \tag{7.1}$$

whose conditional expectation is written as

$$E[Q_{t+1}(\theta)|F_t] = \theta \mu_{t+1} + (1 - \theta)(\sigma_{t+1}^2 + \mu_{t+1}^2) \tag{7.2}$$

where we write $\mu_{t+1} \overset{\text{def}}{=} E[X_{t+1}|\mathcal{F}_t]$ and $\sigma_{t+1}^2 \overset{\text{def}}{=} \text{Var}[X_{t+1}|\mathcal{F}_t]$. If we were to consider this in a data-generating process decomposition of the form:

$$X_{t+1} = E[Q_{t+1}(\theta)|\mathcal{F}_t] + \epsilon_{t+1} \tag{7.3}$$

with ϵ_{t+1} being a martingale difference, we can easily see that this would be a very simple nonlinear autoregressive process within the θ-realm.

The choice of the θ-parameter is the one to consider last. All analysis so far, in the past papers and in this monograph, assumed that it is a parameter indeed, i.e. a constant. Expanding the methodology to account for a (possibly slowly varying) θ_t is also within the range of future research, again with the caveats we mentioned earlier, i.e. not to deviate considerably from the simplicity of the method.

In the end, the θ-method is the prototype of an expectation in a game of chance, a weighted average with θ acting as a constant probability and the time series observations and its trend component acting as the payoffs: sometimes we get closer to one, sometimes to the other. The past and present of the method has shown that in this game the θ-method plays well. Only future research can tell us what else we can do with it – but, unfortunately, future research results cannot possibly be predicted, not even with the θ-method!

References

Andreasen, A.R. (1978). The ghetto-marketing life cycle: a case of underachievement. *Journal of Marketing Research* 15: 20–28.

Armstrong, J.S. and Collopy, F. (1993). Casual forces: structuring knowledge for time series extrapolation. *Journal of Forecasting* 12: 103–115.

Armstrong, J.S., Brodie, R., and McIntyre, S.H. (1987). Forecasting methods for marketing: review of empirical research. *International Journal of Forecasting* 3: 335–376.

Assimakopoulos, V. (1995). A successive filtering technique for identifying long-term trends. *Journal of Forecasting* 14: 35–43.

Assimakopoulos, V. and Nikolopoulos, K. (1999). The Theta model. In: *Proceedings of the 5th International Conference* (4–7 July 1999), 584–586. Athens: Decision Sciences Institute.

Assimakopoulos, V. and Nikolopoulos, K. (2000). The "Theta model": a decomposition approach to forecasting. *International Journal of Forecasting* 16 (4): 521–530.

Bass, F.M. (1969). A new product growth model for consumer durables. *Management Science* 15: 215–227.

Clemen, R. (1989). Combining forecasts: a review and annotated bibliography with discussion. *International Journal of Forecasting* 5: 559–584.

Collopy, F. and Armstrong, J.S. (1992). Rule-based forecasting. Development and validation of an expert systems approach to combine time series extrapolations. *Management Science* 38: 1394–1414.

Cox, W.E. (1967). Product lifecycles as marketing models. *The Journal of Business* 40: 375–384.

Darroch, J. and Miles, M.P. (2011). A research note on market creation in the pharmaceutical industry. *Journal of Business Research* 64 (7): 723–727.

Easingwood, C. (1987). Early product life cycle forms for infrequently purchased major products. *International Journal of Research in Marketing* 4: 3–9.

Fildes, R., Hibon, M., Makridakis, S., and Meade, N. (1998). Generalising about univariate forecasting methods: further empirical evidence. *International Journal of Forecasting* 14: 339–358.

Forecasting with the Theta Method: Theory and Applications, First Edition.
Kostas I. Nikolopoulos and Dimitrios D. Thomakos.
© 2019 John Wiley & Sons Ltd. Published 2019 by John Wiley & Sons Ltd.

Gardner, E.S. Jr. and McKenzie, E. (1985). Forecasting trends in time series. *Management Science* 31: 1237–1246.

Goodwin, P. and Lawton, R. (1999). On the asymmetry of the symmetric MAPE. *International Journal of Forecasting* 15 (4): 405–408.

Fiorucci, J.A., Pellegrini, T.R., Louzada, F., and Petropoulos, F. (2015). The optimised theta method. Arxiv Working Paper http://arxiv.org/abs/1503.03529.

Fiorucci, J.A., Pellegrini, T.R., Louzada, F. et al. (2016). Models for optimising the theta method and their relationship to state space models. *International Journal of Forecasting* 32 (4): 1151–1161.

Hyndman, R.J. and Billah, B. (2003). Unmasking the Theta method. *International Journal of Forecasting* 19 (2): 287–290.

Hyndman, R.J. and Khandakar, Y. (2008). Automatic time series forecasting: the forecast package for R. *Journal of Statistical Software* 27 (3): 1–22.

Hyndman, R.J., Koehler, A.B., Snyder, R.D., and Grose, S. (2002). A state space framework for automatic forecasting using exponential smoothing methods. *International Journal of Forecasting* 18 (3): 439–454.

Kahn, K.B. (2002). An exploratory investigation of new product forecasting practices. *Journal of Product Innovation Management* 19: 133–143.

Kvesic, D.Z. (2008). Product life cycle management: marketing strategies for the pharmaceutical industry. *Journal of Medical Marketing* 8: 293–301.

Lilien, G.L., Rao, A.G., and Kalish, S. (1981). Bayesian estimation and control of detailing effort in a repeat purchase diffusion environment. *Management Science* 27: 493–506.

Makridakis, S. and Hibon, M. (2000). The M3-competition: results, conclusions and implications. *International Journal of Forecasting* 16 (4): 451–476.

Makridakis, S., Andersen, A., Carbone, R. et al. (1984). *The Forecasting Accuracy of Major Time Series Methods*. Wiley.

Makridakis, S., Wheelwright, S., and Hyndman, R. (1998). *Forecasting Methods and Applications*. New York: Wiley.

Mentzer, J.T. and Moon, M.A. (2005). *Sales Forecasting Management: A Demand Management Approach*, 2e. Sage Publications Ltd.

Miller, D.M. and Williams, D. (2003). Shrinkage estimators of time series seasonal factors and their effect on forecasting accuracy. *International Journal of Forecasting* 19 (4): 669–684.

Nikolopoulos, K. and Assimakopoulos, V. (2004). Generalizing the Theta model. International Symposium on Forecasting ISF 2004, Sydney, Australia (4–7 July 2004).

Nikolopoulos, K. and Assimakopoulos, V. (2005a). Fathoming the Theta model. National Technical University of Athens Working paper.

Nikolopoulos, K. and Assimakopoulos, V. (2005b). Theta model: decomposition approach or just SES with drift? *International Symposium on Forecasting ISF 2005, San Antonio, TX, USA (12–15 June 2005)*.

Nikolopoulos, K., Syntetos, A.A., Boylan, J.E. et al. (2011). An aggregate - disaggregate intermittent demand approach (ADIDA) to forecasting: an empirical proposition and analysis. *Journal of the Operational Research Society* 62 (3): 544–554.

Nikolopoulos, K., Buxton, S., Khammash, M., and Stern, P. (2016). Forecasting branded and generic pharmaceuticals. *International Journal of Forecasting* 32 (2): 344–357.

Petropoulos, F. and Nikolopoulos, K. (2013). Optimizing theta model for monthly data. *Proceedings of 5th International Conference on Agents and Artificial Intelligence - ICAART 2013*.

Petropoulos, F. and Nikolopoulos, K. (2017). The theta method. *Foresight* 45: 11–17.

Petropoulos, F., Makridakis, S., Assimakopoulos, V., and Nikolopoulos, K. (2014). 'Horses for Courses' in demand forecasting. *European Journal of Operational Research* 237 (1): 152–163.

Rao, A.G. and Yamada, M. (1988). Forecasting with a repeat purchase diffusion model. *Management Science* 34: 734–752.

Stern, P. (1994). Prescriptions for branded and generic pharmaceuticals. *Journal of Brand Management* 2: 177–182.

Tashman, L.J. (2000). Out-of-sample tests of forecasting accuracy: an analysis and review. *International Journal of Forecasting* 16 (4): 437–450.

Thomakos, D. and Nikolopoulos, K. (2014). Fathoming the theta method for a unit root process. *IMA Journal of Management Mathematics* 25: 105–124.

Thomakos, D. and Nikolopoulos, K. (2015). Forecasting multivariate time series with the theta method. *Journal of Forecasting* 34: 220–229.

Wind, Y., Mahajan, V., and Cardozo, R.N. (1981). *New Product Forecasting*. Lexington, MA: Lexington Books.

Index

Forecasting with the Theta Method: Theory and Applications, First Edition.
Kostas I. Nikolopoulos and Dimitrios D. Thomakos.
© 2019 John Wiley & Sons Ltd. Published 2019 by John Wiley & Sons Ltd.